Always

Fr. Mark Burger

Cover art and design by John Metz Art

ISBN: 978-1-716-39907-7

Library of Congress Control Number: 2020923500

Copyright © 2020 by Fr. Mark Burger. All rights reserved.
No part of this publication may be reproduced or utilized in any form or by any means, electronic or mechanical, including photocopying, recording, or by any information storage and retrieval system, without written permission from the copyright owner.

Published in the United States of America by Fr. Mark Burger

This book is dedicated to all of those people who daily go into that inner room, that personal shrine in their hearts to listen intently to God's quiet voice.

January

January 1
Come, Go Deeper

Recently I was flipping through some old magazines when I came across a picture of a statue of Jesus that caught my attention. The statue is in the harbor in Genoa, Italy, and is called the Christ of the Deep. It is in the form of those classic statues of Jesus with his arms outstretched, and he is looking up. When I first saw it, I could hear him in my mind saying something like, "Come deeper, come deeper so that you can rest, all you who labor and are heavy laden, and I will refresh you and give you rest for your soul."

The statue was originally placed beneath the surface of the water in the harbor, into the depths of the ocean, as a memorial to all of those who died at sea. However, I think it can serve us in a different way. That wonderful image of Jesus so far down in the water is an invitation for each of us to go deeper in our relationship with God. It is also a very striking image of a God who is willing to be with us in the depths of our life. I recommend that you go online to see an image of the Christ of the Deep and then take that with you when you pray.

If you are tired, overwhelmed, lost, or feeling all alone without much hope, perhaps God is saying, "Come, go deeper, and be with me."

January 2
Life Is Too Short

Here is a story of a very smart man who was very clever at finding ways to get out of trouble. Even as a very young boy he could devise ways to keep out of trouble with his parents when he had been careless or done something that could make his very stern father angry.

One day, when he was about nine years old, the boy found himself in a very difficult position. He had been running through the house with his younger brothers when he ran into a table, and his father's very precious teacup went crashing down on to the floor and shattered into many pieces. Hearing the footsteps of his father, he quickly gathered up the pieces and held the pieces of the cup behind his back. When his father appeared, the boy asked, "Father, why do people have to die?"

"This is a natural part of life," explained the older man. "Everything has to die and has just so long to live. It cannot be helped but only accepted."

With a great sigh of relief, the boy showed the shattered pieces of the teacup and added, "It was time for your cup to die."

The story ends there and does not tell us what the father's reaction was when he saw his precious teacup in pieces. We are left wondering.

What is your reaction to the story? What do you think is the moral of this story? Does it teach us to be clever in not taking responsibility for the mistakes we make or the sins we commit? Perhaps there is more to learn here.

These are a few questions that might help to go deeper into the meaning of this story: Do you find it easy to let go of the "broken" things in your life? Do you possess your things or do your things possess you? Like the father in the story, do you think it is only natural that people and things have a limited time, and that this cannot be helped or changed? Perhaps then, the moral of the story is to remind us to cherish fully both the people and the things we have in a life that we often find is too short.

January 3
Ah, Now I See!

One day a man went to his local priest and said, "Father, I want to go really deep in my prayer and maybe even see God's face. I study the Scriptures, I say prayers, I have deep conversations with others about social justice and other important ideas, but I cannot seem to go deeper in my spiritual life.

The priest just smiled at the man but said nothing. This made the man feel a bit uncomfortable, so he spoke again to the priest. "I know, father, that I said almost this very same thing two weeks ago when I met you for lunch. You told me then that I should meditate and work to empty my mind. I have tried what you said but this silly emptying of the mind just does not work. Why must I do that?"

The priest replied, "Perhaps the best way for me to explain this to you is to show you. Come tonight after dark and met me in my garden."

That night, when the man arrived in the garden, the priest was already there waiting for him. "So, father, tell me now what I must do to go deeper in my prayer," the man said.

"I will show you," said the priest, taking a bucket of water deeper into the garden. The night was cool and clear, and there was a full moon. "Now, as I stir the surface, what do you see?"

"I see something like strands or ribbons of light," answered the man.

"Now just wait," said the priest as he set the bucket down. Both men watched the calming surface of the water in the bucket for almost 20 minutes. Then in a very quiet and calm voice the priest asked, "Now what do you see?"

"The moon reflected in the water," replied the man.

"Just as the calming of the water made the moon appear more clearly, so too the only way to go deeper in your prayer and maybe even see the face of God is through a calm and settled mind and heart."

"Ah, now I begin to understand," said the man. "And now may you begin to go deeper and to see," said the priest.

January 4
With Both Eyes

When was the last time you learned something new? When was the last time you tried to learn or master a new skill? I ask these questions because one of the things that I learned when I was studying spirituality is a simple, spiritual truth: when we stop learning we start dying. I remember our teacher telling us that when you stop learning you first go dead from the neck up and then the rest of you follows suit until you walk around dead on the inside! He then told us the following story to encourage us not only to keep learning but also to not rush through the process of learning new things.

One day a young but earnest student went to his Zen Master and asked, "If I work very hard at it, how long will it take for me to be a good practitioner of Zen meditation?"

The Master thought about this, then replied, "About ten years."

The student then said, "But what if I work very, very hard and really apply myself to learn fast, how long then?"

Replied the Master, "Well, maybe twenty years."

"But if I really, really work at it, how long then?" asked the student.

"In that case, certainly thirty years," replied the Master.

"But I do not understand," said the disappointed student. "Each time I say I will work harder you say it will take me longer. Why do you say that?"

Replied the Master," When you have one eye on the goal, you only have one eye on the path. Doing meditation well requires both eyes on the path and not one on finishing the meditation."

When was the last time you learned something new and had both eyes on the path of learning?

January 5
The Flow

Have you ever been traveling and all at once, it begins to dawn on you that you are utterly lost? Most of us have at one time or another found ourselves in an unfamiliar place with no idea of how we got there nor how we will ever find our way home again. We can find ourselves in this condition lout on the road, or in the woods, or even in our spiritual life, family life, or the world of our work. It does not matter in which world we are lost; we still know that being lost is not a pleasant experience.

The idea of being lost reminds me of a story that I came across when I was studying spiritual direction. According to that story, two terrified city dwellers found themselves completely lost in a forest. After wandering around in circles for a whole day and night, they came upon an old hermit, who looked a bit deranged but seemed friendly enough.

"How do we find our way back to civilization?" they asked the hermit.

The hermit looked at them and laughed hysterically. This unnerved the poor city folks, but they waited for his instructions.

"I could tell you, but you'd still get lost," replied the hermit.
"What should we do?" they asked.

"Put yourself in God's hands and simply go with the flow," he said.

"I beg your pardon?" one of the city boys asked.

"Go with the flow. You see that stream over there? Just follow it. Streams go into creeks, creeks go into rivers, and rivers go through towns. Also, along the way you will have water to drink and berries to eat. No need to worry. Go with the flow," the hermit said, looking a bit more serene.

"Is that what you crazy holy people mean when you say, 'go with the flow'?"

"Yes and no," replied the hermit, grinning as he walked by them and proceeded along his way.

If you are at a point in your life right now where you feel lost, confused, or befuddled, perhaps that deranged hermit's advice to "put yourself in God's hands and simply go with the flow" may very well be good advice for you, too. Go with the flow!

January 6
The Music of Friendship

Many happily married couples will say that the secret of their love and happiness lies in the truth that the two of them are not only spouses but also best friends. Some friends of mine who are married for over fifty years told me that they feel their friendship is like a beautiful piece of music that transforms you as soon as you hear it.

That reminded me of something I had read about friendship. A long time ago, in China, there was a married couple who were not only spouses but also true friends. One played the harp skillfully and beautifully while the other one listened skillfully and beautifully.

When the one played and sang about a mountain, the other would say, "Oh, I can almost see the mountain before us." When the one played about water, the listener would say, "Ah, here is the running stream!" Theirs was a beautiful friendship.

Sadly, the listener fell sick and died. The first friend cut the strings of his harp promising never to play again until the two were reunited in the next world. Since that time, in some parts of China, the cutting of harp strings serves as a sign of the close of a deeply intimate friendship.

Have you ever had the blessing of a friendship like that? Do you have such a friendship with your spouse? Do you think it is possible to have such a friendship with God?

January 7
Running from Spiders

Here is a kind of spiritual riddle or parable that comes from Tibet. Before you read it, pause for some quiet prayer and ask God to teach you what you need to learn through this story.

While meditating in his room, a young monk believed he saw a spider descending in front of him. He tried to dismiss it from his mind but each day the menacing creature returned, growing larger and larger each time. The young monk grew so worried and frightened that he went to his teacher to report his situation. He said he planned to place a knife in his lap during meditation, so that when the spider appeared, he could kill it.

The teacher listened attentively and advised him against this plan. Instead, he suggested the young monk bring a piece of chalk to meditation, and when the spider appeared, mark an "X" on its belly.

The young monk was then to report back to his teacher.

The student returned to his meditation. When the spider again appeared, he resisted the urge to kill it, and instead did just what the teacher had suggested. When he later reported back to the teacher, the teacher told him to lift up his shirt and look at his own belly. There, on the student's belly, was the "X."

Having prayed first and then read the parable, is there an "X" on your belly?

January 8
A Splendid Fat Fish

During a visit to the art museum the other day, I heard one of the docents tell a story to a group of students from an art academy. As she told the story, I noticed the art students were paying very close attention and smiling as they listened. Here is the story she told them.

There was a gifted young painter of extraordinary talent who had been apprenticed to a renowned painter, who, when he saw the boy's gifts, became intensely jealous. It did not take long for that jealousy to blossom into some intense behaviors.

"No, that is not the way to do it!" he would shout. "You will do better painting houses than pictures." Slowly the boy's confidence began to fade. No matter how hard he tried, the teacher always found fault and humiliated the boy in front of the other students.

One day the class's painting assignment was to render a goldfish. The boy closed his eyes and saw quite clearly in his mind a splendid fat fish from his uncle's pond. He painted the fish exactly as he had imagined it.

"No. No. No!" screamed the teacher and threw the boy's picture out the window and into a flowing stream just below the school. Everyone was shocked at the display of anger made by the teacher.

A deep silence descended upon the class. All of the sudden an amazing thing happened; the students would later call it "an amazing grace." In the midst of that awkward silence one by one each student was amazed to see that painted, fat fish joyfully swimming down the stream!

When the docent finished telling her story, there was a bit of a pregnant pause. Then all at once the art students began talking enthusiastically about the story. Finally, one of the art students asked, "Why did you tell us that story?"
The docent replied, "I just want you to remember that no matter how hard others may try to quash your talents, you need not be afraid to let them show. Your talents are a living thing, and they will find a way to burst out on their own. Never let anyone diminish the gifts that are in you!"
Have you ever allowed anyone to quash the goodness that is in you?

January 9
Tyranny

One day the abbot of a local monastery sent three of his young monks out to practice their meditation. He told them to go sit near the lake and spend the afternoon in deep meditation. He instructed them to pay close attention to what God might be saying to them. Finally, he warned them not to be so competitive and jealous of one another's talents.

The three monks did as they were told and went out of the monastery and sat by the lake. Soon they were in deep in meditation.

After about fifteen minutes the profound silence was broken when one of the young monks stood up and said, "I've forgotten my bible! I can't meditate properly without it." Stepping on to the waters before him, he walked across the lake to the other side, where their monastery stood.

As soon as he returned, the second monk said, "I just remembered I was supposed to sweep out the chapel!" Like his fellow monk, he too walked calmly across the water to the other bank, and he returned in a few minutes the same way.

The third monk watched both of them intently. Figuring that they were just showing off and that this was a test of his own skills, he loudly declared, "So you think you are so holy and that your abilities are better than mine! You people just watch me! What you can do, I can do!" and he scurried to the edge of the riverbank. No sooner did he put his foot on the water than he fell into waist-high water.

Unfazed, he waded out, ran at the lake, and tried again to walk across the lake as his fellow monks had done. And repeatedly, he sunk to the bottom. After watching this performance in silence, one of his fellow monks turned to the other and asked, "Do you think we ought to tell him where the stepping stones are?"

A basic spiritual principle is that although we are all on the same road to God, we are not in competition with each other. The Desert Fathers would warn each other about what they called "the tyranny of comparison." They taught that once you begin to compare yourself to another and try to compete with them in life, you will have begun to lose your peace of heart and mind.

January 10
What Are You Bringing?

Two brothers were sitting on the front porch one Sunday night having some coffee. The last of the out-of-town guests to their family reunion had just left, and most of the commotion that goes with having such a large family event had calmed down. As the two men stared into their coffee cups one spoke up and said, "Thank God we took that old mule with us on the picnic because when one of the boys got injured, we used the mule to carry him back."

"Oh, I wondered how you were able to carry him all the way back up to the house. How did he get injured anyway?"

The other brother paused for a moment, then grinned and said, "The mule kicked him."

Both brothers laughed for a long time, and then one commented. "You know, as I think about my life, almost all of the trouble I've faced through the years has often been the trouble that I brought with me to the party!"

If you took a few minutes to think about it, is what that one brother said true for you? Have a lot of the troubles you have faced in life been from the trouble you actually brought to the party? How often has an argument between you and a loved one been the result of the attitude you brought to the conversation before the argument? Has the attitude that you have brought home from work ever caused you to misjudge or falsely accuse your spouse? Has your tone of voice ever frightened your children? Perhaps today might be a good day for all of us to do a kind of self-assessment to determine just what we are bringing to the party of our lives.

January 11
Keeping Your Feet on the Ground

There once was a rabbi whom everyone in his community loved dearly, and they loved everything he said and most of what he wrote. The rabbi did have one friend, however, named Aaron who just did not accept everything the rabbi said or did. In fact, the rabbi sometimes would say that Aaron was one of the most irritating friends he had. Aaron never missed an opportunity to contradict the rabbi or to point out the mistakes the rabbi made. They often had words but remained steadfast friends.

One day Aaron caught cold, got sick, and quickly died. No one was more bereft than the rabbi was over his death. He wept for days and just looked terrible. Other members of the community gathered to comfort the rabbi over his loss, but they really could not understand him. They asked, "Rabbi, why are you so sad? We noticed that Aaron often found fault with you and even criticized your thinking. You yourself said that he was the most irritating friend you had. Why are you so sad?"

The rabbi looked at them and said, "I am not sad for my friend for I know he is happy in heaven. I am just so terribly sad for myself because without my friend Aaron I have no one to force me to keep growing and to keep me from taking myself too seriously. I feel lost without him."

Is there an "Aaron" among your family or friends who, by the way they treat you, forces you to keep growing and keeps you humble with your feet on the ground? They are worth their weight in gold for the good that they do you. Even though such folk might irritate you from time to time, are they not truly a blessing to you? Do you appreciate them enough to thank them?

January 12
The Light of Experience

There once was a Sufi holy man who was lying in the shade of an ancient walnut tree. His body was at rest, but, befitting his calling as an imam, his began to meditate on deeper things. He looked up into the huge tree and as he did so, he considered the greatness and wisdom of Allah.

"Allah is great, and Allah is good," he said to himself, "but was it indeed wise that such a great tree as this be created to bear only tiny walnuts as fruit? Just look at the stout stem and strong limbs. They could easily carry the great pumpkins that grow from spindly vines in my field, vines that often cannot bear the weight of their own fruit. Should not walnuts grow on weakly vines on the ground and pumpkins on sturdy trees?"

This was the holy man's thinking, as he dozed off into a peaceful sleep, only to be startled awake by a walnut that fell from the tree, striking him on his forehead.

"Allah be praised!" he exclaimed, seeing what had happened. "If that had been a pumpkin that fell on my head, it would have killed me for sure! God is merciful! He has rearranged nature just this way in order to spare my life!"

Have you ever found yourself questioning what someone (even God) has done on only to find out later, when you have had more experience in life, that what that person had done was actually exactly the right thing? The story of the Sufi holy man who questions God can be a good reminder for us to take a second look at our thinking. Sometimes we jump to conclusions without having all the facts and insights we need to make a good choice. There is nothing quite as good as life experience to give us a light by which we can begin to consider our choices.

January 13
Praying for Evil People

Sitting in a hospital room visiting one of my parishioners, I noticed several old prayer books stacked up on the woman's bedside table. "I see that you have brought your prayer books with you to the hospital," I said, as she noticed me glancing over at them.

"Yes, I take them wherever I go because you never know when you might need to pray for somebody. There are prayers for just about everything and everybody in those books!" she said with a laugh.

She picked them up and handed them to me. As I flipped through the pages, I realized that she was right: there were prayers for just about every possible situation and person you could think of. Then, on a scrap of paper in the back of the oldest looking book, I found the following remarkable note. I copied it down and have it in my bible.

The following prayer was found amongst the personal belongings of a Jew who died in a concentration camp: "Lord, when you come in your glory, do not remember only the men of good, but remember too the men of evil. And on the Day of Judgement, do not remember only the acts of cruelty, inhumanity, and violence that they carried out, but remember, too, the fruits that they produced in us because of what they did to us.

"Remember the patience, courage, brotherly love, humility, generosity of spirit, and faithfulness that our executioners awoke in our souls. Then, Lord, may those fruits be used to save the souls of those men of evil. Amen."

January 14
Wouldn't It Be Great?

Probably one of the most important things that any of us could ever learn is the wisdom of paying attention to one's own attitudes. Our attitudes play a major role in whether or not we do well in life or not. This was brought home to me recently when, as pastor of my parish, I was called to visit some of our parishioners who live in nursing homes.

As I walked into the lobby on the morning of my visit, two elderly women invited me to have coffee with them in the dining room. The director of the home joined us at the table and gave each of us a copy of an article she had written for her staff. The article described one of the newest residents of the facility, and she wanted everyone to know about this new 92-year-old arrival. As she handed the article to each of us, she said, "Oh, wouldn't it be great to be like her?"

Here is some of what she wrote:

A 92-year-old, petite, cute, and proud lady, who is fully dressed each morning by eight o'clock, with her hair fashionably coifed and makeup perfectly applied even though she is legally blind, has moved into our assisted living section. Because her husband of 70 years recently passed away, and because her recent eye surgery did not produce the best results, she has decided that these circumstances have made the move necessary.

The lady smiled sweetly when she was told her room was ready. As she maneuvered her walker to the elevator, I provided a visual description of her tiny room, including the color of the walls, carpeting, and draperies.

"I love it," she stated with the enthusiasm of an 8-year-old having just been presented with a new puppy. "Mrs. Jones, you haven't seen the room yet. Just wait until I show it to you."

"That doesn't have anything to do with it," she replied. "Happiness is something you decide on way ahead of time. Whether I like my room or not does not depend on how the furniture is arranged or what color the walls are or if there is carpet. More importantly, it is how I arrange my mind about these things. I already decided to love it and I am sure that I will love it until the day the Good Lord calls me home.

"I make a decision every morning when I wake up. I have a choice; I can spend the day in bed recounting the difficulty I have with the parts of my body that no longer work or I can get out of bed and be thankful for the ones that do. Each day is a gift, and as long as my eyes open, I will focus on the new day and all the happy memories I have stored away for exactly this time of my life. I am happy right now, even though I don't see too well, because I choose to be happy."

Wouldn't it be great to be like her?

January 15
Nobody

There is an ancient story told of a holy man who came upon a large banquet hall. There he entered a formal reception area and seated himself at the foremost elegant chair. The Chief of the Guard thought this was rather odd, so he approached and said: "Sir, those places are reserved for our guests of honor."

"Oh, I am more than a mere guest," replied the holy man confidently.

"Oh, so are you a diplomat?"

"Far more than that!"

"Really? So, you are a minister, perhaps?"

"No, much bigger than that too."

"Oh, so I see it now! So, you must be the king himself, sir," said the chief even more sarcastically.

"Higher than that!" the holy man said.

"What?! Are you higher than the king? Nobody is higher than the king in this kingdom!"

"Now you have it. You have it exactly! I am nobody!" said the holy man, grinning broadly.

What do you suppose the holy man was trying to teach everyone about the king? Is it true that nobody is higher than the king or is it that the king is higher than nobody?

January 16
Do You Need This Cure?

Many years ago, in China, a girl got married and went to live with her husband and mother-in-law. Not too long after the wedding that the young wife found that she could not get along with her mother-in-law at all. They were very different people.

Mostly it was little things. The young wife felt crowded in her own home and angered by many of her mother-in-law's habits. In addition, her mother-in-law criticized constantly. As these kinds of situation often develop, days passed days, and weeks and even months passed with little change. The two women never stopped arguing and fighting. But what made the situation even worse was that, according to ancient Chinese tradition, a young wife had to bow to her mother-in-law and obey her every wish.

At the same time, all of the anger and unhappiness in the house was causing the young husband great distress and agitation. He let his wife know that he had had quite enough.

Finally, the young wife could not stand her mother-in-law's bad temper or her manner of dictatorship any longer, and she decided to do something about it.

She went to see her father's good friend, a wise man who sold herbs. She told him the situation and asked if he would give her some herbs with which to poison her mother-in-law so that she could solve the problem once and for all.

The herbalist thought and pondered about the situation for a while, and finally said, "Young one, I will help you solve your problem, but you must listen to me and obey what I tell you.

The young wife said, "Yes sir, I will do whatever you tell me to do."

The herbalist went into the back room and returned in a few minutes with a package of herbs. He gave her these instructions: "You can't use a quick-acting poison to get rid of your mother-in-law, because that would cause people to become suspicious. Therefore, I have given you a number of herbs that will slowly build up poison in her body. Every other day prepare some pork or chicken and put a little of these herbs in her serving. Now, in order to make sure that nobody suspects you when she dies, you must be very careful to act very friendly towards her. Don't argue with her, obey her every wish, and treat her like a queen."

The young wife was very happy to have a solution. She thanked the herbalist and hurried home to start enacting her plot of murdering her mother-in-law.

Weeks went by, months went by, and every other day, the young wife dutifully served the specially treated food to her mother-in-law. She remembered what the herbalist had said about avoiding suspicion, so she controlled her temper, obeyed her mother-in-law, and treated her like her own mother. All seemed to be going well.

After six months had passed, the whole household had changed. The young wife became very good at controlling her temper, so much that she found that she almost never got mad or upset. She had not had an argument in six months with her mother-in-law, who now seemed much kinder and easier to accept.

The mother-in-law's attitude toward her changed and she began to love her almost like her own daughter. She kept telling friends and relatives that she was the best daughter-in-law one could ever find. The young wife and her mother-in-law were now treating each other like a real mother and daughter.

The young husband was very happy to see what was happening and was no longer agitated.
One day, the young wife went to see the herbalist to ask for his help again. She said, "Most kind sir, please help me to keep the poison from killing my mother-in-law! She completely changed into such a nice woman, and I love her like my own mother. I do not want her to die because of the poison I gave her."

The herbalist took a deep breath and nodded his head. Looking around to make sure no one was listening, he whispered to her, "Young one, there's nothing to worry about. I never gave you any poison. The herbs I gave you were vitamins meant to improve her health. The only poison I could see was in your mind and your attitude toward her. But now that has been all washed away by the love which you gave to her."

January 17
How Poor?

If you were to compare your life with the lives of most of the people in the world, would you consider yourself rich or poor? I have been thinking about this recently because someone told me a story that their grandfather had related to them.

The story tells of a father who took his son on a trip through the country with the firm purpose to show him how many of the world's people are truly very poor people. He wanted to make sure that his son appreciated how blessed he was to be in the family he was in, and how materially wealthy he was.

In the first part of their journey, they spent a day and a night on the farm of a very poor family. When they returned home from their trip, the father asked his son, "How was the trip?"

"Very good Dad I loved it and I have learned a lot!"

"Did you see how poor people can be?" the father asked.

"Yeah!"

"And what did you learn?"

Pausing to collect his thoughts, the son answered, "I saw that we have a dog at home, and they have four. We have a pool that reaches to the middle of the garden; they have a creek that has no end. We have imported marble lamps to light up the garden at night; they have the stars. Our patio reaches to the front yard, but they don't have a patio. Instead they have the whole horizon!"

When the boy was finished, his father was speechless. Then the son added one more thing, "Thanks, Dad, for showing me how poor we are!"

January 18
This Is Good!

There is a story told in Africa that I like very much, a story about a local king and one of his best friends. These two friends were inseparable and they both felt that nothing could ever ruin their friendship. One thing the king never understood, however, was how his friend was always so positive about everything. In fact, that friend had the habit of saying the same sentence whenever anything happened. It did not make any difference whether it was a positive thing or a negative thing that happened, the friend always had the same comment. What was that comment? Three words: "This is good!"

Those three words came between the king and his friend one day; here is what happened. The king and his friend were out on a hunting expedition. The friend would always load and prepare the guns for the king. On this one occasion, the friend apparently did something wrong in preparing one of the guns, for after taking the gun from his friend, the king fired it and his thumb was blown off. The king was in great pain and was instantly angry.

Examining the situation, the friend made his usual remark, "This is good!" to which the king replied, "No, this is NOT good!" and proceeded to have his friend arrested and sent to jail. It appeared that their long friendship was at an end.

Nearly about a year later, the king was hunting in an area that he should have known to stay clear of. Cannibals captured him and took them to their village. They tied his hands, stacked some wood, set up a stake, and bound him to the stake.

As they came near to set fire to the wood, they noticed that the king was missing a thumb. Being superstitious, they never ate anyone that was less than whole. Untying the king, they sent him on his way. The king could not believe his good fortune.

As he returned home, the king remembered the event that had taken his thumb and felt remorse for his treatment of his friend. He went immediately to the jail to speak with his friend. "You were right," he said, "it was good that my thumb was blown off." Then he proceeded to tell the friend all that had just happened. "And so, I am very sorry for sending you to jail for so long. It was bad for me to do this."

"No," his friend replied, "This is good!" "What do you mean, 'This is good?' How could it be good that I sent you, my friend, to jail for a year?"

"If I had NOT been in jail, I would have been with you and both of us would have ended up being supper for the cannibals!"

Are you able to find the good in the things that happen in your life?

January 19
A Friend Like Jim

One of the greatest treasures that life offers us is a good friend who you can always count on to be there for you. There is a famous story from the days of World War I that illustrates this very well.

Horror gripped the heart of the soldier as he saw his lifelong friend fall in battle. Caught in a trench with continuous gunfire whizzing over his head, the soldier asked his lieutenant if he might go out into the "no man's land" between the trenches to bring his fallen comrade back.

"You can go," said the lieutenant, "but I don't think it will be worth it. Your friend is probably dead already and you may just be throwing your own life away."

The lieutenant's words did not matter to the soldier, and he went to find his friend. Miraculously he managed to reach his friend, hoist him onto his shoulder, and bring him back to their company's trench.

As the two of them tumbled in together to the bottom of the trench, the officer checked the wounded soldier and noticed that he was dead. He then looked kindly at his friend.

"I told you it wouldn't be worth it," he said. "Your friend is dead, and you are not going to survive your wounds. Was it really worth your own life?"

"It was worth it, sir," the soldier said.

"How do you mean, 'worth it'?" responded the lieutenant. "Your friend is dead!"

"Yes sir," the private answered. "But it was worth it because when I got to him, he was still alive, and I had the satisfaction of hearing him say, 'Jim, I knew you'd come.' I am so glad I went."

Do you have a friend like Jim who you know you can always count on to be there for you when you find yourself stranded in a "no man's land?" Are you a friend like Jim to anyone in your life?

January 20
Free Money

This is a story worth knowing because it teaches an important lesson for us all. We are told about a small boy who, when walking down the street one day, found a brand-new copper penny. It was so shiny that the sun's reflection off it caused the boy to wince in pain. He was so excited that he had found money and it did not cost him anything.

This experience led him to spend the rest of his life walking with his head down; eyes wide open, looking for treasure. He kept his head down so that he would not miss a thing. To tell you the truth, the boy certainly didn't miss much. During his lifetime he found 296 pennies, 48 nickels, 19 dimes, 16 quarters, 2 half dollars and one beat up dollar bill -- for a total of $13.96. The boy had gotten money for nothing and he was thrilled. He also found many bent nails, some nuts, and some bolts.

There was a downside to the boy's view of things, however. By spending his days looking down for free money, he missed the beauty of 31,369 sunsets, the colorful splendor of 157 rainbows, and the fiery beauty of hundreds of maples after autumn's frost. He never noticed the white clouds drifting across blue skies, shifting into various wondrous formations. Birds flying, sun shining, and the smiles of a thousand passing people are not a part of his memory. By always looking down, the boy did find some free money. But what did that free money cost him?

If you were to check your own way of looking at life and your own way of living your life, do you suppose there might be some wonderful things you are missing? Are you open to all that life might be offering you?

January 21
A Visiting Angel

A holy man prayed to God for help. The man prayed with these words, "O most loving God, I am so terrified of what will happen to me if I live my life the way you want me to live it. How can I overcome my fears and become your faithful follower? I do not know what to do. Would you kindly send me an angel to show me the way? O loving one, please do not send me a frightening angel or an angry or mean one. Send me an angel I can welcome and love and from whom I can learn how to overcome my fears."

When the holy man finished his prayers, he simply waited for an angel to show up. He waited a whole two days and still no angel came. He prayed again asking for an angel. Then all at once, the holy man felt thirsty. He knew there was a river nearby, so he made his way there to get a drink.

As he was making his way to the river a big dog suddenly appeared next to him and it too was making his way toward the river. The holy man could tell that the dog was as thirsty as he was. When they finally arrived at the river, the dog looked into the river, and saw another dog there -- his own image -- and became terribly afraid. He would bark and run away, but his thirst was so strong that he would come back. Finally, despite his fear, he just jumped into the water, and the image disappeared. The dog drank fully from the river and was content.

When he saw all of this happening, the holy man knew that God's kind angel had just arrived bringing a message from God: no matter what, one has to jump in spite of all fears. The holy man never forgot that wonderful angel that God had sent him.

January 22
Unexpected

One day a Muslim holy man was giving a lecture on how God often instructs us in unexpected ways and through unexpected people. He said that God had once instructed him through a small child. This is how he told the story: "One day, I entered a town and saw a child carrying a lit candle. He was going to the mosque to put the candle there.

'Just joking,' I asked the boy, 'have you lit the candle yourself?' He said, 'Yes sir.'

Then I asked the boy, 'There was a moment when the candle was unlit, and then there was a moment when the candle was lit. Can you show me the source from which the light came?'

And shaking his head the boy laughed, blew out the candle, and said, 'Now you have seen the light going. Where has it gone? Can you tell me?'

And it was then that I knew that God was speaking to me through a small child. God was telling me to realize that I have much to learn yet about God's world. I must always be a student, always ready for what God might show me next in many unexpected ways."

January 23
When Weakness Is Strength

Have you ever felt powerless and overwhelmed, and that you have very little to offer? That is a terrible feeling to have, yet many people feel they are weak and just don't measure up. Many are tempted to give up on life because they fear they don't have what it takes to succeed. Perhaps they should think again.

There is a remarkable story of a 10-year-old boy who was in a horrific traffic accident. He was seriously injured and lost his left arm as a result. The boy recovered physically, but he was very depressed and thought that he would never be able to do much in life. He felt he was doomed to be an invalid.

One day a neighbor who had heard that the young boy was despondent came to visit with him. The neighbor happened to be a sensei, or teacher of martial arts. After a brief introduction, the sensei asked the boy if he wanted to learn judo. The boy's face lit up, "Yes, I would love to study judo but how can I with no left arm?" he asked.

The sensei said, "You leave that to me."

The boy began lessons with the sensei. The boy was doing well, so he could not understand why, after three months of training, the master had taught him only one move.

"Sensei," the boy finally said, "Shouldn't I be learning more moves?"

"This is the only move you know, but this is the only move you'll ever need to know," the sensei replied.
Not quite understanding, but believing in his teacher, the boy kept training.

Several months later, the sensei took the boy to his first tournament. Surprising himself, the boy easily won his first two matches. The third match proved to be more difficult, but after some time, his opponent became impatient and charged; the boy deftly used his one move to win the match. Still amazed by his success, the boy was now in the finals.

The boy began to be a bit worried because his opponent was bigger, stronger, and more experienced. It looked to everyone there that the boy appeared to be overmatched. Concerned that the boy might get hurt, the referee called a time-out. He was about to stop the match when the sensei intervened.

"No," the sensei insisted, "Let him continue. Trust me."

Soon after the match resumed, his opponent made a critical mistake: he dropped his guard. Instantly, the boy used his move to pin him. The boy had won the match and the tournament. He was the champion.

Now on the way home, the boy and sensei reviewed every move in each match. Then the boy summoned the courage to ask what was really on his mind.

"Sensei, how did I win the tournament with only one move?"

"You won for two reasons," the sensei answered. "First, you have mastered one of the most difficult throws in all of judo. Second, the only known defense for that move is for your opponent to grab your left arm. The one thing you thought made you vulnerable really is your strength."

January 24
What Solomon Learned

A friend of mine told me that there is an ancient tale told about King Solomon. As the story goes, one day Solomon decided to humble Benaiah ben Yehoyada, the man who was his most trusted minister.

The king said to him, "Benaiah, there is a certain ring that I want you to bring to me. I wish to wear it for Sukkot, which gives you six months to find it."

"If it exists anywhere on earth, your majesty," replied Benaiah, "I will find it and bring it to you. But what makes it so special?"

"It has magic powers," answered Solomon. "If a happy man looks at it, he becomes very sad, and if a sad man looks at it, he becomes happy."

Now the truth of the matter was that Solomon knew that no such ring existed in the world, but he wished to give his minister a little taste of humility.

Spring passed and then summer, and still Benaiah could not even think to know where he could find the ring. Realizing that his time was almost up, on the night before Sukkot, he decided to take a walk in one of the poorest quarters of Jerusalem. He passed by a merchant who had begun to set out the day's wears on a shabby carpet.

Taking a chance on the man, he asked the merchant, "Have you by chance heard of a magic ring that makes the happy wearer forget his joy and the broken-hearted wearer forget his sorrows?" The old merchant nodded to him. He watched the grandfather take a plain gold ring from his carpet and engrave something on it.

When Benaiah read the words on the ring, his face broke out in a wide smile for he had done it! He had found the ring that King Solomon wanted.

That night the entire city of Jerusalem welcomed in the holiday of Sukkot with great festivities. "Well, my friend," said King Solomon, "have you found what I sent you after?"

All of the other ministers laughed as did King Solomon because they all knew that no such ring existed on the earth.

To everyone's surprise, Benaiah held up a small gold ring and declared, "Your majesty, here it is!"
Everyone was stunned into silence. As soon as King Solomon examined the ring and read the inscription on the ring, the smile vanished from the king's face. The merchant had written three Hebrew letters on the gold ring: gimel, zayin, and yud, which began the words "Gam she ya'avor." The words mean, "This too will pass."

At that very moment, King Solomon realized that all of his wisdom and fabulous wealth and tremendous powers were but fleeting things, for one day, they, like everything else in this life, will pass.

January 25
Returns

A Native American medicine man would often gather the youngest members of his tribe in order to pass on some important spiritual teachings and traditions. He often used parables to help the young ones remember what he taught them. Perhaps one of his parables, which follows below, will be of help to you in your spiritual life.

A father and his son were walking in the mountains. Suddenly, his son falls, hurts himself and screams: "Boy, does that ever hurt!"

To his surprise, hears a voice repeating, somewhere in the mountain: ""Boy, does that ever hurt!"

Curious, he yells: "Who are you?"

He receives the answer: "Who are you?"

Angered by the response, he screams: "Coward!"

He receives the answer: "Coward!"

He looks to his father and asks: "What's going on?"

The father smiles and says: "My son, pay attention." And then he screams to the mountain: "I admire you!"

The voice answers: "I admire you!"

Again, the father screams: "You are a champion!"

The voice answers: "You are a champion!"

The boy is surprised, but still does not understand.

Then the father explains: "People call this *echo*, but really, this is *life*. Remember that *echo* or *life* gives you back everything you say or do. Our life is simply a reflection of our actions. If you want more love in the world, create more love in your heart. If you want more understanding in our family, you must become more understanding. This relationship applies to everything, in all aspects of life: just like echo, life will give you back everything you have given to it."

January 26
That Way

Out of India comes a story of a man who meets a guru in the road. Hoping to make something of himself, the man decides to ask for some advice. He stops the guru and says, "Can you tell me the way to find success?"

The guru does not speak a word to the man, but he does turn and points to a place far off in the distance. The man, thrilled by the prospect of quick and easy success, rushes off in the direction pointed out by the wise man. Suddenly, there comes a loud "Splat!" and then complete silence follows.

In about a half hour, the man limps back, tattered and stunned. Assuming he must have misunderstood the guru's instructions, he repeats his original question to the guru, who again points silently in exactly the same direction.

Shaking his head, the man obediently walks off once more into the area pointed out by the guru. This time the splat is deafening, and when the man crawls back, he is a bloody, broken, tattered, and irate mess.

"I asked you which way is success," he screams at the guru. "I followed the direction you indicated. And all I got was splatted! No more of this pointing! Talk to me!"

Finally, the guru does speak, and what he says is this: "Success is always that way. Just a little after the splat."

January 27
Angry?

The big day came for a young man when his father asked him to chair the Board of Directors meeting the family business. During the discussion of the third agenda item, a heated debate arose over a company policy. At one point in that conversation, the young man lost his temper and said some harsh and sarcastic things. The proposal he was supporting was promptly defeated.
When the meeting ended, the young man wondered what his father thought of how he had run his first board meeting. He took his father aside and asked, "How did I do, dad?"

"It was a good first meeting. You have some things to learn about people and how to treat them, but for a first meeting, you did alright," his father replied.

The next morning, when the son arrived at his desk, he found an envelope from his father. When he opened it, he found a letter in which his father said, "Last night as I was falling asleep, I thought of you chairing yesterday's meeting. I was proud to see you taking your place in our family work. I want to share with you something your grandfather shared with me after I chaired my first board meeting. It is a quote from Aristotle: 'Anybody can become angry -- that is easy, but to be angry with the right person and to the right degree and at the right time and for the right purpose and in the right way -- that is not within everybody's power and is not easy."

The father concluded his letter by adding, "If you want to be a good leader, a good friend, spouse, or father you must certainly learn how to handle your anger. Your mother lovingly taught me that I had to learn how handle my anger. I thank God for her every day because I think I have learned a great deal about it over the years. I hope you listen to Aristotle and maybe even to me. Just remember, if you ever want a coach to help you, I am ready to be of service to you."

January 28
Roses

Did you ever hear a story about someone that just made you feel glad to be alive, and able to love and care for others? I heard such a story not too long ago and I have enjoyed thinking about it ever since. The story is about the famous comedian, Jack Benny:

On the day after Jack Benny's death, in December of 1974, a single, long-stemmed red rose was delivered to Mary Livingstone Benny, his wife. They had been married for 48 years.

When another rose was delivered the following day and continued to arrive every day, day after day, Mary called the florist to find out what was happening and who sent them.

"It was quite a while before Jack passed away," the florist told her. "He stopped in to send a bouquet to somebody, paid the bill, and made for the door. As he was leaving, he suddenly turned back and said, 'If anything should happen to me, I want you to send Mary a single red rose every day. They are her favorite.'

There was complete silence on Mary's end of the line, then weeping, she said, "Goodbye."

Subsequently, Mary learned that Jack had actually included a provision for the flowers in his will, one perfect red rose daily for the rest of her life. He said he wanted her to know that his love for her did not end when his life did but continued on into eternity.

January 29
Faults

In ancient Greece, one of Socrates' students asked him if he could help him understand human beings better. The philosopher thought for a moment and is said to have replied by saying, "Every man is born into the world with two bags suspended from his neck: a big bag in front full of his neighbors' faults, and a large bag behind filled with his own faults. That is why people are quick to see the faults of others, and yet are often blind to their own failings. Look to your own faults and perhaps you will have a better insight into your neighbor's life."

One of the Desert Fathers would often tell the story above. He would then ask his disciples to be quiet for a few moments so they might ponder this question: "Whose faults do you spend the most time thinking about?"

If you were to take some time to be quiet, how would you answer that question?

January 30
Taking Time

A police officer in a small town stopped a motorist who was speeding down Main Street. "But officer," the man began, "I can explain."

"Just be quiet," snapped the officer. "I have had a long week dealing with idiot drivers and I am not willing to hear your lame excuses. I'm going to let you cool your heels in jail until the chief gets back."

"But, officer, I just wanted to say..." "And I said to keep quiet! You're going to jail!"

A few hours later, the officer looked in on his prisoner and said, "Lucky for you that the chief's at his daughter's wedding. He'll be in a good mood when he gets back."

"Don't count on it," answered the fellow in the cell. "I'm the groom."

That story can serve as a good reminder of the importance of listening to people when they are trying to tell us something. Failure to listen is probably one of the biggest causes of pain in our families and among our friends. It's usually at the core of most broken relationships.
One of simplest yet most profound ways we can improve the world is simply to be willing to take the time to listen.

January 31
Patience

Saint Anthony the Great, one of the first of the Church's Desert Fathers, often gave his spiritual disciples passages from the bible or other writings to use in their meditations. He would have them memorize a quotation and then ask them to, as he put it, "turn it over again and again in their minds." It was his hope that his disciples would grow in wisdom and in grace by spending time with "wise words."

Every so often, when I am doing spiritual direction with someone, I will give him or her a quote to memorize or at least to copy down and take with them. I ask them to let the quotation be what they think about as the settle into some quiet time with God. Here is a quote from Abraham Lincoln that I often give people. They have told me that it has born much fruit in their meditation, so I want to offer it to you:

"A man watches his pear tree day after day, impatient for the ripening of the fruit. Let him attempt to force the process, and he may spoil both fruit and tree. But let him patiently wait, and the ripe fruit at length falls into his lap."

Is there someone or some situation in your life right now that needs your patience? Perhaps the time has come for you to be calm and to wait.

February

February 1
Like a Fox

I was recently having breakfast with a friend of mine who is an insurance salesman. In the course of our conversation that morning, I asked him about his work. I said, "Isn't it difficult to sell people insurance these days?" He just laughed at me and said, "A good salesman sees every prospect as a wonderful challenge. I enjoy sales because I enjoy sizing up a customer and discovering what the key to understanding that potential customer might be. A good salesman, is an observant student of human nature. If you know people, you will be a great salesman." Then after a pause, he quietly added, "It is really so much fun to see if people respond to the story, I present them about me and about what I am selling."

Finally, I asked him to give me an example of what he meant. He said, "Let me give you an example of what I mean by the story I present about me and what I am selling; "A young salesman walked up to the receptionist and asked to see the company's sales manager. Ushered into the office, he said, "I don't suppose you want to buy any life insurance, do you?"

"No," replied the sales manager curtly.

"I didn't think so," said the salesman dejectedly, getting up to leave. "Wait a minute," said the sales manager. "I want to talk to you." The salesman sat down again, looking very nervous and confused.

"I train salesmen," said the sales manager, "and you're the worst I've seen in a really long time! You'll never sell anything until you show some semblance of confidence. You had better learn to accentuate the positive. Now, because you're obviously new at this, I want to help you out by buying a hundred-thousand-dollar policy!"

After the sales manager had signed on the dotted line, he said helpfully, " Now, young man, one thing you'll have to do is develop a few standard organized sales talks. You know, talks that allow you to manipulate potential customers' egos so that they end up buying from you when they really don't need insurance in the first place!"

"Oh, yes, I know that. My dad taught me that and I have," replied the salesman, smiling. "This is my standard organized sales talk for sales managers."

When my friend had finished telling that story, I remarked about how impressed I was by his understanding of human nature and how to appeal to it.

His reply has stayed with me. He said, "I think every truly good person wants to help out someone who appears to be struggling to do something. I believe that most people are really good at heart. As a good salesman, I have to know how to appeal to that goodness."

I told him I was impressed by his wisdom. He laughed. Then he said, "I often let people think that I am dumb. That's not too difficult. They may think I am dumb, but I prefer to think of myself as dumb, dumb, like a fox! Foxes always get their prey!"

February 2
A Simple Solution

If a friend of yours came to you troubled by family relationships and they were seeking advice from you, what would you say to them? You may feel unqualified to give advice, but there you are with someone you care about who is looking for help. Do you have any "golden rules" that you live by which could be of help to others?

I knew an old priest who was like a kind old grandfather to the members of his congregation. Parishioners flocked to him to get his advice, especially when they had family disputes or heart-breaking divisions. He had what he called his "simple solution," which was a short "saying" that he would ask them to write down and then spend time reflecting on it.

Here is his simple solution: "When you have a talking mouth, you have no listening ears. When you have listening ears, you have no talking mouth. Think about this carefully. Does my situation need a talking mouth or listening ears?"

Would that old priest's "simple solution" be the kind of advice, you might give a friend or loved one if they came to you for your good counsel? Would that simple solution be something, you could apply to your own life? Why not spend some time with the old priest's words and see where they take you?

February 3
What Are You Doing?

Here is a question that spiritual masters often ask people when they come for direction or instruction: do you know what you are doing? Spiritual guides ask this question because very often people do so many things so quickly and intensely that they really lose sight of what they are doing. A simple question like, "What are you doing?" can often bring them to their senses. It reminds me of a story. When you finish reading it, ask yourself, "What am I doing?"

A wise, modern, spiritual master would often say, "When you eat, just eat. When you read the newspaper, just read the newspaper. Don't do anything other than what you are doing." These words sounded very wise to the man's students, who tried to take them to heart and follow them. The students repeated the phrase, "Don't do anything other than what you are doing" repeatedly. They committed these words to memory and did their best to live by them.

This was fine until something rather surprising happened one day. Several of the man's students were quite taken aback when they saw him reading the newspaper while he was eating. Confused, one student approached his master and a bit sheepishly asked him if this did not contradict his teachings.

The master looked at the student for what seemed like a very long time. Finally, the master said, "When you eat and read the newspaper, just eat and read the newspaper!"

February 4
A Drop of Water

I once attended a class on meditation. The first thing the teacher did was tell us a story that he said came from a Zen master who had opened his eyes and seen how to live a truly spiritual life.

According to this story, the Zen master asked a young student to bring him a pail of water to cool his bath. The student brought the water, and after cooling the bath, threw the remaining few drops of water out on the ground. Having finished his chore, the student made his way out when the master held up his finger and said to the boy, "Think. You could have watered the temple plants with those few drops you have thrown away. Those few drops of water, small as they were, could have brought new life to those plants."

All at once, in a flash of insight, the young student understood the spiritual in a way he had never known until that exact moment. He changed his name to Tekisui, which means drop of water, and lived to become a wise and great spiritual master himself.

When our teacher finished telling the story, one of the students asked him, "So, what does that mean for us?" The teacher replied, "You will find God not so much in the big events and questions of life as you will in the small drops of experience that will bring you to life in God.
Savor the small events and the small people of life. The greatest things you will ever see and do will be in the small things you do with love."

February 5
Are You Ready?

I have a story for you that someone gave me recently. The person who gave me the story told me they liked it because it reminded him of how precious time is, that we should never waste it and always use it wisely.

As the person handed me a copy of the story he said, "I just lost a really good friend to cancer. I had not seen him in years, so his death came as a shock. I wish I had had a warning or something." We sat and talked for quite a long time. When we finished, he told me that I should pass the story on to others, and I assured him that I would. Here it is:

"There was once a man who was always afraid of death. He was afraid that death would suddenly overtake him and find him unprepared, and he just could not bear the thought of death sneaking up on him. To his great surprise, one day Death himself showed up in his office.

"Have you come to carry me off?" the man said in a trembling voice.

"Oh no, it is not your time yet. I just came to meet the man that everyone tells me is so frightened of me. Why are you so afraid of me?" Death asked him.

"Because I am afraid that you will come when I am not prepared and not ready to go. I am afraid that you will sneak up and pounce on me and carry me away!"

Death laughed. That laughter did not make the man feel any better. In fact, Death's laughter made him even more frightened. Then Death said, "Perhaps we can come to some agreement."

That is exactly what they did. The man gladly made a bargain with the Grim Reaper. According to the agreement, death promised that he would give the man clear, repeated notices before he would come.

Years later, however, unannounced and altogether unexpectedly, Death did appear to the man to demand his life.

"How could you break your pledge?" the man protested bitterly. "You sent me no warnings. You said you would send me clear and repeated notices. I have had no notices from you!"

Slowly the skeletal figure of Death turned toward him and replied, "But how about your failing eyesight, your dimmed sense of hearing, your gray and thinning hair, your lost teeth, your wrinkled face, your bent body, your dwindling physical strength, and your weakened memory? Were these not clear and repeated notices and truly unmistakable warnings? I sent each one as a reminder that time is short, it takes its toll, and it is very precious. Have you spent your time wisely? Were you too preoccupied to pay attention? Are you prepared for me now?"

The questions that Death asks in the story above are questions he could very well put to you. How would you answer?

February 6
The Look

Years ago, I went to our cathedral to hear a talk given by Mother Teresa. As she spoke of her work with the abandoned people of Calcutta, she told us about how she often sits with each person she finds on the street, comforts them with kind words, and then says the Prayer of St. Francis with them. She told us that the simple words of that prayer brought great peace and comfort to those who were experiencing such terrible suffering.

As she spoke, a great and profound quiet settled over the audience. Mother Teresa looked up and around the room. She did not interrupt the quiet but simply smiled. Just as she was about to speak, someone spoke out and asked, "Mother Teresa, when you are alone with God and when you pray, what do you say to God?"

She said, "I don't talk, I listen."

Then someone else in the crowd asked, "What does God say to you?"

Mother Teresa replied, "He doesn't talk. He listens. In our listening, we are one. You may not understand this; and if you don't understand that, I can't explain it to you."

No one asked any more questions. There was a minute or two of silence and Mother Teresa bowed humbly, thanked everyone, and then left the podium.

Her comments reminded me of some of the teaching of another famous Teresa, St. Teresa of Avila. She taught her sisters that in prayer there is a place of union, of communion, that goes beyond human language. She called it the prayer of "the look." What she meant was that, although this kind of prayer has no words, much is communicated by looking at one another. We look at God and God looks at us.

February 7
Wising Up

Have you ever beaten yourself up because of the mistakes you have made in the past? Many people find it difficult to forgive themselves when they have failed, yet, failure is part of life. Very few can get through life without some failures, so it is important to know what to do with mistakes, errors, and failures.

When I think about failures or mistakes, I often remember the story of a truly wise man who knew just what to do with such things. According to the story, that wise man, an old country doctor, was honored one day with a banquet. That old doc was much loved by many because he was extraordinarily kind, and also for his many years of service and his wise counsel. Many people had benefitted from his keen insight, his gentle medical care, and his sense of humor. People came from all over to seek him out, to get his advice and pick his brain for ideas.

The good doctor gave a speech after dinner that was filled with very practical wisdom. The crowd gathered there hung on his every word. Finally, there was time for questions.

"Dr. Barker," a young man asked, "how did you get to be so very wise?"

The doctor answered, "Well, I suppose it came a little bit at a time over the years. For one thing, I have good judgment. How did I get good judgment? Well now, good judgment can come from experience," he continued. "And experience -- well, that comes from having bad judgment. There is nothing quite like bad judgement to get your attention. Once you are paying attention, then you start wising up!"

February 8
Light and Water

A severe storm struck a small town in the Midwest, leveling many houses and destroying a local greenhouse. The owners of that greenhouse knew that they had no choice but to start over and build a new greenhouse. The owners hired the best people to plan and build a state-of-the-art structure. The results were outstanding. There was never a more beautiful building than that new greenhouse.

The family that owned the greenhouse held a dedication ceremony during which the local Catholic priest walked through the building, blessing it with holy water. When the blessing was finished, the owners unveiled a beautiful bronze plaque that contained these words:

"Plants grow best when we pay attention to them. That means watering, touching them, putting them in places where they will receive good light. They need people like us around them to notice if they are drooping from lack of water or if they are looking particularly happy in the sunlight. The more attention a plant receives, the better it will grow. Let us all make paying attention to the plants growing here our way of living."

What difference would it make if we had such a plaque posted in our homes that reminded us to pay attention to the people around us? Such a plaque could be a real blessing because we all need to be noticed in the same way. If we notice a family member or friend is drooping, perhaps we can pay some special attention to him or her.

All of us need someone to care about how we are and to take the time to listen to us. We can share and deepen someone's happiness by simply noticing and talking about it. We help the people around us to grow by listening to them on their droopy days as well as on their bright days. People need this as much as plants need light and water.

February 9
Within

There is a story among the Sioux that their holy men use to teach the young about growing into the realm of spiritual things:

The Creator gathered all of Creation except for humanity and said, "I want to hide something from the humans until they are ready for it. It is the realization that they create their own reality. If they are miserable, it will be because they have made themselves so by their choices. If they are happy, they will be so because they choose to be in harmony with me."

The creatures thought hard about this for quite some time., then some of them began to offer suggestions to the Creator.

The eagle said, "Give it to me, I will take it to the moon."

The Creator said, "No. One day they will go there and find it."

The salmon said, "I will bury it on the bottom of the ocean."

"No. They will go there too."

The buffalo said, "I will bury it on the Great Plains."

The Creator said, "They will cut into the skin of the Earth and find it even there."

It was at this point that Grandmother Mole, who lives in the breast of Mother Earth and who has no physical eyes, but only sees with spiritual eyes, said, "Put it inside of them."

And the Creator said, "Ah, yes, it is done! From now on, when they are ready, I will tell them to look within.

February 10
Thistles and Flowers

Here is something to consider. When your time on earth has ended and you have peacefully died, what is it that you would want people to remember about you? I have been thinking about this for some time now because in reading a biography of Abraham Lincoln, I came across his thoughts on the matter. Evidently, he had spent a great deal of time thinking about what he hoped people would remember about him. Here is what he said:

"Die when I may, I want it said by those who knew me best that I always plucked a thistle and planted a flower where I thought a flower would grow."

I am sure that Abraham Lincoln plucked many thistles and planted quite a few flowers in his day. I think we have all benefited in some way from his striving to do so. So take a moment to think about it: How do you want to be remembered?

February 11
Life's Battles

In Japan, there is an ancient story that is part of Japanese military tradition. It is taught to those training to be officers. According to the story, during a momentous battle a Japanese general decided to attack even though his army was greatly outnumbered. It looked to everyone that the battle was all but lost. The general was confident they would win, but his men were filled with doubt and certain that they would lose.

On the way to the battle, the general made them stop at a religious shrine. After praying with the men, the general took out a coin and said, "I shall now toss this coin. If it is heads, we shall win. If it is tails, we shall lose. God will now reveal the future."

He threw the coin into the air and all watched intently as it landed. It was heads.

The soldiers were so overjoyed and filled with confidence that they vigorously attacked the enemy and were victorious.

After the battle, one of the lieutenants remarked to the general, "No one can change what God wants."
"Quite right," the general replied as he showed the lieutenant the coin -- which had heads on both sides.

Do you suppose the general's army would have been as successful in battle had they not stopped at the shrine to pray or had not seen the results of the coin toss? This story can certainly serve as a great reminder for us all of the importance of how we choose to see the world around us. What we choose to see around us and how we choose to see ourselves has a major role to play in the outcome of so many important battles in life.

February 12
Fretting?

Do you ever worry? Most people worry at times, yet others seem to worry quite a bit.

Recently a young college student asked to speak with me. He said he needed to talk because he wanted to find peace of mind enough so that he could at least get a good night's sleep.

I asked him what he thought about as he was trying to fall asleep. Without a pause he blurted out, "All of my troubles!" He was literally shaking with worry. I said I had one question for him. He said, "Are you going to ask me to list my troubles?" I said no, then asked, "How many of those troubles of yours have ever actually happened?"

I asked him that question because a priest mentor of mine once told a story about Winston Churchill when I had asked the old priest about my troubles. My mentor told me that Churchill was a very big worrier who would fret over many things. He told me that the famous Brit had at one time been nearly overwhelmed by his worries. Had a friend not helped Churchill through it, he would have been lost.

My mentor added, "Churchill was asked to help a friend overcome some anxiety and worry. In response, the prime minister wrote to the friend listing some of his own trouble, and then added this statement: 'When I look back on all these worries of mine, I remember the story of the old man who said on his deathbed that he had had a lot of trouble in his life, most of which never happened. Stop fretting, your troubles may never happen.'"

February 13
Wealthy and Blessed?

Do you consider yourself wealthy or even blessed? Most folks would not see themselves as being wealthy, yet they probably are better off than most of the world.

Here are some rather interesting facts to consider:
If you woke up this morning with more health than illness, then you are more blessed than the over two million or so people in the world who will not survive this day.
If you have never experienced the danger of being in battle, the loneliness and isolation of being in prison, the agony of torture, or the pangs of starvation, then you are ahead of the almost 500 million people who have experienced these things.
If you have food in the refrigerator, clothes on your back, a roof overhead, and just a simple place to sleep, then you are richer than 75% of our world.
If you have money in the bank, in your wallet, and some spare change in a dish somewhere, then you are among the top 8% of the world's wealthy.
If you can read even a little, you are more blessed than over two billion people in the world who cannot read at all.

So, considering just these few facts, are you a wealthy and even blessed person?

February 14
Change

When I lived as a hermit in the desert of Israel, I learned many things. The desert experience taught me that in every change you experience in life, there will be times when you will wonder if you can endure it. Yet I learned from the desert fathers that we all must learn to accept and expect changes in life.

You will eventually learn that facing each difficulty one by one is not as hard as you think. It is when you do not deal with change that it can come back to cause you great harm.

Change is sometimes very painful, but it teaches us that we can endure and even become stronger through change. Living with and trying to understand the changes that life brings will teach you something very profound, that everything which comes into your life has a purpose.

The outcome of the changes we face and endure will show itself in the actions we take. It pays to be wise enough to be willing to endure and face the challenges of change that will come your way.

February 15
What the Bear Said

If someone were to ask you what to look for in a good friend, how would you answer that question? I was asked that question a few years ago when I was invited to give a talk at a high school religious retreat.

I spent a lot of time praying about what I should say at the retreat. In the end I just decided to tell the retreatants an old story that I call, "What the Bear Said." When I studied philosophy, I found that teachers in ancient Greece had used a version of this same story. Perhaps you might find the story helpful as you choose friends. Here is that story:

Two men were traveling together, when a bear suddenly met them on their path. One of them climbed up quickly into a tree and concealed himself in the branches. The other, seeing that he was about to be attacked, fell flat on the ground. When the bear came up to him, felt him with his snout, and smelled him all over, he held his breath and played dead as much as he could. The bear soon left, for it is said that bears will not touch a dead body.

When he was quite gone, the other traveler descended from the tree, and making fun of his friend, inquired what it was the bear had "whispered" in his ear. "He gave me this advice," his companion replied: "Never travel with or keep a friend who deserts you when you are most in danger."

February 16
Do You See Where You Are?

A young man went to a holy hermit out in the desert of the Holy Land and asked him, "Abba, I have been told that you are a holy man and that you can teach me how to be close to God. I have come to ask you to teach me."

The hermit replied, "I will share what I have learned on my journey with God, but it will take quite some time for me to do so."

"I am willing to do whatever you ask of me and I will do it for as long as it takes," the young man responded.

The hermit was pleased by the young man's response, so he began training him right away. "I will give you a question to ponder for two weeks," the hermit said.

"And what is your question?" the young man asked.

"For the next two weeks, every morning, noon, and night I want you to ask yourself this one simple question: 'What can I do to attain God?'"

The young man wrote the question down so as not to forget it, and then left the hermit. When the two weeks were completed, the young man returned to the hermit.

"What have you learned in these past two weeks?" asked the holy man.

"Not a thing!' replied the young man.

"I see where you are, then," the hermit replied. Then he said, "I will give you another question to ask yourself for two weeks' time: 'What can I do to make the sun rise?'"

"I am willing to do whatever you ask of me, and I will do it for as long as it takes," the young man responded.

Two weeks later the young man returned to the hermit. "What have you learned in these past two weeks?" asked the holy man.

"Not a thing!" replied the young man.

"Once again, I see where you are, then," the hermit said.

The young man was not happy at this response. "Abba, for a month now I have been doing nothing but asking myself two questions that have gotten me nowhere! Why aren't you teaching me holy sayings or methods of prayer? What good are these two silly questions?" the young man asked indignantly.

The hermit calmly replied, "To make sure you're awake when the sun rises, of course. What can you do to attain God? Nothing. What can you do to make the sun rise? Nothing. What can you do? Be awake! Do you see where you are?"

February 17
Are You?

I attended a prayer service in which the rabbi told a story about two brothers who went to their rabbi to settle a longstanding feud. These two brothers just could not get along. After a long afternoon of heated discussions and fierce argumentation, the rabbi got the two to reconcile their differences and shake hands.

Feeling good about all the hard work he done that afternoon, as they were about to leave, the rabbi asked each one to make a wish for the other in honor of the Jewish New Year.

The first brother turned to the other and said, "I wish you what you wish me."

At that, the second brother threw up his hands and said, "See, rabbi, he's starting up again!"

The rabbi concluded his story by telling us that just saying you are reconciled and shaking hands does not actually mean you are reconciled. "Only when you have truly chosen to no longer find hurt where none is intended, and once you have stopped trying to win rather than understand will you ever truly be reconciled with those you love," he said.

A kind of silence fell over the crowd as we considered what he had said to us. The rabbi then looked around and asked us one question: "Are you truly reconciled with those you love?"

So, I ask you, are you truly reconciled with those you love?

February 18
Gandhi Wondered

I have recently been re-reading the autobiography of Mahatma Gandhi. In his book, Gandhi wrote that during his student days, he read the Gospels seriously and was set on converting to Christianity. He was a Hindu, but he believed that in the teachings of Jesus he could find the solution to the caste system that was dividing the people of India.

One Sunday he decided to attend services at a nearby Christian church and talk to the minister about becoming a Christian. When he entered the church building, however, the usher refused to give him a seat and suggested that he go worship with "his own people."

Gandhi left the church and never returned. He said, "If Christians have caste differences also, I might as well remain a Hindu." That usher's prejudice not only betrayed Gandhi but it also betrayed Jesus.

Although the Mahatma never became a Christian, he did lead the people of India through a passive resistance that ended in their liberation from British domination. Gandhi said that he based his methods on the person and activities of Jesus. He told his followers that if they followed the way of peace and freedom that Jesus taught, certain things were sure to happen. He said, "First they laugh at you, then they fight you, then you win."

Gandhi often wondered how many Christians have ever really tried to live the way of peace and freedom that Jesus taught.

February 19
Be Kind

One of the famous stories that rabbis often tell their young Hebrew students is about God and his friend Abraham. This traditional Hebrew story is meant to illustrate how God often uses us to help him do his work.

According to the story, Abraham was sitting outside his tent one evening when he saw an 80-year-old man, weary from age and journey, coming toward him. Abraham, a very hospitable man, rushed out, greeted him, and invited him into his tent. There he washed the old man's feet and gave him food and drink.

The old man immediately began eating without saying any prayer or blessing. Now this made Abraham a little miffed, so Abraham asked him, "Don't you worship God?"

The old traveler replied, "Hell no! I worship fire only and reverence no other god."

When he heard this, Abraham became incensed, grabbed the old man by the shoulders, and threw him out of his tent into the cold night air.

Now when it had been a long time since the old man had departed, God called on his friend Abraham and asked where the stranger was. Abraham replied, "I forced him out because he did not worship you."

God answered, "I have suffered him these eighty years although he dishonors me. I was hoping that by being with you that he might be convinced to believe in me. I've endured him for 80 years. Could you not endure him one night?"

The rabbis conclude this story by telling their students to always be kind because God might need you to tend to someone he wants to befriend.

February 20
Broken Windows

Do you ever worry about crime? Do you ever think about the state of your neighborhood or city when it comes to crime rates? I think many people do worry about these things.

I have been thinking about this lately because I was reading an article the other day about how to minimize crime in neighborhoods. The article said that many years ago, two criminologists, James Q. Wilson and George Kelling, formulated a theory about how a neighborhood or community slowly gives in to increasing crime rates. They called it the "broken window" theory.

Wilson and Kelling said that crimes are more likely to be committed in areas where it appears that the residents have lowered their standards and no longer care about their community. If a window is broken and left unrepaired, people start to assume that no one cares about maintaining that building. More windows will get broken. As the building becomes more dilapidated, there is a growing assumption of lawlessness by the residents. People assume that they can lower their standards of behavior, because no one will notice or care. This is when a neighborhood begins to go bad.

It occurred to me after I read that article that the "broken window" theory could also apply to our spiritual life. What are the broken windows in your life that seem to multiply and break down your relationship with God?

February 21
What You Owe

Here is a question for your meditation: "Do I have any debts?" This story from the teaching tradition of Islam may give you new insights.

A Hodja (teacher) was selling olives at the market and business was slow. He called to a woman who was passing by and tried to encourage her to buy some olives. She shook her head and told him she did not have any money with her.

"No problem," the Hodja grinned. "You can pay me later."

She still looked hesitant, so he offered her one to taste. "Oh no, I can't, I'm fasting," she responded.

"Fasting? But Ramadan was 6 months ago!"

"Yes, well, I missed a day and I'm making it up now. Go ahead and give me a kilo of the black olives."

"Forget it!" shouted the Hodja. "If it took you 6 months to pay back a debt you owed Allah, who knows when you'll get around to paying me!"

Do you have any debts? If you stop to think about it, every one of us owes God a great deal. When was the last time you got around to paying back what you owe to God? Are there people in your life who are still waiting for you to pay back what you owe them?

February 22
Sharing with the Stranger

When a stranger comes to you and asks for your help, are you ever hesitant to do so? Some people say they are hesitant to help when someone asks because they are afraid the person may be a con artist attempting to steal from them. Others say that they don't like being "pressured" to give, and so they refuse most requests from strangers. One person said that they do not help strangers because strangers simply frighten them, so they just avoid them.

When I was living as a hermit in Israel, I remember meeting strangers when I was out walking in the desert. They were always very friendly, and often offered me water, fruit, or nuts "to help you on your journey," they would say. When I would thank them for their generosity the response was always the same: "If any of us is going to thrive here in the desert we all must share what we have."

A story from the deserts of Africa tells of a Bedouin who was walking with his dog in the desert, carrying jugs of water on his shoulders, crying pitifully as he went along. When asked by someone why he was crying, he replied, "Because my dog is dying of thirst."

"Why don't you give him some of your water, then?" the questioner asked.

"Because I might need the water myself."

The questioner grew sad and said, "Then you are both doomed because failing to share leads to death for everybody."

February 23
Camels

Do you ever get mad at God? When you pray for something and it doesn't happen the way you asked God to do it, are you angry with him? Have you ever had a bad day and then spent the evening grumbling against the Almighty? Perhaps a story from Islam may be of help to you as it has been for me.

According to this tale, there was once a man who was on his way back home from market with his camel. Because he'd had a good day, he decided to stop at a mosque along the road and offer his thanks to God. He left his camel outside and went in with his prayer mat and spent several hours offering thanks to Allah, praying and promising that he'd be a good Muslim, help the poor, and be an upstanding pillar of his community. He concluded by asking Allah to continue to be good to him.

Having said all he had come to say, the man concluded his prayers and got up to leave. When he emerged, it was already dark. Lo and behold, he realized that his camel was gone!

The man immediately flew into a violent temper and shook his fist at the sky, yelling: "You traitor, Allah! How could you do this to me? I put all my trust in you and then you go and stab me in the back like this!"

A passing Sufi holy man heard the man yelling and chuckled to himself. "Listen," he said to the man, "Trust God, but you know, you have to remember to tie up your camel. Remember your camels!"

February 24
Second-Guessing God

Sometimes horrible things happen to us and we just cannot understand why. We look for reasons, but they seem to elude us. I remember once speaking to an old priest, a mentor of mine, about this very thing. After he had listened to my tale of woe, he tried to reassure me and then said that I should listen to the story he was about to tell me:

An ailing king summoned a physician, whom he had heard was very wise about the body, the mind, and the soul, to come and treat his illness. The wise old doctor refused to come.

The king had his soldiers seize the physician and bring him to the palace. He said, "I have brought you here because I am suffering from a strange paralysis that no one has been able to cure. If you cure me, I will reward you. If not, I will kill you."

The wise and holy physician said, "In order to treat you, I need complete privacy."

So the king sent everyone out of the room. Then the physician took out a knife and said, "Now I shall take my revenge for your threatening me." He advanced on the king wielding the knife.

Terrified, the king jumped up and ran around the room, forgetting his paralysis in his need to escape the seemingly crazed physician.

The wise yet holy physician fled the palace one step ahead of the guards. The king never realized that he was cured by the only method that could have been effective. The wise doctor knew this, of course.

When my priest mentor had finished telling the story, he added, "Sometimes God uses the horrors of life to scare us enough to get us moving in the right direction. Remember that and stop second-guessing God!"

February 25
Cake

Here is a teaching from a great Zen master about the importance of living in the present moment. As you begin this reading, as you begin this day, at this time, be present to only what is before you. Here is the teaching:

A Zen master was very close to death. His students brought him a piece of his favorite cake. They circled the master's deathbed and watched him eating his cake. As the dying master was nibbling on the cake, one of the students asked the master, "Do you have a final message for us?"

The dying master feebly replied, "Yes. This cake is delicious." Then he smiled and died."

Will you be able to truly "taste the cake" that this day offers you?

February 26
The True Value

A certain young man was always speaking against those who believe in and worship one God. He would berate believers and make fun of them. This disturbed everyone. One day, after the young man had belittled a believer, a local holy woman took the ring from her finger and gave it to the man.

"Now, I want you to take this to the market and sell it for a dollar," she said.

The young man took it to the market and tried to sell it, but not even one person would give him more than 10 cents for it. The young man shrugged his shoulders and quickly returned to holy woman with the news that the ring was worthless.

The woman said, "Now, I want you to take the ring to the jewelers and see what they price it at." The jewelers carefully examined the ring and priced it at $7,000 dollars.

The young man ran back to the holy woman with the news about the great value of her ring. She looked at the young man and said to him, "You know as much about believing in one God as those people in the marketplace knew about this ring. It is time for you to discover the true value of faith."

February 27
Now They Understood

Some very strict yet puzzled Jews went to see their rabbi. "Rebbe, we are puzzled. It says in the Talmud that we must thank God as much for the bad days as for the good. How can that be? What would our gratitude mean if we gave it equally for the good and the bad? It is confusing to us and we need an answer."

The rabbi replied, "Go to the rabbi in our neighboring town, he is a good friend of mine and he will have an answer for you."

The puzzled Jews undertook the journey. Arriving in next town, they looked everywhere for the rabbi. At last, they came to the poorest street of the city. There, crowded between two small houses, they found a tiny shack, falling down with age.

When they entered, they saw the rabbi sitting at a bare table, reading a volume by the light of the only small window.

"Welcome, strangers!" he said. "Please pardon me for not getting up; I have hurt my leg. Would you like food? I have some bread. And there is water!"

"No. We have come only to ask you a question. Our rabbi, your friend, told us you might help us understand: Why do our sages tell us to thank God as much for the bad days as for the good? We are puzzled by this teaching."

"The rabbi sent you to me, did he? He proceeded to laugh hysterically. "Me? I have no idea why your rabbi sent you to me." He shook his head in puzzlement. "You must understand, I have never had a bad day. Every day God has given to me has been filled with miracles. I open my eyes, I see, I give thanks!"

It was at this point that the puzzled Jews were no longer puzzled. Now they understood.

February 28
Real or Fake?

Years ago, some students of the famous rabbi Baal Shem Tov came to him one day with a question. "Every year we travel here to learn from you. Nothing could make us stop doing that. However, we have learned of a man in our own town who claims to be holy and of God, a true righteous one. If he is genuine, we would love to profit from his wisdom. But can you tell us how we will know if he is a fake?"

The Baal Shem Tov looked at his very sincere disciples. "You must test him by asking him a question," he said, then paused. "Tell him that you have had difficulty with stray thoughts during prayer. Tell him that you try to think only of your holy intentions as you pray, but other thoughts come into your minds. Tell him that you have tried many methods not to be troubled by them. Finally, ask him *the* way to stop such thoughts from entering your minds."

The Baal Shem Tov smiled. "If he has an answer, he is a fake."

February 29
Somewhere Else

One day in the synagogue, the rabbi was observing a group of his students as they prayed. When they were finished, he approached them with a hearty greeting, "Shalom aleichem!"

They looked startled and a bit shocked to hear their rabbi pronounce the greeting that traditionally is only given after returning from a long journey. "But rabbi," they said, "we have not been anywhere!"

The rabbi walked among them to shake hands with them, as though they really were travelers arriving in a new town. He said, "From your faces it was obvious to me that your thoughts were in the grain market far from here or in one of the local bars or cafes. None of you were actually here while you said the prayers, so I am glad to welcome you back once I got your attention and brought you back."

When you were last in church, were you there or was your mind and heart actually somewhere else?

March

March 1
He Will Let You Find Him

Nearly two centuries ago a renowned holy man named Rabbi Barukh told his disciples a story that he said was essential for their spiritual growth and development.

The rabbi said that his grandson David was once playing hide and seek with another boy. He hid himself well and waited for his playmate to find him. When he had waited for a very long time, he came out of his hiding place, but the other child was nowhere to be seen. It began to dawn on David that his friend had not looked for him from the very beginning. This made him cry. He continued to cry as he ran to his grandfather and complained about his mean friend who had hurt him so terribly.

Tears then brimmed down Rabbi Barukh's cheeks and he said: "God has told me that he says the same thing: 'I hide, but no one wants to seek me.'"

The rabbi told his grandson David that he must seek God every day of his life, because on some special days, God will actually let you find him!

March 2
Is It Time?

I recently read about a psychologist who was asked to do an evaluation of a top executive who had been acting oddly. The CEO was doing something everyone thought was destructive, and the Board of Directors wanted to intervene before his behavior reflected badly on the company or destroyed his home life.

The man's executive assistant, who kept his calendar, had noticed that every Wednesday afternoon, this hard-charging, hard-working man would leave his office for a 3:00 P.M. appointment, and he did not return until Thursday morning. He never told anyone where he went, but because the executive assistant had observed him entering a nearby apartment building, it was assumed that he was visiting a mistress.

The psychologist made an appointment with the executive for the evaluation. When the psychologist explained why he was there, the man smiled, then broke out into a full belly laugh.

The executive explained his weekly habit quite easily to the psychologist. Inside Apartment 2B waited not a young mistress, but a professional woodworking shop that he had set up, where he labored happily every Wednesday to turn out furniture and knickknacks. The executive explained that he kept this special appointment with himself faithfully because it was his way of recovering from the demands and pressures he lived with day in and day out. He needed this chance to be alone with himself, to be creative, to work with his hands and to engage in an activity that took his mind far from the job and focused his attention in a calming way.

After the evaluation, the psychologist made his report to the Board of Directors. He pronounced the CEO to be eminently healthy and a model for others. He concluded his report by saying that the company was truly blessed to have such a man at the helm and added a postscript: "You can expect big things to come from the calm, quiet man who is obviously in touch with himself and with his Creator. You would all do well to be more like him."

How do you cope with the day-to-day pressures and stresses of life? Do you ever "make an appointment with yourself" to be calm, recharge, and recover from what life is throwing at you these days? Is it time that you did so?

March 3
Who Are You?

I recently read an amusing story. Back in 1934, the famous Cunard line of ships was getting ready to name its great, new ocean liner, but the committee in charge of naming the vessel was quarreling over the name. Finally, they voted and decided it should be named after Queen Elizabeth I. The committee said it was only fitting since undoubtedly, she was the greatest queen in the long history of England.

Using a royal name required permission from the royal family, and a high official from Cunard was sent to have an audience with King George V. When the King asked what the committee needed from him, the company official said, "Your Majesty, we need your permission concerning the naming of a ship. We would like to name the ship after England's greatest queen.

"Well," said King George, "I shall have to ask her."

The company official immediately answered the king saying, "Yes, Your Majesty, please tell your wife that the ship will be named the Queen Mary!"

There was no one more surprised than the naming committee when they read in the paper that the newest ship of the Cunard line would be called the Queen Mary! They had not taken into account that in King George's mind, the greatest queen in England's long history was certainly his own wife. No matter how great any other queen could be, none would be greater than the love of his life.

If you were to consider who the greatest people in the short history of your life were, whom would you name? Who is it that has had the greatest influence on you for good? Are there people who have had a bad influence on you? Who are the people who have had a hand in forming you into the person you are today?

March 4
Reading John Steinbeck

Not too long ago I got a telephone call in the middle of the night. It was from a college student who was thinking about ending his life. He called to say that he felt like such a loser that he thought he would never find happiness. He asked if I could see anything in him that was good at all. I said a quick prayer to the Holy Spirit to give me the right words for this guy because I could hear the desperation in his voice.

I felt a calm come over me, and I just asked the young man if I could pray for him. He said yes. As I began to pray, he began to cry. As I finished praying, an image came to me that I felt God wanted me to share with him.

The image that came to me was from a story that John Steinbeck had written called "The Pearl". In the story a man finds a tremendously beautiful pearl. The problem is that while the man knows it is a valuable pearl, he also notices that there is a tiny flaw on it. He thinks to himself that if he could just remove that tiny flaw, the pearl may not only be beautiful and valuable, it would be perfect as well. So, the man begins to peel off the top layer of the pearl. After he peeled off that first layer, he noticed that the flaw was still there. Thinking the flaw would disappear if took off the next layer, he removed that layer and a third one as well. The flaw still remained. He continued taking off layer after layer until finally he had no pearl left at all. The flaw was gone, but so was the pearl.

When I finished telling that story, the college student screamed into the phone, "That pearl is me! I am completely screwed up; I am one big flaw!" I said, "No, you are not one big screwed up flaw, you are really a very valuable pearl that happens to be human and therefore imperfect. No one is without a flaw or two, what makes us who we are is both our good qualities and even our flaws."

When I had finished speaking there was just silence on the other end of the phone. Then he said, "So you are telling me that I have to stop picking myself apart?" "Exactly!" I said.

An hour later that young man had calmed down and decided not to take his life. Before he hung up, he said, "I guess I should read John Steinbeck."

March 5
Accept the Pardon

I read an interesting thing the other day when I was flipping through an historical novel. According to that novel, back in the 1830s there was a man by the name of George Wilson, who was convicted of robbing the U.S. Mail. In those days it was a capital offense to rob the mail service, and he was sentenced to be hanged.

On hearing about the case, President Andrew Jackson issued a pardon for Wilson, thinking that the sentence was far too severe. That should have been the end of the matter, but it turned out there was more to come. Although the President of the United States had issued a pardon to Mr. Wilson, the man refused to accept it.

The warden at the prison where George Wilson was being held did not know what he was supposed to do when the day of the execution arrived. And so, the case went back to court, and actually ended up at the U.S. Supreme Court. The matter went to Chief Justice John Marshall, who wrote the court's final decision.

The Chief Justice concluded that Wilson would have to be executed. "A pardon is a slip of paper," wrote Marshall, "the value of which is determined by the acceptance of the person to be pardoned. If it is refused, it is no pardon. George Wilson must be hanged." That is how the case ended.

Evidently, George Wilson, although pardoned by the President of the United States, could not find a way to forgive himself. The burden of his guilt was so heavy for him to carry that death was his only way to be free of it.

Isn't that a sad story? Have you ever been unable to forgive yourself for some past sin or mistake? Do you know anyone who, like George Wilson, is unable to see beyond his or her past, and ends up lost forever?

It is important to remember that there is always pardon, forgiveness, and healing available to us from Jesus. With Jesus, there is no unforgiveable sin. We are always loved and cared for no matter how bad our sins may be. Jesus is always ready and willing to forgive us and heal us.

If you are feeling guilty or lost, please accept the pardon that Jesus wants you to have.

March 6
Need Glasses?

I saw a billboard the other day that advertised the services of a group of eye doctors. The sign had just one question, painted on it in blurred letters: "When was the last time you had your vision tested?"

You know, I almost ran off the road as I drove by that billboard because I wanted to check if the letters were really blurred or if I truly did need to have my eyes examined! I laughed as I got my car back in control. That sign was very effective. It got me to check my vision.

Later in the day, when I was meeting with a group of people who wanted to plan for the future of our parish, I told them about that sign. I told them how I had almost crashed my car looking at the sign, and everyone laughed. Then someone spoke up, and looking around the room, said, "So, if we are going to plan for the future, shouldn't we "check our vision?"

That question got everyone thinking, and there was a long quiet pause in the conversation. One woman then told us about something she had just read:

Many years ago, an inventor had a daring vision for a better kind of watch. After working on his idea for some time and building a prototype, he decided to go to Switzerland, the world capital of watchmaking, to seek backing for the manufacture of his new design.

When the renowned Swiss watchmakers examined his invention, they said, "This is not a watch. It does not have hands to tell time. It just has little numbers. You have to have a big hand and a little hand to make a watch." When they opened the back, they were even more negative. "This thing doesn't even have gears or springs or jewels. It's just a lot of electronic parts. This is not a watch!" The Swiss watchmakers would have nothing to do with the man's invention.

The inventor then took his revolutionary idea to Japan where he found industrialists who weren't as sure as the Swiss watchmakers what made up a watch, and they agreed to manufacture his idea. Of course, as you know, the rest is history. As a result of the man's invention, most watches today are electronic and are made in the Asia instead of in the Alpine confederation.

Someone else in the group then quoted a biblical proverb that reads, "Where there is no vision, the people perish" (Proverbs 29:18). The person who spoke paused and looked around. When no one said anything, she added, "Without a vision, we have no future. We had better check our vision!"

When was the last time you checked your vision for life? Do you need some new spiritual glasses?

March 7
Complaining About the Noise

One day last week I remembered something from an education course I took in college. As part of the class we were asked by our facilitator to recall a teacher who influenced our lives.

One of the students in that class told us about a high school teacher who changed her life. A main highway ran next to the school along the side of the building where this teacher's classroom was located. The student said that traffic never seemed to stop throughout the day; sometimes it became quite loud, especially when emergency vehicles raced by. At the beginning of each class, the teacher would complain to the students about the noise from the traffic. The sirens from the emergency vehicles especially annoyed him, and he would even cuss a bit when there seemed to be too many.

Our college classmate continued her story: "One morning, the teacher same in and said he wanted to apologize to the class. We wondered why he needed to apologize to us. Then he told us that over that weekend, his pregnant wife had an emergency and went into premature labor. The teacher said that he never knew how beautiful a siren could sound until he heard one that was bringing help to his wife and unborn child. He said that the help the ambulance provided saved his wife's life and his baby's life, and told us, 'I want to apologize because I was listening to the noise instead of thinking about the lives. I will never hear a siren again and be indifferent.'"

The woman then said that her mom always told her to say a prayer whenever you hear a siren because it almost always means someone needs help. I remember my mom saying that to me when I was little, too, and since then I have continued to pray whenever I hear a siren.

The question this memory raised for me was a simple one. It is a question we probably should ask ourselves on a regular basis: "Do I hear the cries for help that may be coming my way, or do I just complain about the noise?"

March 8
The Hardest Kind of Work

Today I thought I would write something about work. As I began to think it, I thought of two very different people who commented on work. The first one was Martin Luther.

When I was studying Lutheran theology, I read an article that used a quotation from Martin Luther that has stuck with me over the years. Whenever I get a bit lazy or feel like I don't want to do the work that is before me, I think of Luther's wisdom. He said, "God had it in mind that we should work. We must remember that God cares for the birds of the sky. He gives every bird food, but he does not throw it into the nest!"

The second person I thought of when it comes to work was Kennan Wilson, the founder of the Holiday Inn chain. When people ask me about balancing work and home life, I usually laugh and quote Kennan Wilson. He said, "I believe to be successful, that you have to work at least half a day -- it doesn't make any difference which half, the first twelve hours or the last twelve hours." Isn't that a great quote? The problem is that many of us who live life that way end up being burned out in a very short time.

As I continued to think about work, I began to wonder what kind of work is the most difficult. There are many different answers to that question, but the one kind of work that we must all do from time to time is the one kind of work we all hate. What kind of work is that? It is simply this: waiting. We all hate to wait.

Why do you suppose we all hate to wait? One of the ancient Greek philosophers, I cannot remember which one it was, said that we hate to wait because when we wait, we have to admit there are some things that are not under our control. We try to kid ourselves into thinking that we are in control. We imagine that we are in charge of our own destinies. We convince ourselves that if we work hard enough, if we just concentrate, we can make life work. And many times, we can -- to a point.

There comes a time in our life when we realize that we all have to do the hard work of waiting. Some things cannot be hurried, things life grief, maturing, recuperation from surgery, or learning responsibility. These things cannot be rushed. You have to take your time.

I really do think that the hardest work we all have to do is the work of waiting. As a man by the name of John Claypool put it, "Let's face it, there are two kinds of reality in this world of ours. There are the things you have to work for, and there are the things you have to wait for."

Why not take some time today to consider slowing down a bit, to wait and see what God might be trying to give you?

March 9
A Deeper Place

Here is a story for you to consider, one that I have used in my prayer for some time. I think I first used it when I lived as a hermit in Israel. This little parable is a reminder that Jesus came to tell us to look inside ourselves and be ready to discover some marvelous things that God himself has put inside us. Why not take this story with you when you sit down for your prayer time? Let it lead you to a deeper place.

A beggar had been sitting by the side of the road for thirty years. One day a stranger walked by. "Spare some change?" mumbled the beggar.

"I have nothing to give you," said the stranger. Then he asked, "What's that you're sitting on?"

"Nothing," replied the beggar, "just an old box. I have been sitting on it for as long as I can remember."

"Ever look inside?" asked the stranger.

"No," said the beggar. "What's the point? There's nothing in there."

"Have a look inside," insisted the stranger. The beggar, reluctantly, managed to pry open the lid. With astonishment, disbelief, and elation, he saw that the box was filled with gold.

Remember, I am that stranger who has nothing to give you and who is telling you to look inside. Not inside any box, as in the parable, but somewhere even closer: inside yourself.

March 10
Seeing God Walk By

There is a story told among Zen monks, which may be of help to you in your meditation today. According to the story, a Zen monk saw a beautiful goose fly by, and he wanted to share this joy with his elder brother, who was walking beside him. Just at that moment, however, the other monk bent down to remove a pebble from his sandal. By the time he looked up, the goose had already flown by. He asked, "What did you want me to see?" but the younger monk could only remain silent.

Have you ever wanted to share a significant event with someone you love dearly, only to see by the look on their face that they cannot even begin to understand how you have been changed by it? At such times we realize, like the younger monk above, that there are no words that can adequately convey what we have seen or experienced. Silence may be the only response we can make.

After all, how can you put what God does into mere words? The change in you that takes place because of the experience may be the only sign of God's movement in our world. Perhaps our silence will open a loved one's eyes to begin to see God walk by.

March 11
A True Friend

In my reading this past week I came upon something that really touched my soul. What I read was written by a man who had lost three of his children in a tragic accident. The man described the horrors of losing his precious children and then described how people came to help him through his ordeal.

He said, "I was sitting there in my living room, torn apart by intense sadness. Some folks came from the church and talked to me of God's dealings and how all of this was God's will. They talked constantly about God things. I guess what they said was true, but I was unmoved by them. I just hoped that they would go home soon. They finally did, and that was a blessed relief. In the afternoon, an old friend came to call on me. He stayed for hours. Did not say much, just sat near me, listened when I spoke, gave me brief answers, said a simple prayer before he left. I was deeply moved and touched. I felt comforted. I hated to see him go. He is a true friend. I am blessed to have him."

March 12
A "Note" about Frustration

One of the most common human experiences that almost everyone can identify with is feeling frustrated. I've been thinking about this because a friend of mine has had trouble sleeping lately. One day his doctor said to him, "Joe, I think the reason you are not sleeping is that you let things frustrate you. I don't think its worry that's keeping you up, it's frustration. Go talk to somebody about it and see if you can get it resolved."

Well, guess who my friend decided to talk with about his sleeplessness? Me, and one day Joe came to see me about this. He sat down, looked at me, and said, "Do you have one of your stories that might explain what my doctor is talking about?"

I thought about it for a minute or two, then one came to mind. Here's the story:

There was a famous composer who had a rebellious son, who used to come in late at night after his father and mother had gone to bed. Before going to his own room, he would go to his father's piano and slowly, as well as loudly, play a simple scale -- all but the final note. Then leaving the scale uncompleted, he would retire to his room.

His father, hearing the scale minus the final note, would writhe on his bed, his mind unable to relax because the scale was unresolved. Finally, in utter frustration and consternation, he would stumble down the stairs and hit the previously unstruck note. Only then would his mind surrender to sleep once again.

My friend said, "So, what does that mean?"

I answered, "You have to decide what 'final note' on the scales in your life are stealing your sleep. Then you have to decide if they are worth the sleep you seem to be losing. That composer had to make a choice: he either had to play the note, or let it go and roll over and go back to sleep."

Is frustration keeping you awake at night? Is there something you can do about that?

March 13
Good Advice from a Sufi Holy Man

There was a Sufi mystic who used to teach his disciples many things. One day, one of his students asked him to share what he thought was the most important thing a person needed to know in order to be a true follower of God.

The Sufi teacher thought for a moment, then said: "When I was young, I thought my mission in life was to change the whole world. So I approached Allah and said, 'Give me energy so that I can change the whole world. Everybody looks wrong to me. I am a revolutionary and I want to change the face of the earth. Please, I beg you, give me this energy.'

"When I became more mature, I started praying a little differently. I prayed this way, 'Oh God, all of this seems to be too much. Life is getting away from me -- almost half of my life is gone, and I have not changed a single person, and the whole world has not been changed for it is too much. So I ask you, God, my family will be enough to change. Let me change my family.'

"And now, when I have become old, I say to the God above, 'I realize now that even the family is too much for me, and who am I to change them anyway?'

"Now I realize that if I can change myself that will be enough, more than enough. So now I pray to God, 'Oh God, I know now that I have come to the right point. At least give me the grace to do this: I would like to change myself."

The Sufi master concluded by telling his student, "If you really seek to change the world, to make your family better, to change the face of the earth, start today by changing yourself."

That is some pretty good advice, isn't it?

March 14
Good Day or Bad Day?

A man had been driving all night and by morning he was still far from his destination. He decided to stop at the next city he came to, and park somewhere where it was quiet so he could get an hour or two of sleep.

As luck would have it, the quiet place he chose happened to be on one of the city's major jogging routes. No sooner had he settled back for a snooze than there came a knock on his window. He looked out and saw a jogger running in place. "Yes?" he said.

"Excuse me, sir," the jogger, said, "do you have the time?" The man looked at the car clock and answered, "8:15." The jogger said thanks and left. The man settled back once more and was just dozing off when there was another knock on the window, and another jogger.

"Excuse me, sir, do you have the time?" asked the jogger. "8:25!" the man replied. The jogger said thanks and left. Now the man could see other joggers passing by and he knew it was only a matter of time before another one disturbed him. To avoid that, he got out a pen and paper and put a sign on his window saying, "I do not know the time!"

Once again, he settled back to sleep. He was just dozing off when there was another knock on the window. "Sir, if you need to know," said a jogger, seeking to be helpful, "its 8:45!"

Have you ever had an experience like that? These situations give you an opportunity to decide if you are going to have a good day or a bad day; that will be determined by your reaction or response to the situation. Either you will be irked all day about the continued interruption of your nap, or you will find yourself laughing at the thought of that last jogger giving you the correct time.

If you found yourself in that situation today, what kind of day do you think you would have?

March 15
What Did it Cost You?

I remember reading about a major disaster that took place in northern England in the 1800s. It occurred in a small fishing village where there had been three or four days of continuously fierce storms with much lightening and howling winds. All of the village's fishermen had been detained in the harbor for a week because the storms were so intense.

One day toward the end of that week, the sun shone out in a clear blue sky. It seemed as if the storms had passed away, and the boats started out for the fishing grounds.

Forty-one boats left the harbor that day. Before they started, however, the harbormaster hoisted the storm warning signal flag, and then went from boat to boat telling each captain that another storm was still coming. He begged them not to go, but they laughed at him and disregarded his warning.

Since they saw no sign of the coming storm, the boats made for open waters. It wasn't but a few hours later that an even more powerful storm blew in and swept down that coast. Very few of the men in the boats survived.

Sailors who definitely knew better ignored the warnings that a very knowledgeable harbormaster had given them. When survivors were asked why they went fishing when they had been warned not to, they all gave the same reply: "We were afraid that we would not be able to feed our families."

The harbormaster's response was simple: "When you let fear make all of your decisions, a disaster is not far away!"

Stop to think for a minute. If you look back through the years, have you ever let fear make your decisions? If you did, how did that turn out? Has listening to your fears ever cost you anything?

March 16
You've Got It!

There was a very famous evangelist by the name of Billy Sunday who was asked one time, "What would I have to do to end up going to hell?"
Sunday grinned at the man and answered, "Nothing. If you want to go to hell, all you have to do is nothing." He went on to explain that in Matthew 25 Jesus told us what we have to do if we want to go to heaven. He then added that if we want to have hell on earth and

hell for eternity, then we would look the other way when people are in need.

When I read about Billy Sunday's answer, I thought about a religion teacher I know who asked her students if they knew what Jesus wanted all of his disciples and friends to do if they were going to be his followers. There was a long period of silence and no one said a word. The teacher looked around her classroom and then said, "Come on now, tell me, what did Jesus want from his friends and what does he want from each of us?" No one said a word. Finally one student put his head down and quietly said, "I guess he would want us to talk to God in prayer and then to do our best to take care of each other. I think that is about it."
The teacher just smiled at him and said, "You've got it!"

March 17
Tomorrow

Do you ever think of the future and wonder what will happen to you as the days pass by? Many folks are a bit nervous about the future because they want to be prepared for anything bad that may be headed their way. The more they think about the future, the more they begin to squirm and become rather restless. This reminds me of a story.

The story is a bit unusual. It tells of a conversation between a man and a nail, but it really is about having a discussion about the future. Here is how the conversation progressed:

The nail said, "I have often wondered, during my years sticking here in this wooden panel, what my fate is to be. What do you think will happen to me in the future?"

The man said, " As I see it, hidden within your situation may be a tearing out with pliers, a burning of wood, the rotting of the plank, or the casting into a garbage pail -- so many things."

Said the nail, "I should have known better than to ask such foolish questions! Nobody can foresee the future, let alone a variety of scenarios, all so unlikely." So the nail decided to wait until someone more insightful came along, someone who would talk intelligently and not threaten him so much.

When you think about it, do you really want to know your fate, or even your present situation? If you are a believer in God, is the future something you look forward to, or something that you dread? Is there purpose in your life and in the direction it is headed? What do you think?

March 18
What Is in Your Heart?

One day a rather judgmental Westerner was watching an Asian gentleman burning paper money before the tablets marking the graves of his ancestors. The Westerner, who considered the Asian man to be a pagan, said, "How can your ancestors benefit at all from the smoke of your paper money?"

The Asian man, who respected all religions, bowed courteously and said, "In the same way in which your dear departed relatives appreciate the flowers you put on their graves."

When the Westerner did not reply, the Asian man bowed again and said, "We both know that it is not what comes from the paper money or the flowers that has any power toward our deceased loved ones. What comes out of our hearts is what makes all of the difference. What comes out of our hearts is based on the attitudes, thoughts, and love that we keep in our hearts."

March 19
Wisdom from the Birds

Have you ever had the experience of becoming a bit depressed because you just don't feel you are as good as the people around you?

I was recently at a support group meeting in which an older woman wanted to tell us all a story that her mother had read to her when she was a little girl. She said that the story had come back to her one night when she was feeling overwhelmed by depression. She told us that she had been feeling isolated, lonely, and bitter. The woman said that she even had begun to entertain thoughts of taking a handful of pills so that she could go to sleep and not wake up: that is how despondent she was.

The woman said she wanted to tell us the story because she believed it had saved her life. She said that even though her mother had told her the story over 60 some years ago, it had the power to reach across the years and convince her not to swallow that handful of pills. Here is how she told it:

The story is about a bunch of birds. One of the birds, a crow, lived in the forest and was absolutely satisfied in life. It was happy as could be until that one day when he saw a swan. "This swan is so white," he thought, "and I am so black. This swan is so much better looking than me. It must be the happiest bird in the world." The crow went and told the swan how he felt.

The swan was a bit taken aback by what the crow had confided in her and said, "Actually, I was feeling that I was the happiest bird around until I saw a parrot, with feathers that are so bright yellow and blue. I now think the parrot has to be the happiest bird in creation."

The crow decided it should go see the parrot. The parrot explained, "I know exactly how you feel! I lived a very happy life until I saw a peacock. I have only two colors, but the peacock has hundreds of colors."

The crow knew there was a peacock in the zoo, so he flew off to visit him. The crow approached the peacock. "Dear peacock," the crow said, "you are so beautiful. Every day thousands of people come to see you. When people see me, they immediately shoo me away. I think you must the happiest bird on the planet."

The peacock replied, "I always thought that I was the most beautiful and happy bird on the planet. But because of my beauty, I am stuck here in this zoo. I have examined the zoo very carefully, and I have realized that the crow is the only bird that is not kept in a cage. So for past few days, I have been thinking that I wish I was a crow. Then, I could happily roam everywhere and anywhere I wanted."

When that older woman finished telling the story, the crowd listening was very quiet. She looked around the room and said, "I realized that we all have things given to us as gifts and we should be happy to have and use those gifts. We do not need to compare ourselves with others and feel cheated because we didn't get their gifts. We must be happy with what we have been given and be happy for those around us for what they have been given. Otherwise we will miss our gifts and end up isolated, lonely, and bitter. Stop comparing yourself to others!"

March 20
It Is Simple

In my reading this past week, I came across a quotation from Ann Landers, the famous newspaper columnist. I was so impressed by it that I decided to use it in my daily prayer all week. If people just tried to do this one simple thing that she suggested, the world would be a much happier place.

Here is what she wrote: "Be kind to people. The world needs kindness so much. You never know what sort of battles other people are fighting. Often just a soft word or a warm compliment can be immensely supportive. You can do a great deal of good by just being considerate, by extending a little friendship, by going out of your way to do just one nice thing or saying one good word."

We often fail to realize how much power each of us has to change the world around us. We assume that only important government leaders, influential people, even famous athletes or musicians change the world. The truth of the matter is, however, that the best changes in the world come through ordinary people doing ordinary kindnesses for each other. Simple kind words offered at the right time, a thoughtful gesture, even just thanking people for the things they do and the people they are can do wonders.

God has created a wonder-filled universe and placed it in our hands. What is the best thing we can do to take care of it and the people in it? It is quite simple. Be kind!

March 21
The Time to Prepare is Now

There was an article in National Geographic recently about the survival of the Alaskan bull moose. As I read the piece, I discovered that the bulls of the species battle for dominance during the fall breeding season, literally going head-to-head with antlers crunching together as they collide. Often the antlers, their only weapon, are broken by the intensity of the fight.

Broken antlers almost always spell defeat for the bull moose. The biggest moose, with the largest and strongest antlers, is the one who wins.

The article went on to say that the real battle occurs not during the actual physical fight, but much earlier than that. Although the physical battle is fought in the fall, it is really won during the summer, when the moose eat continually. The bull that eats the best diet for growing antlers and gaining weight will be the most likely one to win the fight. Those bulls that eat poorly end up with weaker antlers and less bulk.

There is a big lesson here for each one of us. When challenges and spiritual battles come our way, much depends on what we do months or even years before that battle comes. The way we live our life and the spiritual practices we use in our daily lives will have a great deal to do with how well we can weather difficult times and the ensuing spiritual crises that often come with them. It's what might be called "the bull-moose principle."

And just what is that principle? It is simply this: enduring faith, strength, and wisdom for the trials that are bound to come into every person's life are best developed before they're needed. The time to prepare for those coming battles is today.

March 22
At the Root

Do you know that there is a big difference between jealousy and envy? The desert fathers described the difference to their followers, and this is how they explained it. Envy is a desire to possess something that belongs to another person. In contrast, jealousy is the fear that something we possess will be taken away by another person.

Although jealousy can apply to our possessions or our reputations, the word more often refers to the fear or anxiety that comes when we're afraid the affections of a loved one might be lost to a rival. We fear that our good friends, our spouse, or perhaps even our children, will be lured away by some other person who, when compared to us, seems to be more attractive, capable, and successful.

The great spiritual masters say that although envy may be difficult to overcome at times, there is nothing that destroys our peace of mind and heart like the tiny seed of jealousy that can be planted deep in our hearts. They would often warn their disciples that if you find your heart begins to be unsettled and you find it difficult to find peace or rest, very often it will be jealousy that is at the root of the disturbance.

March 23
Service

Here is something extraordinary from the life of President Franklin Roosevelt. The extraordinary thing is that there was one man who did more for the United States and for President Roosevelt than any other person in the world. That person was Roosevelt's closest adviser during much of his presidency, a man named Harry Hopkins.

During World War II, when his influence with Roosevelt was at its peak, Hopkins held no official cabinet position. Not only that, Hopkins's closeness to Roosevelt caused many to regard him as a shadowy, sinister figure. As a result, he became a major political liability to the president. A political enemy asked Roosevelt, "Why do you keep Hopkins so close to you? You surely realize that people distrust him and resent his influence and are angry at you because of him."

Roosevelt replied, "Someday you may well be sitting here where I am now as President of the United States. And when you are, you'll be looking at that door over there and knowing that practically everybody who walks through it wants something out of you. You'll learn what a lonely job this is, and you'll discover the need for somebody like Harry Hopkins, who asks for nothing except to serve you. He needs nothing else."

Harry Hopkins was one of the most powerful people in the world because he had the ear and complete trust of *the* most powerful person in the world. That power never went to his head because he knew his real power came from serving, not leading. Winston Churchill said that Hopkins, whom most of the world never heard of, was one of the half-dozen most powerful men in the world in the early 1940s. Then Churchill added a final thought by saying, "I am certain that the sole source of Hopkins's power was his willingness to serve."

Now here are a couple of important questions to consider. First, Is there a "Harry Hopkins" in your life right now? Is there someone wo utterly and completely has your back? And just one more question: is God asking you to be a "Harry Hopkins" for someone?"

March 24
Sophomores

If you were asked to define what a sophomore is, you would probably say that, in high school or college, a sophomore is a second-year student. You would be correct, but did you know that the word "sophomore" has another, more profound meaning?

The word "sophomore" is derived from two Greek words, *Sophos*, which means "wise," and *Moros*, which means "fool." Literally, then, a sophomore is a wise fool. Sounds kind of harsh to call a second-year student a fool, doesn't it? So why do we call second-year students sophomores?

Greek scholars in the ancient world realized that often, when we are young and have a little bit of knowledge, we can think we know everything. To counter this, the Greek teachers would give the same lecture each year on the first day of a student's second year. Here is what they taught: "You are all wise fools! We say that as a compliment because a true 'wise fool' knows enough at least to know that he does not know everything. That knowledge is the actual beginning of true wisdom. We implore you to be good sophomores! Good sophomores know that there is always more to learn."

Are you a good sophomore?

March 25
A Good Look

In these days of the coronavirus pandemic, we are all closed up in our homes. Many folks are spending a lot of time alone, and I have been hearing from lots of people who are finding it difficult to spend so much time alone.

How we see ourselves is important in dealing with feelings of isolation. Like most things, this present situation reminds me of a rather famous Sufi teaching story. I really like the story because no matter how often I hear it or read it, it always makes me laugh. Here it is:

A man was living with his family in the thick forests of Africa. One day, while walking in the woods, the man found a mirror. He had never seen anything like this before! When he looked into it, he felt he was looking at a photo of his father.

The man took the mirror to his home and started talking to it daily. That made his wife suspicious. One day when the husband was not at home, she took the mirror in her hands and wondered, "So this is the hag he is talking to daily. Let me show this to my mother-in-law, who thinks he is so perfect!"

When her mother-in-law looked at it, she said, "Don't worry. She is an old fragile lady. Very soon she will die."

How do you see yourself? Do you feel good about the person you have become through the years, or do you find yourself wishing you had made better decisions? Perhaps these challenging days, or any day for that matter, can be an opportunity for each of us to take stock, maybe even decide to make changes. After all, there is nothing like a good look in a mirror to get your attention.

March 26
The Best Advice

A few years ago, I was asked to give a talk to a group of college students who were part of a leadership course. In my talk, I was to answer the following question: "What is the most important thing to remember when dealing with people?"

A week or so before I was to give that talk, I had breakfast with one of my parishioners, who owns his own construction company. I told him about the talk on leadership and what my topic was. He looked at me and said, "Do you want to know how I would answer that question?" I said that I would really appreciate his opinion.

The man didn't have to think too long to respond. He put it this way: "I follow what my dad taught me. He called it the 'triple A principle.' My dad said that everyone who works for you, and in fact, anyone you ever meet, will feel better and do better when you give them these three things: attention, affirmation, and appreciation. That is the best advice I ever got on how to treat folks." That "best advice" became the main theme of my talk at the leadership course.

I think that is certainly some of the best advice I have ever heard not only on being a good leader, but also on being a good friend and on living what Jesus taught. If we truly care for someone, we will make sure to give them those "triple A's."

March 27
Winning

A few weeks ago, I was trying to help a young couple work through some of their differences. They had been married for about a year and a half, and they had come to an impasse in their relationship. The main problem was that they each felt they had to win every argument, no matter what consequences that might bring. As I listened to them talk, I kept asking God to give me an image or an insight that might help them see just what kind of consequences such an attitude can bring.

At that point that I remembered a story. It was about a foreman in a construction company who always worked very hard and was probably the most conscientious worker in the entire company. The odd thing was that even though he was such an excellent employee, he never got promoted.

One of the younger employees noticed that the foreman seemed to be unjustly treated by management. So, one day, as the crew was eating lunch, the young man asked the foreman why management seemed to treat him so unfairly. The foreman, a man who was older and wiser than most of the workers sitting there having lunch, explained it this way: "Here's the thing. Many years ago, I had an argument with my supervisor. It was a nasty disagreement. In the end, I won." No one asked any more questions.

I finished telling the young couple that story and simply added, "When you get into arguments, especially nasty ones, can you really afford to 'win?'"

March 28
Is It Spring Yet?

Recently I had to make a major decision for my parish. No one decision seemed to be the right one. I felt a bit depressed and was full of doubt. So, I went to my prayer place at home and simply said to God, "You will have to point me in the right direction. I just don't know what to do. I have no clarity on this."

There was a period of quiet, and then a feeling of peace came over me. As that peaceful feeling was filling me, I happened to notice an article that I had cut out of a magazine to read at a later date. I had actually forgotten to read it, but now something told me to pick it up.

The article was by a Protestant minister who was writing about his life and the difficulty he had making decisions! In the article he told of a winter at home on the family farm, when his dad needed firewood. He found a dead tree and sawed it down.

In the spring, to his dismay, the minister's dad found that new shoots had sprouted from the trunk. He said to his son, "I thought for sure it was dead; the leaves had dropped, the twigs snapped, it seemed as if there was no life there. But now I see there is still life at the taproot of the old tree."

The father looked at his boy and said, "Joe, don't forget this important lesson. Never cut down a tree in the wintertime. Never make a negative decision when you are in a low time. Never make your most important decisions when you are in your worst mood. Wait. Be patient. The spring will come. When spring finally comes, then you will know what choice to make."

When I finished that article, I knew I had my answer. It wasn't "spring" yet. It wasn't time for me to make the decision. I had to be patient and let things develop.

I learned a lot in that prayer session. The Lord used my inability to make a decision to get my attention so that I would turn to him for direction. If you find yourself at an impasse in your life, not sure of the decisions you need to make, perhaps it isn't "spring" yet. If you find that it isn't, be patient. Spring will come in due time and then you will know what to do.

March 29
A Greater Savior

I discovered something from the life of a man named John Newton, who wrote the famous hymn "Amazing Grace."

When Newton was an old man his past kept creeping up on him, making him feel tremendous guilt and fear and dread. In his earlier life he had been a slave trader and had done horrendous things that now worked their way into his mind and heart, leaving him terrified and unable to pray. In addition to that, Newton was beginning to feel very weak and was also growing a bit confused. He was losing his memory.

One day, however, he had a spiritual breakthrough while speaking with a local woman who was known to be very pious. Newton was telling her of his troubles, fretting about losing his memory and about the thoughts of his evil past. The woman's response was to reassure Newton by saying, "There are only two things you need to remember: you are a great sinner and you have a greater Savior. Those are the two most important memories an old slave trader turned friend of Jesus needs to have."

John Newton died completely at peace, trusting in his greater Savior.

March 30
How Big Is Your God's Heart?

Are you at a time in your life when you are becoming more and more aware of your needs? Do you ever feel that you just cannot keep up with all of the things you have to do, and all of things you need to have in order to do them? If that is true, then today is the day you need to come to God in deep prayer to lay your needs before him.

Today, when you settle down to pray, ask yourself: How generous is the God I love and who loves me? Then, after you have thought about that, consider this: God is more than generous, but am I able to accept his true generosity? If you bring God a cup, he will fill it. If you bring God a bucket, he will fill that. If you bring God a fifty-gallon drum, he will fill that too.

So, which best describes how generous you really think God wants to be with you: a cup, a bucket, or a fifty-gallon drum?

March 31
Sage Advice

If you were to think back to your school days, can you remember something one of your teachers said to you that you still recall today? Did any of your teachers say something profound enough for you to carry with you up to this very day?

I was giving a retreat to a group of Catholic school principals and I asked them this same question: Had any of their former teachers left them with good advice or sage wisdom? Just asking that question sparked a lot of discussion. Many of those educators had stories to tell about a favorite teacher who might have been very tough but who made a profound impression on them.

There were many wise sayings that were shared during our time of discussion, but there was one in particular that everyone loved. The saying was from a principal who recalled her days at Notre Dame University, where she majored in English. She said that on the first day of one of her classes, the professor said, "There are two kinds of people who don't have much to say: those who are quiet and those who talk a lot. In my class, if you don't have much to say, please be the quiet kind." The other principals at the retreat loved this saying so much they were going to use it with their students -- maybe even with their faculty members during faculty meetings.

I think that qualifies as sage advice, don't you?

APRIL

April 1
Acid

Here is something to ponder. A few weeks ago, I was meeting with a fathers' group at a local Catholic parish. As part of that morning's discussion, one man was talking about his anger. He was explaining to the group how his anger had always been his downfall. He said that even as a little boy, his anger would get the best of him and he would always end up hitting, biting, or at least, hurting the feelings of his brothers and sisters. Then he added, "Both at work and at home, even today, I spend a great deal of time apologizing for losing my temper. I just seem to have this rage somewhere down deep inside that finds its way out of me, and I end up hurting the people around me."

After the man had finished speaking, there was a rather long period of silence. Then, one of the men spoke up. "I guess I am the oldest man here. I am 89 years old and those long years have taught me a lot. When I was a younger man, my anger got me in lots of trouble, too. I tried just about anything and everything to try to overcome it. Then, when I was in the Marines, I got in trouble for hitting a sergeant. I was locked up for a week or so.

"The Marine chaplain came to see me. I told him about my anger. He told me I was a real ass and that I had better learn the most important thing there is to know about anger before it kills me. When I asked what that was, he said he was going to write down a quote from Mark Twain. He wrote down, gave it to me, then told me to memorize it and never forget it. I did what he said, and I still remember it all these years later. It did the trick. I changed. I stopped being an ass and got control of my anger."

When the elderly man stopped talking, everyone shouted all at once, "What was the quote?"

The man laughed and said, "Oh! Here's what old Mark Twain said: 'Anger is an acid that can do more harm to the vessel in which it is stored than to anything on which it is poured.'" Then the man added, "I finally learned that the one person I was hurting the most with my anger was me! It turned me into an unlovable, lonely person. I couldn't' stand that, so I changed."

April 2
Life's Aquarium

While on vacation a few years ago, I went to visit a huge aquarium. I paid for a guided tour of the major aquarium and all of the smaller ones as well.

The tour guide took us first to what he called the most popular fish that everyone wants to see up close. He turned around and pointed us to the shark exhibit. He told us that if you capture a shark from the ocean and then put it in an aquarium, it will not grow very much because sharks grow in proportion to the size of their environment. He told us that they have sharks in some of their smaller aquaria that are fully mature but only six inches long.

Then he said, if you were to put the shark back in the ocean and set it free, it would quickly grow to be over eight feet long. After he explained all of that to us tourists, he invited us to come forward to get a closer look at the sharks. When we had finished looking, the tour guide said something that has stuck with me ever since. He said, "Remember, the environment you live in day after day determines how well you grow."

There is great truth in what the tour guide said to us that day. I have thought about that ever since and have had some great meditations on what he said. I have become so grateful as I look back at the family environment I grew up in because it was a wonderful place to be nurtured to maturity. I think of the wonderful environment I was in when I was with my various friends over the years.

The list of good environments I was blessed to be a part of is quite long. I bet that may be true for you too. Why not take some time right now to consider what kind of "aquaria" you have grown up in over the years? Just how have your life experiences shaped your growth over the years?

April 3
A Grace-Filled Experience

I had a very interesting conversation recently with a man who told me he practices meditation from a Buddhist perspective. He said that he takes time to let some of the teachings or sayings of Buddha to sink into his heart and then asks God to let those wise sayings transform his heart. When I asked him if he found it made his prayer life better, his face lit up and he said, "Absolutely! It is so good for my soul that I want to teach you how to do it too. It will open up a new level of prayer for you."

With that, he reached into a plastic bag he had with him and brought out two candles. He gave them to me and said, "These are for you to use in your prayer time. I am going to ask you to do two separate prayer sessions. Here is what you are to do: First, take one of the candles and light it. Hold the lighted candle and look at the flame as you read and consider the following saying from Buddha: 'Just as one candle cannot burn without fire, so one cannot live without a spiritual life.'"

"Spend a half hour letting those words sink into your heart, then ask God to show you what they mean for your life. He may lead you into deeper waters in your spiritual life. Just be attentive to what God might say to you. When your prayer time is obviously over, you can discard what is left of the first candle," he instructed me.

The man told me to do the prayer right then as he sat across from me, and I did what he asked me to do. When he saw that I was finished with my meditation and prayer, he took my candle. The he said, "Now tomorrow, I want you to take the second candle I gave you and do the same kind of meditation, except here is some more wisdom from Buddha to take into your heart." He handed me an index card with this quotation from Buddha: "Thousands of candles can be lit from a single candle, and the life of that candle will not be shortened. Happiness never decreases by being shared."

I did exactly as my friend had instructed. The prayer was a profound and grace-filled experience. I recommend it to you. Thousands of candles can be lit from a single candle, and the life of the candle will not be shortened. Happiness never decreases by being shared.

April 4
Troubles

Have you ever felt that your whole world was falling apart? I think just about everyone at some time or other has felt that way. When both of my parents were beginning to decline and their health began to fail them, I found myself feeling inadequate to help them no matter how hard I tried. I felt that their needs were so great and my abilities to make things better so small that I found myself feeling rather lost.

One thing I did know was that learning to cope with those difficult times would take help from above. So, I took a weekend and went off to a Trappist monastery in Kentucky.

On Sunday morning of that weekend, I was sitting in the monastery garden reading. The abbot came up to me and sat down next to me. He put his hand on my shoulder and said, "I have noticed you praying during Mass and at the liturgy of the hours. It is obvious to me that you are carrying a heavy load. So, in my prayer I asked God to give me the words he wants you to have as you go through whatever you are going through."

The abbot continued: "God answered my prayer. When I opened my Bible this morning, a holy card fell out on to my lap. When I picked it up, I noticed that it had a quote from Saint Teresa of Avila. When I read it, I knew it was directly from the Lord and that I was to give this to you with the instructions that you keep this with you to help you through your difficult times. I think this is God's remedy to help you take care of whomever it is you are worried about." The abbot then handed me the holy card, got up, smiled at me, and said, "God knows how you feel. He cares very deeply for you."

Here is the quote that was on that holy card: "Let nothing trouble you, let nothing frighten you. All things are passing; God never changes. Patience obtains all things. He who possesses God lacks nothing. God alone suffices."

I kept that holy card. It provided me with all of the patience, courage, and perseverance I needed to be there for my parents in their declining years. In the end I was so grateful to God for allowing me to be there to care for them as best I could.

If you ever feel that your world is falling apart, perhaps the wisdom of St. Teresa of Avilla will help you as it did me.

April 5
First Impressions

Here is a story from ancient sources that is meant to remind us about how evil can present itself. The ancient teachers told it this way: There once was a man who met another man. The other man was handsome, intelligent, and even a bit elegant. The first man asked him who he was. The other said, "I am sometimes called the Devil, sometimes I am called Satan."

"But you cannot be," said the first man, "for the devil, I have heard, is evil and ugly and gross."

"My friend," said Satan, "it sounds like you have been listening to my detractors."

The ancient teachers would immediately tell their students that they must realize that when you first meet and get to know Satan, he will be very pleasant, even kind, and full of helpful suggestions. Most will find him handsome and lovable. But after time has passed, you will discover that, as you look back and see what has come from your time with Satan, he is quite ugly in hindsight. You will discover that what seemed to be good and beautiful was really ugly and vicious and destructive. Head on, the devil almost always looks good, but when you dig below the surface you will find how sly the Evil One really is.

April 6
Finding Your Way

Every religion or faith has much wisdom to share with us. Among Muslims, many look for deeper wisdom in the tradition of the Sufis. Some of that wisdom comes from the stories that have been handed down through the ages, from one generation to the next.

A friend of mine recently told me that he had just come through a rather dark period in his life that was full of self-doubt, fear, and anxiety about the future. He shared a Sufi wisdom story with me that he said was very helpful to him in overcoming his difficulties. I used that story in my own meditation and also found it helpful. Perhaps you will too.

Once a Sufi master was asked, "Who guided you in the Path?"

The master answered: "A dog. One day I saw him, almost dead with thirst, standing by the river's edge. Every time he looked at his reflection in the water, he was frightened and withdrew because he thought there was another dog. Finally, such was his necessity that he cast away fear and leapt into the water -- at which point the other dog vanished."

"The dog found that the obstacle, which was himself, was the barrier between him and what he sought. When he jumped into the water the obstacle melted away. In this same way, my own obstacle vanished when I knew that what I feared was what I took to be my own self. My Way was first shown to me by the behavior of a dog."

April 7
Beauty Within

Here is an interesting story that you may find helpful. One day a sparrow complained to God, "You gave beautiful colors to the peacock and a lovely song to the nightingale, but what did you give to me? I must be the ugliest of birds. As you can see, I am plain and unnoticed. Why did you make me have to suffer like this?

Very patiently and with a very soft voice God said, "I did nothing to make you suffer. It is not my will for you to suffer. You suffer because you make the same foolish mistake that human beings make. You compare yourself with others."

"I would advise you to be yourself. When you do that, you will no longer suffer, for in that there is no comparison and no pain. By being yourself, you will discover an even deeper beauty within your own heart."

April 8
Jealousy

Aesop told a fable about two beautiful eagles. Although both birds were quite beautiful, one of them could fly much higher than the other one.

The lower-flying eagle soon became jealous of his high-flying friend. Whenever he saw his friend soaring so beautifully far above him, that jealous eagle would pluck out one of his strongest and sharpest feathers and shoot it at that high-flying bird above him. Of course, the first feather he plucked failed to reach the bird above. In fact, none of the twenty other feathers he shot up at that soaring eagle made it to the target.

That jealous eagle plucked more and more feathers out of himself in an effort to wound or kill the soaring eagle. But in the end that jealous eagle not only could not fly as high as the other eagle, he couldn't fly at all because now he didn't have enough feathers to fly. In a jealous effort to hurt someone else, he only hurt himself. Aesop taught that this is the way it always goes when we give in to jealousy.

This fable reminds me of something that the famous New York Yankees baseball player, Yogi Berra, once said about jealousy: "Boy, was I ever angry and jealous of one of my teammates who could bat either right or left-handed whenever he wanted. I could not do that. So, in the end, I told God, 'I'd give my right arm to be ambidextrous!'"

April 9
Seeds or Bullets

I read about a rather interesting law that was enacted by the Pennsylvania legislature in 1794.
Here is what that law said: "If any person of the age of 16 years or upwards shall profanely curse or swear by the name of God, Jesus Christ, or the Holy Ghost, every such person shall pay 67 cents for every such curse or oath. And whosoever shall curse or swear by any other name or thing than as the aforesaid, shall pay the sum of 50 cents for every curse or oath. The truth being that a good person should use good language."

When I read that law to some of my friends at breakfast one day, they all laughed. Someone asked if one could have a running tab, or did you have to pay after each offense. Although that law may cause us to laugh, it can also cause us to consider our language and our use of words. I often remind the kids in our parish school to pay attention to the words they use. I tell them that our words can be seeds for making people feel good about themselves, or they can be like bullets that wound or even kill.

The best line in that 1794 Pennsylvania law is the one that says, "a good person should use good language."

April 10
God's Touch?

Do you ever wonder if God is real? Do you ever wish you still had the complete trust you had as a little child that God was real because your mother had taught you so? I ask you that question because while I was at the library the other day, I read a short story by John Updike. I can't recall the name of that story, but the image he described in it has stuck with me.

The story centers around a young guy who, for many years, had rejected the faith of his childhood. He thought it was just some fable his mother had told him. But one night, while the young man was in bed trying to fall asleep, he decided he would like to have that childhood faith back. So, in one last ditch effort, he lifts his hands into the darkness above him and asks God to simply reach down and touch them. He asks for just the slightest contact or touch, saying that it would be enough for a lifetime.

The man keeps his hands in the air waiting for that touch. He hopes. He feels something. He begins to be excited and he can feel his heart leap. He can feel something, but he is not sure whether it is the movement of the air, or maybe just the blood pulsing through his veins. Or maybe it is truly God's touch. He cannot be certain, but there is something.

So, in your own life, from your own experience, what would you tell that young man if he asked you about his experiment?

April 11
Wise Words for the Day

When I was at prayer this morning, thinking about all of the turmoil going on all over the world and in our own country, I asked God to show me what attitude I ought to take as I move into this new day. I sat in silence for quite a while when something I had read the night before in an e-mail from a friend came back to me.

My friend had sent me a prayer request and then said that she had found a quote I might like and find useful. She was right. I did like it and it became very useful in my morning prayer. It was like God was giving me a direct answer to my prayerful question about how I should enter the day. Here's that quote, and I hope you find it helpful as you enter this day.

"What is an optimist? The man who says, 'It's worse everywhere else. We're better off than the rest of the world. We've been lucky.' He is happy with things as they are and he doesn't torment himself. What is a pessimist? The man who says, 'Things are fine everywhere but here. Everyone else is better off than we are. We're the only ones who've had a bad break.' He torments himself continually."

Those wise words are from the writings of Aleksandr Solzhenitsyn in his book, *Cancer Ward*. That quote came to me at exactly the right time. It gave me a lot to think about and ponder.

April 12
Start Doing Good

Centuries ago, a very wise and holy man, a rabbi, was concerned about what he had observed his students doing. He noticed that they were not doing the good things they were capable of doing, rather, they spent most of their time thinking and analyzing what is the best good thing to do. They were so concerned about the perfect good thing that they did no good thing.

The rabbi called his students together and said, "Please listen to this story which our God has told me to share with you: A little bear cub was confused about how to walk. 'What do I do first?' he asked his mother. 'Do I start with my right foot or my left? Or both front feet and then my back feet? Or do I move both feet on one side and then both feet on the other?' His mother answered, 'Just quit thinking and start walking.'"

When he finished telling the story, the rabbi whispered to his students, "God says this to you: stop thinking, stop analyzing, and start doing good."

April 13
The Order of Things

What is the biggest blessing you have discovered in your life? I have been thinking about my own blessings, and in doing so, recalled an ancient story that can serve as a reminder of how important we all are to each other. The story is sometimes called "The Proper Order of Life," but I have seen it recounted with other titles. It comes from the tradition of Zen Buddhism. Here is the story:

A rich man asked a Zen master to write something down that could encourage the prosperity of his family for years to come and encourage them to see the blessings that life offers. So, on a large piece of paper, the master wrote, "Father dies, son dies, grandson dies."

The rich man became angry when he saw the master's work. "I asked you to write something down that could bring happiness and prosperity to my family. Why do you give me something like this?"

"If your son should die before you," the master answered, "this would bring unbearable grief to your family. If your grandson should die before your son, this also would bring great sorrow. If your family, generation after generation, disappears in the order I have described, it will be the natural course of life. This is true happiness and prosperity."

When Zen students are given this story, they are asked how the proper order of things can be a real blessing. Can you see the wisdom of that idea?

April 14
When You Grow Up

What do you want to be when you grow up? Every child is asked that question quite often and I always enjoy hearing its responses to that question. I just read about a little girl's response to that question that literally did make me laugh out loud.

Here is the story: A woman had just returned from a meeting of the National Organization for Women (NOW) when her five-year-old daughter greeted her with the news that she wanted to be a nurse when she grew up. "A nurse!" her mother exclaimed. "Listen, Lisa, just because you're female doesn't mean you have to settle for being a nurse. You can be a surgeon, a lawyer, a banker, President of the United States. You can be anything!"

The daughter looked a little dubious as she asked, "Anything? Anything at all?" As she thought about it, her face was filled with ambition and real enthusiasm. "All right," she said. "I'll be a horse."

I love that story. The reason I start with that story is that I want to give you a question to consider for your future. The desert fathers would not ask you what you want to be when you grow up, they would tell you to ask a different question if you want to grow spiritually. They would ask you to ask yourself this question: "What am I becoming?" Hopefully, you are not becoming a horse!

April 15
A Little More, A Little Less

Just yesterday I was reading a short story by Mark Twain. I haven't read anything by him since my college days and I remembered just how enjoyable it is to read his writings. So I took out my trusty Kindle and read more of his writings.

There was one quote I came across that I found really interesting. Evidently, he had been asked to answer a reporter's question as to what Twain thought was the secret to living a good and happy life. Here is what he said:

"A little more kindness, A little less speed, A little more giving, A little less greed, A little more smile, A little less frown, A little less kicking a man while he's down, A little more 'We,' A little less 'I,' A little more laugh, A little less cry, A little more flowers, On the pathway of life, And fewer on graves, At the end of the strife."

Isn't that a wonderful quote? I used it in my prayer by simply asking myself, "What do I need a little more of in my life right now, and of what do I need a little less?" It was a great way to do a kind of spot check on how I am choosing to live my life. I would encourage you to ask yourself the same questions the next time you settle in for your prayer time.

April 16
Becoming a Good Person

Just about everyone knows or at least has heard of Confucius, but there are probably very few who have ever heard of his grandson, Zeng Shen. Although he was one of the youngest of Confucius's grandsons, it was he who won the highest praise from the old sage.

One of the sayings for which Zeng Shen became famous even in his own lifetime was something like this: "Every day I ask myself three questions. The first is, 'Have I sinned in my thoughts and actions toward others?' The second is, 'Have I broken faith in any of my friends?' The third is, 'Have I tried to teach anything to others I have not fully learned and understood myself?'"

Confucius said that his grandson's three questions are a roadmap to becoming a good person. Do you think Zeng Shen's three questions could provide a map for you in your life today?

April 17
The Key

What do you think is the key to everything in life? There are probably many answers that could be given in response to that question, but I would like to suggest just one for your consideration.

When I was studying Zen meditation, I was given something to take with me for my meditation time. It was a little paper card made of a very high-quality rice paper, with these words calligraphed on it: "The method of trying to conquer hatred through hatred never succeeds in overcoming hatred. But the method of overcoming hatred through non-hatred is eternally effective. That is why that method is described as eternal wisdom." The words were from Buddha himself.

We were asked to take the saying of Buddha to our hearts as we sat in quietude to begin our meditation and prayer. When I finished my meditation, I remembered something I had read in a magazine about the assassination attempt on President Ronald Reagan. It was something that Patti Davis, the daughter of the President, had said. She wrote that her dad made a lasting impression on her the day after the assassination attempt in 1982: "The following day my father said he knew his physical healing was directly dependent on his ability to forgive John Hinckley, the assassin. By showing me that forgiveness is the key to everything including physical health and healing, he gave me an example of Christ-like thinking. It was eternal wisdom he gave me that day."

April 18
Your Time

I have a true story to tell you, and after you have read it, I have a question to ask. Here is that story:

A woman in the hospital was weeping after being told she was terminally ill with cancer. She fell into a very deep depression and no matter who came to see her, no matter what words of comfort they offered, she could find no peace. Finally, the medical staff asked a hospital chaplain to stop by and visit with the woman to see if he might find a way to bring her some peace.

When the chaplain came to see the woman, she explained why she could not find peace by saying, "I'm not weeping because I'm dying. I'm weeping because I never lived. When I think of all of the precious time that I have wasted throughout my life, I could just kick myself in the butt! When I start to think about all the time I wasted being angry with my family over nothing important at all, I just get so angry at myself! Then I think of all the time I wasted staying in my own little world when in reality, my kids or my husband really needed me to pay attention to them! I think of that and I just get so angry!"

When the woman paused to take a breath, the chaplain put up his hand to indicate that he wanted her to stop talking. When she looked at him, she noticed that there were tears flowing down his face. Then he whispered very softly, "God has sent me to tell you to stop wasting these last days of your life being angry at yourself. Use these days to embrace those you love and those who love you. God sent me to say these words, which are from him: Be calm! Be still! I am with you. And when you are calm enough and still enough, I will give you peace and one day, very soon, lead you home to be with me. Don't waste this valuable time. Be at peace."

Here is the question I have for you: How are you using your time?

April 19
Open Some Windows!

In my private prayer this past week I have been reading the Bible and praying with the story of the Prophet Daniel. As a kid I always loved hearing about the story of Daniel being thrown into the lion's den. How did he get himself thrown into that terrifying place? Well, on one occasion, Persian king Darius made an edict that for thirty days no one in all of his kingdom should make any prayer to

any god except to himself, the king. Good old Daniel had other ideas and plans. Now the scriptures tell us, knowing full well that the king had issued the edict, Daniel "went to his house where he had windows in his upper chamber opened them toward Jerusalem; and he got down on his knees three times a day, bowed his head, and prayed and gave thanks to God, as he had done all of his life."
It was for this reason, of course, that Daniel was tossed into the lions' den. But the thing that is important to know is that Daniel wasn't too worried -. He had his windows open - this is what mattered most. He had them open in the right direction, toward Jerusalem, and the holy the temple of God. It was Daniel's custom to have his windows open on the Jerusalem side of his house. No matter what King Darius and his edicts demanded, Daniel kept those windows open, all of the time. They were his path to God's heart. When I read about Daniel's windows, I began to understand what he meant by keeping the way to God's heart open. When Daniel did that, he was able to accept God's help, strength and wisdom. So, I would ask you to take some time with good old Daniel. Ask yourself some questions. Questions like, "Are my windows open to God?" Or another question may be important to ask as well: " Whatever may be threatening to overwhelm me right now, am I keeping the windows open on the God-ward side of my life?

I am sure that every one of us has "lions" that we face every day. Daniel teaches us that whatever befalls us, we must make sure that our windows are open, open wide, so wide that whatever happens to us today, we will have a way open to God's own heart.

April 20
Only by Love

I have spent a lot of time in my 40 years of ministry as a priest working with and befriending alcoholics and drug addicts. For some reason unknown to me, God has brought me into the lives of so many truly good men and women who have become overwhelmed by life, or suffering, or depression, or feelings of despair and loneliness, failure and loss.

The most important thing they have taught me over the years is that none of us can get through this life without love from above. So many folks working programs to overcome their addictions refer to the "higher power" they need to whom they can give over their life and will. I almost always tell them that their higher power is not some force or thing, it is a person of tremendous love and affection for them. It is the God who loved them into existence and will never abandon them.

One very famous addict was Edgar Allan Poe. He often was so overwhelmed by life that he turned to things he thought could numb the pain he was living in. Here is how he described it: "I have absolutely no pleasure in the stimulants in which I sometimes so madly indulge. It has not been in the pursuit of pleasure that I have periled life and reputation and reason. It has been the desperate attempt to escape from torturing memories, from a sense of insupportable loneliness and a dread of some strange impending doom."

Addictions of any kind are horrible because over time, they can rob us of everything and everyone who is important to us. I think that God has brought addicts into my life and me into their lives so we can learn from each other. We are all both teachers and learners. We can all come to know, through the pain and suffering life can bring, that there is someone bigger than any pain, suffering, or despair that may befall us.

The higher power whom addicts are taught to "turn their life over to" is really a person who is filled with a higher, unconditional love for each one of us. Addiction is a spiritual disease that can only be healed by God. Addictions are only conquered by love -- God's love.

April 21
I Am with You

One of my parishioners sent me a thank-you card in which they included a little story. The card said, "Please read the enclosed story. Once you have read it, please know that you have been my grandfather." Once I read the story, I realized what a compliment they were giving me.

I invite you to read this little story and then ask yourself this question: "Who are the 'grandfathers' in my life?

An elderly gentleman was out walking with his young grandson. "How far are we from home?" he asked the grandson. The boy answered, "Grandpa, I don't know." The grandfather asked, "Well, where are you?" Again, the boy answered, "I don't know." Then the grandfather said good-naturedly, "Sounds to me as if you are lost." The young boy looked up at his grandfather and said, "Nope, I can't be lost. I'm with you."

Ultimately, that is the answer to our feeling lost, too. We can't be lost because God is with us.

April 22
Created Not Constructed

In my prayer this morning something I had read last night came back to me in a wonderful way. It happened when I picked up the readings for daily Mass and discovered that the first reading was the story of Creation from the Book of Genesis.

As I prayed with that story, I was struck by how much care God took in creating each part of our world, especially when he stopped to create us. What came back to me in my prayer was a quotation from Charles Dickens that I had read before bed last night. Here is what Dickens wrote:

"The whole difference between construction and creation is exactly this: that a thing constructed can only be loved after it is constructed; but a thing created is loved even before it exists."

That is a marvelous thought to spend time with: God loved us even before we came into existence. God did not construct us; he created us. God didn't build us into existence; God loved us into being.

April 23
Fear Motivates

Here is something to ponder today as you think about what motivates you in life. The story is about a man who was the most successful bill collector in the whole country. Other bill collectors marveled at how successful he was with just about any client. If truth be told, he could collect old debts from people upon whom all the other collectors had given up years before.

Someone asked him how he did it. The man's answer showed real insight into people: "Oh, it's quite simple really. I just write them one letter, and in that letter, I tell them just one thing. That one thing is this: if you don't pay this bill immediately, what you are most afraid will happen -- will happen. Once they get my letter, they almost always pay up in a day or two!"

That bill collector was, of course, pretty sure that most people have some fear of something in the future, and the mere suggestion that it might happen makes them do what must be done as soon as they can.

Is there any fear in your life that causes you to do what needs to be done right away?

April 24
Sharing Your Best

There was a great wise man who knew that his days were coming to an end. He decided to call together all of his children, their spouses, and their children so he could give them some important knowledge to help them live lives of meaning and significance.

When all of them were gathered around him, the great man began to thank them for all they had done for him, and he thanked them for making his life such a blessing by sharing their gifts with him. "My hope for each of you is that you never stop sharing the best that is in you. I pray that you will always offer the people around you and the whole world, for that matter, the best that is in you. Never stop sharing your best with the world."

As his children and grandchildren listened to him, tears began to flow. Then the wise man said, "Let me tell you a story that will help you remember my request and my prayers for you." Then he told this story:

A great festival was to be held in a village. Each villager was asked to contribute by pouring a bottle of their best wine into a giant barrel. One of the villagers had this thought: "If I pour a bottle of water in that giant barrel, no one will notice the difference." But it didn't occur to him that everyone else in the village might have the same thought.

When the banquet began and the barrel was tapped, what came out was pure water. No one had given their best, and so there was no wine at the festival. There was no joy because no one had shared their best.

April 25
Two Rabbits

Here is something to ponder. How does the following episode from the life of a great sage apply to your life right now?

One day, a martial arts student approached a well-respected and wise teacher with a question. "I'd like to improve my knowledge of the martial arts. In addition to learning from you, whom I have been told is the greatest martial arts teacher of all time, I'd like to study with another teacher in order to learn another style. What do you think of this idea?" The great sage answered, "The hunter who chases two rabbits catches neither one."

In your life right now, are you chasing two rabbits?

April 26
In the Room with You

Have you ever felt that fear had complete control of you? Recently, I was speaking with a guy who was getting ready to go off to Notre Dame to begin his college career. I don't think I have ever met a person who was filled with as many fears as this young man. He was afraid he would have no friends; he was afraid he would end up with the wrong roommate. He was afraid that he wasn't going to be able to handle the academics, and he was afraid that maybe he just wasn't cut out for college. In short, he was, as he put it, "a hot mess." Then, before I could say anything, he added, "I guess I should tell you that I have anxiety issues too."

My first response was to suggest that we just sit in quiet for a few minutes. He was very nervous, and I said, "Let's just sit and try to feel the peace that is in this room." He said, "Is there peace in this room?" I said, "I know there is. Do you know how I know that?" He shook his head and said, "No."

I told him that I knew there was peace in the room because I knew that Jesus was in the room with us. I reminded him that Jesus promised to be with us always. Then I told him that Jesus especially comes to be with us when we are afraid, and that since he was so afraid, I knew Jesus had to be in the room with us. Then I asked him to close his eyes, be quiet, and try to picture Jesus sitting with us.

It wasn't long before the guy was calm. As the quiet time came to an end, he slowly opened his eyes, smiled, and said, "I feel like he is right here!" I said, "It feels that way because he *is* here with us." His eyes opened wide as he looked at me and said, "Are you telling me that you can feel him too?" I shook my head. Finally, he said, "Hey, I am not afraid right now!"

When our time together was over, the young man turned to me and said, "Can I come back here when I need to be calm? Can I come and get the feeling that Jesus is right here?" I said, "You know, Jesus will go home with you. You don't have to be here to find him. He is with you here, at your home, and he will be with you there at Notre Dame too!" He paused and quietly said, "I just have to remember that, don't I?"

If you find yourself overwhelmed by fear, perhaps it is time for you to sit quietly for a short time and recall that the peace you are seeking is not far away in some distant, exotic land. It is right in the room with you. How do I know that peace is in the room with you? I know because I know that Jesus is in the room with you.

April 27
A Good Question

There was a famous chaplain in the British army during the First World War, named Geoffrey Studdert Kennedy. The soldiers he served loved him because he would do anything to serve them. He would stay with them when they were wounded, and he would remain with soldiers as they lay dying.

Kennedy was asked one time what he said to comfort the soldiers who were near death. He said, "I tell them about the judgment to come, and I tell them to be assured that God loves them. He added, "I always tell the men that I believe there will be just one question asked of me on that day when I appear before my Maker. I believe that God will say to me, 'What did you make of it?' And then I will say to God, 'What did I make of what?' And then, God will say to me, 'This gift of life, which I, your Heavenly Father, have given you. What did you make of it?'"

The chaplain said he would tell the men who were watching him as he spoke with dying soldiers that if there is one thing they should learn from their war experiences, it is that life is precious. Then he would tell them that a good thing for all of them to take home with them after the war is that one question God will ask of them: "What did you make of it?" The chaplain would then tell the young men, "From now on, every night before you go to sleep answer God's question but apply it just to the day you have completed. Imagine God saying to you 'This gift of life, which I, your Heavenly Father, have given you. What did you make of it?'"

April 28
What I Have

There is a Spanish proverb that is supposed to be the key to happiness. It is said that if a Spanish mother hears her children whining about what they have or what they cannot have, she will sit down with them and make them memorize this proverb: "Remember, one cannot always get what one would like, so one must learn to like what one can get."

When I first heard that proverb, I was immediately reminded of a poster I saw in the waiting room of a doctor's office. At the top of the poster were two words: Please Note. Below those two words was an arrow that pointed to a picture of a post-it note with these words written on it:

With feet to take me where I'd go,
With eyes to see the sunset's glow,
With ears to hear what I would know;
I'm blessed indeed. The world is mine;
Oh God, forgive me when I whine!

April 29
Grateful?

A man was headed home from work one night when another man approached him and proceeded to rob him. A week later as he described his ordeal to his friends, one of them asked him how the robbery had affected him. The man thought for a few minutes and said, "The whole affair has made me very thankful."
Confused by that answer, one of his friends asked, "How in the world could you ever be thankful for having been robbed?"

"Well, I can see four reasons to be grateful," the man replied. "First, because I was never robbed before, second, because although they took my wallet they did not take my life, third because they did take all that I had on me, they did not take my life, and fourth, that I was the one robbed and not the one so desperate that I had to rob someone."

If you were robbed, could you be as grateful for the experience as the man above?

April 30
Turmoil

I was in the public library recently when I saw a book on display that caught my attention. I had read the book years ago and remembered that it had a huge impact on me. The book, *The Gulag Archipelago*, by Aleksandr Solzhenitsyn, is full of real wisdom.

When I first read the book, I knew the author had true wisdom that had come from his own life experience and his own suffering. As I browsed through the book again, I came across a quote that I have been meditating on since and using in my prayer for the world. Here is what Solzhenitsyn said his life experience had taught him:

"Over a half century ago, while I was still a child, I recall hearing a number of old people offer the following explanation for the great disasters that had befallen Russia: 'Men have forgotten God; that's why all this has happened.' Since then I have spent well-nigh 50 years working on the history of our revolution. In the process I have read hundreds of books, collected hundreds of personal testimonies, and have already contributed eight volumes of my own toward the effort of clearing away the rubble left by that upheaval. But if I were asked today to formulate as concisely as possible the main cause of the ruinous revolution that swallowed up some 60 million of our people, I could not put it more accurately than to repeat: 'Men have forgotten God; that's why all this has happened.'"

If you were to stop and think about your own life experience so far, what has it taught you? What does it tell you is the reason the world is often in such utter turmoil?

May

May 1
How Has Life Been for You?

One of my favorite rabbinic stories comes out of Hungary. According to the story, in a little village near Budapest, a man goes to his rabbi and complains, "My life is completely unbearable. There are nine of us living in one room. What can I do?"
The rabbi answers, "Take your goat into that room with you." The man in incredulous, but the rabbi insists. "Do as I say and come back in a week."
A week later the man comes back looking more distraught than before. "We cannot stand it," he tells the rabbi. "The goat is filthy. Please help us!"
The rabbi then tells him, " Now, I want you to go home and let your goat out. And come back in a week."
A radiant man returns to the rabbi a week later, exclaiming, "Our life is beautiful! We all enjoy every minute of it now that there's no goat, only the nine of us."
The rabbi concludes, "Remember, as bad as things are, they could be worse. As bad as things have been, there is always something we can do to change things."

May 2
When Sadness Comes

I have been thinking about kindness because one day last week I had a very difficult day. I was rather depressed and a bit forlorn, so n my way home I decided to stop at a little restaurant for supper. As I looked over the menu, the server came over, sat down at my table across from me, and said, "Why are you so sad?"

I was really surprised by her question, but as I looked at her and she looked back at me, I realized I was sad. Rather than give her a direct answer, my first reaction was a heavy sigh, to which she responded, "Can you tell me about it?"

She said those words to me with such tenderness and kindness that I immediately began to tell her about the family I had visited with that afternoon. The mother of that family, who was just 45 years old, had died right after I had baptized her. Her husband, her children, her extended family, and many of her friends were all there as she took her last breath.

As I continued talking, I noticed that the server was looking back at me with eyes full of tears. She reached across the table, took my hand, and said, "I always tell my kids, 'Never try to carry sadness or sorrow by yourself.'"

I said, "I think God sent me here so I would hear you say that!"

She smiled at me and then said, "You know, I have not told anyone this, but I found out a few months ago that I have a terminal disease. When I think of my husband and my kids, I just get so sad."

I looked across the table at her and said, "In all of my years as a priest, one of the best pieces of advice I have every received came from a very kind and caring woman."

She said, "And what was the advice she gave you?"

I leaned across the table and whispered to her, "She said, 'Never try to carry sadness or sorrow by yourself!'"

May 3
A Good Question

There is a story from the days of Queen Victoria that I found rather interesting. According to the story, on more than one occasion the queen would go out among her subjects, choose to drop in on someone, and ask to have some tea with them.

One afternoon, Queen Victoria decided to visit the widowed mother of one of her dressmakers. The queen and the dressmaker's mother had a very pleasant afternoon drinking tea and sharing stories. The queen enjoyed the visit and so did the widow.

The following Sunday afternoon, the local parson and many of the widow's neighbors came to visit her and congratulate her on having the queen come to see her. As they were all sharing tea, one of her neighbors happily asked, "Who is the most honored guest you've ever entertained, Granny?"

The widow answered, "Her Majesty the Queen, of course!"

The parson said, "Did you say the queen? Surely, you are mistaken. Isn't Jesus Christ the most honored guest in this house? If he is not, he should be, shouldn't he? After all, he is frequently a guest in my house!"

The widow's answer was strong and sure. Looking the parson straight in the eye, she said, "No! Indeed! Jesus is no guest in my house. He lives here all of the time!

When I first read that story, I asked myself, "Is Jesus an honored guest in my house from time to time, or does he live there all of the time?" It's a good question to ask oneself.

May 4
Where to Put Your Trust

Here is an important lesson from ancient China. Centuries ago, the emperor of China wanted to protect his people from the invading hordes to the north. Therefore, he put thousands of people to work building what we now call the Great Wall of China. He believed the wall was perfect because it was too high to climb over, too thick to break down, and too long to go around. Peace and security had been achieved!

Yet during the first hundred years of the wall's existence, China was indeed invaded three times. Was the wall a failure? Not really. Not once in those three invasions did the barbaric hordes climb over the wall, break it down, or go around it.

Just how then did they get into China, then? The answer lies not in the wall but rather, in people. China's enemies did not destroy the wall; they simply bribed a gatekeeper and then marched right in through a gate. The fatal flaw in the emperor's defense was placing too much trust in a wall and not putting enough effort into building up the integrity and character of the people he chose to be the gatekeepers.

Building walls can only do so much; building character brings real security and trust.

May 5
The Stars

Here is a thought to consider as you go about the busyness of the day. The famous philosopher
Soren Kierkegaard used to tell a parable about a wealthy man who was driving along the road at night. The man was inside a very well-lighted carriage, looking comfortable and feeling completely content. As Kierkegaard told it, there was so much light in his carriage and he was so wrapped up in his own little world that the man never noticed the majestic beauty of the stars overhead.

A little ahead on the same road, however, traveled a peasant who had no fancy, well-lighted carriage, only a small cart. He was not in his own little world, he was traveling through God's world and so he had the stars!

Now here is the thought to consider: As you go through life, do you exist only in your own little world, or do you, like the peasant, have the stars?

May 6
Sound Advice

I had breakfast recently with a group of elderly men, all of whom had been friends since high school. The youngest in the group was 83 and the oldest was 98 years old. Because I was getting ready to give a high school retreat talk, I asked the men what one sentence or piece of advice they would want to tell high school seniors that might help them to be happy in life

I heard many answers from the group, but by far my favorite answer was the one given by a 95-year-old retired teacher. He said, "Here's my advice if you want to be truly happy: You should do something every day to make other people happy, even if it's only to leave them alone."

Isn't that some sound advice?

May 7
A Good Ship

Recently I had a conversation with a good friend in which she was telling me about all of the difficulties she and her family had been through in the last six months. She said, "It has been so difficult that my husband and I are afraid of what tomorrow might bring. We wonder what we can rely on to get us through all of this."

As she talked to me, my mind began to wander to something I had read in an old book found at a used books store. The book was written by the well-known Protestant minister Dr. Norman Vincent Peale. In one chapter I read, Peale told of encountering a hurricane while on a cruise in the Atlantic. After the captain managed to sail around the danger, he and Dr. Peale were visiting with one another.

The captain said he always lived by a basic truth, namely, that if the sea is smooth, it will get rough; and if it is rough, it will get smooth. Thinking for a moment, he then added something worth remembering: "With a good ship," the captain said, "you can always ride it out."

When my friend finished speaking, I immediately told her about that passage from the book. I said, "You and your family have been through some rough times and some smoother times. It sounds to me like you have been on a pretty good ship."

She said, "You mean that God has been our good ship that gave us the ability to ride it out?" I nodded and said, "I could not have said it better myself."

May 8
Reading You

I often lead classes in Bible study. Because of that a woman in my parish sent me a story that she thought I should use whenever I am about to begin teaching the Bible or preaching about it. She told me that the story came to her through a missionary in East Africa.

According to the story, there was a pious woman who was accustomed to walk around with her bulky Bible. She was never without it. It wasn't long before the villagers began to tease her: "Why always the Bible?" they asked. "There are so many other books you could read." The woman never really gave them an answer, yet she continued living with her Bible, neither disturbed nor angered by all the teasing.

Then very unexpectedly one day, she knelt down right in the midst of all of those who laughed at her. She held up the Bible, high above her head, and said with a great smile, "Yes, of course there are many books that I could read. Now, I want one of you to tell me, can any of those books do what the Bible can do for me? I want you all to realize that in all of my years, having read many, many books, no other book except the Bible has been able to read me!"

When was the last time you sat down and read the Bible? When was the last time you discovered that the Bible was reading you?

May 9
What a Worm Taught Me

I was eating an apple this morning for breakfast when I discovered that there was a worm in that apple. That was a rotten way to start the day! As I was looking at the apple, I wondered just how a worm gets inside an apple in the first place, and I was curious enough to go to the Internet and look it up.

Here is what I discovered: You would think, of course, that if there is a worm in the apple, it must have burrowed in from the outside. That is not what usually happens. No, scientists have discovered that the worm comes from inside. So how do you suppose he gets in there? Well, in truth, it is rather simple! An insect lays an egg in the apple blossom. Sometime later, the worm hatches in the heart of the apple, then eats his way to the outside.

As I thought about that, I came to see that it is a perfect metaphor for what happens in our hearts when some person lays an egg of resentment in the center of our heart. It grows and eats at our hearts until it bursts out into full-fledged anger or hatred. It occurs to me that the little egg of resentment can be down deep in our hearts growing and eating at us without our ever being aware of it. Scary, huh?

Do you know what the antidote is to such "eggs" planted deep in our hearts? One word: gratitude. A heart filled with gratitude will leave no room for an egg of resentment to grow.

May 10
Good Leaders

Some years ago, I was part of a youth retreat that had as its focus the study of good leadership. The retreat was designed for young leaders, and it was meant to help them discover the skills they would need to develop into the leaders of the future.

One of the retreat team members had invited his dad to give a talk on leadership. His dad was a West Point graduate and a career military officer. He gave a vibrant and fascinating talk about the famous World War II leader, General Dwight Eisenhower.

That dad spoke very softly, but he had every participant and leader of the retreat in rapt attention. He told us that cadets at West Point were taught about Eisenhower's leadership skill set. He said that the general would gather all of the sergeants and first lieutenants in his army to do some leadership training.

General Eisenhower demonstrated the art of leadership with one long piece of string. He would put the string on a table and say: "*Pull* it and it will follow wherever you wish. *Push* it and it will go nowhere at all. It's just that way when it comes to leading people. They need to follow a person who is leading by example and who knows where he is headed. You must be that kind of leader or this army will be defeated quickly!"

After a long pause, General Eisenhower would look around the room and say, "You do not lead by hitting people over the head -- that is nothing more than assault. That is not leadership. A leader finds the best in his men and pulls it out of them."

If you were to take a few minutes to consider your own leadership skills and ability, how would you assess them? Are you a good judge of talent and personal qualities? Can you encourage and get the people you work with or live with to see their gifts and talents? Are you a good leader?

May 11
Drifting?

There is an old story that one of my parishioners was eager to tell me. His wife was from Ireland, and he said that his father-in-law used to tell him this story whenever they were getting ready to go to church. He said that he would always invite his father-in-law to join them for church, but the man always refused, saying that he had his reasons and the following story would explain them.

The story was about an Irish sea captain who was out of fellowship with the Lord. One day the captain was out fishing with his godless companions when a storm came up and threatened to sink their ship. His friends begged him to pray, but he shook his head, saying, "It's been a long time since I've done that or even entered a church." At their insistence, however, he finally cried out, "O Lord, I haven't asked anything of you in 15 years, and if you help us now and bring us safely to land, I promise I won't bother you again for another 15!"

That story always makes me laugh. It can serve as a reminder but also as a warning for how easy it is for us to drift away from our prayers and our relationship with God. It happens little by little, without even noticing how far we are drifting and just how long it's been since we last talked to God -- even more importantly, since we last listened to God.

May 12
Your Inventory

During the Civil War, back in the 1860s, Abraham Lincoln became aware that the nation needed to do something about healing itself. He thought that the nation needed to find a "higher power" who could bring some order to the terrible chaos that was consuming the country. His solution was to proclaim what he called a national day of fasting, humiliation, and prayer. When he issued the proclamation, he included his rationale for calling the nation to prayer. Here is what he wrote:

"We have been the recipients of the choicest bounties of heaven. We have been preserved, the many years, in peace and prosperity. We have grown in numbers, wealth, and power, as no other nation has ever grown. But we have forgotten God. We have forgotten the gracious hand which preserved us in peace and multiplied and enriched and strengthened us; and we have vainly imagined, in the deceitfulness of our hearts, that all these blessings were produced by some superior wisdom and virtue of our own. Intoxicated with unbroken success, we have become too self-sufficient to feel the necessity of redeeming and preserving grace, too proud to pray to God who made us. It behooves us, then, to humble ourselves before the offended Power, to confess our national sins, and to pray for clemency and forgiveness."

As you read through Lincoln's words, did they make you stop to consider the blessings that you enjoy? Did his words serve as a reminder to you of just how you have arrived at all of your blessings? When was the last time that you made an inventory of your blessings?

May 13
How Deep?

I read something about Albert Einstein that I found rather fascinating. When the German-born mathematician looked at what happened to his homeland just before the onset of the second world war, he was deeply saddened by what he saw as his homeland give in to Adolf Hitler's fascist dictatorship.

Einstein wondered if any Germans were going to stand up and oppose Hitler. Here is what he said about it: "When Hitlerism came to Germany, I expected the universities to oppose it. Instead, they embraced it. I hoped for the press to denounce it, but instead they propagated its teachings. One by one the leaders and institutions which should have opposed the Nazi philosophy bowed meekly to its authority. Only one institution met it with vigorous opposition and that was the Christian church. The very group which I once despised I now love with a passion I cannot describe."

It is certain that the commitment of the Christians in standing against evil made a profound impression upon Albert Einstein. Those individuals in the 1930s understood the cost associated with their actions, and they did not back down. Many hid Jewish families in their homes, others stood up and publicly spoke against Hitler, and many gave their lives. They were completely committed. The question we must ask ourselves today is, "How deep is our commitment to living the Gospel?"

May 14
Compromise?

Are you good at compromise? Whether or not you consider yourself good at it or not, it is a very important skill to have. One of my favorite stories about compromise comes from Russia. Modern Russian hunters are fond of telling their version of the story as they warn younger hunters on the danger of trying to compromise with a bear. Here's that old story:

A hunter raised his rifle and took careful aim at a large bear. When he was about to pull the trigger, the bear spoke in a soft, soothing voice, "Isn't it better to talk than to shoot? What do you want? Let us negotiate the matter."

Lowering his rifle, the hunter replied, "I want a fur coat."

"Good," said the bear, "that is a negotiable thing. As for me, I only want a full stomach, so let us come to a compromise!"

They sat down to negotiate, and after a time the bear walked away alone. The negotiations had been quite successful. The bear had a full stomach, and, in a way, the hunter had his fur coat.

May 15
Are You Making a Difference?

One of the truly great spiritual men of the nineteenth century in England was William Wilberforce. He had experienced a profound religious conversion that led him to do great works of charity and kindness. In addition to those great works, he became a very strong, loud, and powerful voice against the evils of England's participation in the slave trade. He was surely one of the most vigorous opponents of the slave trade in England during the early 1800s.

As he surveyed the terrible moral and spiritual climate of his day, he did not lose hope. In fact, he had tremendous hope that his fellow Christians could make a difference. He wrote, "My own solid hopes for the well-being of my country depend not so much on her navies or armies nor on the wisdom of her rulers nor on the spirit of her people, as on the persuasion that she still contains many people who love and obey the gospel of Christ. I believe that their prayers may yet prevail. Their prayers will have great influence."

Within a few years after he made this statement, the country he loved experienced one of the greatest religious awakenings in modern times, bringing faith to thousands and producing widespread social changes. One of the most important of those social changes, the end of the slave trade in England, came about because of Wilberforce's strong words in Parliament and the way he lived his daily Christian life.

It was Wilberforce's words and his actions that brought about some much-needed change in the world in which he lived. How do you think your words and actions are affecting the world in which you live? In other words, are you making a difference?

May 16
All of the Time

Here is a story that goes all the way back to the time of the American Civil War.

On one particular Sunday morning near the end of the war in 1865, a black man from the South was bold enough to enter a fashionable church in Richmond, Virginia. There was much grumbling in the church that morning. Then, when communion was served, he walked down the aisle and knelt at the altar. A rustle of resentment swept the congregation. How dare he! After all, believers in that church used the common cup. There was no way that they would share the cup with that black man.

Suddenly a distinguished layman stood up, stepped forward to the altar, and knelt beside the black man. The congregation was absolutely quiet. With Robert E. Lee setting the example, the rest of the congregation soon came forward and knelt next to Lee and the black man, following Lee's lead.

Later that day, when Lee was asked about his actions, he replied, "I did that because a leader must always be a good leader, just as a good Christian must always be a good Christian."

Robert E. Lee's example can serve as a reminder to each of us that we are called to be good Christians all of the time, not just when it is easy, but especially when it would not be appreciated by the world around us.

May 17
Getting the Frantic Out of Your Life

I read about a national survey that showed most people today find they are not only busy but living frantic lives. The survey indicated that people say they are racing the clock all of the time. The results of that survey reminded me of something I learned at a seminar more than twenty years ago.

I don't remember the speaker's name, but I can still see her face. She had the most pleasant expression and she smiled a lot. The main theme of her talk was that if we want to live a less frantic life, we must begin with living more by the calendar than the clock. She told us if we make an effort to live a day at a time and not an hour at a time, we would immediately feel more peaceful.

I remember taking lots of notes at her talk because she spoke from the heart and gave such simple, down-to-earth advice. She gave us six things we needed to know to "get the frantic" out of our lives. I wrote them down on a piece of paper and put them in my Bible.

Here is the wisdom she shared that day: 1. Do your best to stop thinking about several things at once. One thought at a time is enough. 2. Listen without interrupting. 3. Read good books. Read things that brings out the best in you. 4. Avoid irritating people. Simply practice kindness every day. 5. Make sure you find some personal quiet time each day. 6. Always remember that things worth being are better than things worth having.

May 18
Humility

When I was in college, I majored in history. When we were studying the American Civil War, I came across a story about something Abraham Lincoln did during the most difficult days of the war that has always stuck with me.

In those dark days, Lincoln got caught up in a situation where he wanted to please a politician, so he issued a command to transfer certain regiments. When the Secretary of War, Edwin Stanton, received the order, he refused to carry it out. He said that the President was a fool.

Lincoln was told what Stanton had said, and he replied, "If Stanton said I'm a fool, then I must be, for he is nearly always right. I'll see for myself." Lincoln made his way over to the war department to talk with Stanton. As the two men talked, the President quickly realized that his decision was a serious mistake, and without hesitation he withdrew it. Lincoln was humble enough and wise enough to realize that he had made a terrible decision based on a need to please someone rather than to do, as Lincoln said, "the best and the right thing."

In your decisions, are you humble enough and wise enough to be able to admit when you have made a decision based on wanting to please others rather than on sound judgement?

May 19
Suffering

I often come across stories of famous people who have truly amazed me, yet there are often those who have horrified me. One story I found falls into that second category. The man I am thinking about was Vladimir Ulyanov, who was born in 1870 to a family that would suffer many tragedies in the years to come. Later, he used the pen name "Lenin" to promote his revolutionary ideas. He was completely wrapped up in himself and in his revolutionary work until he lost almost all capacity for human compassion. His friends said that there was no tenderness in him at all. Just about everyone who knew him said he was the most miserable man on earth.

He was married, but Lenin gave very little love to his wife, Krupskaya. One night she rose, exhausted from her vigil beside her dying mother, and asked Lenin, who was writing at a table, to awaken her if her mother needed her. Lenin agreed and Krupskaya collapsed into bed. The next morning, she awoke to find her mother dead and Lenin quietly at work on his writings. Distraught, she confronted Lenin, who replied, "You told me to wake you if your mother needed you. She died. She didn't need you. She doesn't matter anyway."

Such a cold-hearted response to human need and suffering is shocking. I remember asking a friend of mine, a woman who was very compassionate herself, how someone like Lenin could be so cruel and heartless. Her response was, "Well, he must have suffered a lot in his younger life. Suffering has the power to do two things to a person. It either makes them bitter or it makes them better. Obviously, the suffering in Lenin's younger life made him bitter."

How has the suffering in your life affected you? Has it made you bitter or better?

May 20
Not Things at All

I had breakfast recently with a group of businessmen. In the course of our conversation, we got to talking about the importance of knowing what really matters in life. One of the men said that he had a story that illustrated how people can miss what is really important.

There was a prosperous, young investment banker who was driving a new BMW sedan on a mountain road during a snowstorm. As he veered around one sharp turn, he lost control and began sliding off the road toward a steep cliff. At the last moment he unbuckled his seat belt, flung open his door, and leaped from the car, which then plummeted to the bottom of the ravine and burst into a ball of flames.

Although he had escaped with his life, the man suffered a ghastly injury. Somehow his arm had been caught near the hinge of the door as he jumped and had been torn off at the shoulder. A passing trucker saw the accident in his rearview mirror, pulled his rig to a halt and ran back to see if he could help.

When he arrived at the scene, he found the banker standing at the roadside, looking down at the BMW burning in the ravine below. Incredibly, the banker was oblivious to his injury and moaned, "My BMW! My new BMW!" The trucker pointed at the banker's shoulder and said, "You've got bigger problems than that car. We've got to find your arm. Maybe the surgeons can sew it back on!" The banker looked where his arm had been, paused a moment, and groaned, "Oh no! My Rolex! My new Rolex!"

We all laughed at the story, but as one businessman said it, "I bet we all know someone who puts things way ahead of what is truly important in life." Perhaps this story can help you look at your own priorities. Or again, as another man at that breakfast put it, in the end, we all will come to realize that the most important things in life aren't things at all.

May 21
Planned Neglect

Consider what for you is the most important thing you do each day. How far into your day are you before you get to doing that most important thing? I ask you this because of something I heard a parishioner tell me. She is in graduate school studying the violin, and she told me that the one thing that has changed her attitude about practicing the violin is a story her professor told her.

A noted concert violinist was asked the secret of her mastery of the instrument. The gifted woman answered the question with two words: "Planned neglect." Then she explained, "There are many things that used to demand my time. When I went to my room after breakfast, I made my bed, straightened the room, dusted, and did whatever seemed necessary. When I finished my work there, I went into the rest of my day doing what needed to be done. Then, when I had finished doing everything else that needed to be done, I turned to my violin practice."

"That system prevented me from accomplishing what I should on the violin. So, I reversed things. I deliberately planned to neglect everything else until my practice period was complete. And that program of planned neglect is the secret of my success."

When it comes to the most important thing in your life, do you need some "planned neglect?"

May 22
Buttons

I heard a clever little parable that I think you'll find helpful in your own spiritual life. It certainly has been in mine. I heard it when I was at breakfast with a father's group from a local parish. The topic for that morning's discussion was what Jesus meant when he told his followers, "Seek first the kingdom of God and his righteousness, and all things will be given you as well" (Matthew 6:33).

Most of the discussion was rather flat until one man in the group said he had a parable for us that explains what Jesus meant better than lots of talk. Here is how he told it:

"Have you ever been in a hurry and buttoned up a shirt with lots of buttons and when you were done, found out that the stupid shirt was uneven? What went wrong? I'll tell you what went wrong. When you don't get the first button in the right hole, all the rest are out of sequence too, right?! That's a parable about life. Jesus said it. If the Lord is not the high priority in your life, then, like the shirt, so many other things in life will be out of whack as well."

That simple story has been a big help in my spiritual life. Since I first heard it, every morning when I button up my shirt, I ask myself if I have Jesus in the right place in my heart. So, the next time you're buttoning up a shirt or a coat or sweater, ask yourself, "Is Jesus in the right place in my heart?"

May 23
Why Do You Do That?

Have you ever taken the time to consider just what your purpose in life really is? It's probably a good idea for all of us to take some time to remind ourselves why we choose to live the lives we live. I was recently reminded of the importance of this when I heard this story from a local doctor.

The story is about a little girl who had a very serious cancer that required some surgery. As she was about to undergo the dangerous operation, the whole surgical team was gathered around her. Just before the anesthesiologist was going to administer the anesthetic, he said, "Before we can make you well, we must put you to sleep." The girl responded, "Oh, if I'm going to go to sleep, then I must say my prayers first." Very reverently she folded her hands, closed her eyes, and said, "Now I lay me down to sleep, I pray the Lord my soul to keep. If I should die before I wake, I pray the Lord my soul to take. And this I ask for Jesus' sake. Amen." Then she added, "Ready!"

The doctor who told the story said there wasn't a dry eye in the operating room. Then he said that someone in the room said very softly, "Now I remember why I got into medicine: to care for the precious lives that God puts in our hands."

May 24
Hidden Greatness

Every so often, I come across an anecdote from history that I really enjoy, usually because it is so human and simple that it is also profound. I like the following story about Calvin Coolidge because it shows what kind of man he was even when no one else was watching. He was a man who noticed suffering and responded to it, even when the injury or wound was minor.

Dwight Morrow, the father of the famous Anne Morrow Lindbergh, once held a dinner party to which Calvin Coolidge had been invited. After Coolidge left, Dwight Morrow told the remaining guests that Coolidge would make a good president. The others disagreed. They felt Coolidge was much too quiet, that he lacked color and personality. No one would like him, they said.

Anne, who was then only 6 years old, spoke up: "I like him a lot," she said. Then she displayed a finger with a small bandage around it. "He was the only one at the party who asked about my sore finger. He is kind and he really cares. And that's why he would make a good president," added Morrow.

If you were to assess the members of your family, or even just the people you know, are you aware of their best qualities, which may be hidden from most people? Do you know anyone who possesses a hidden greatness?

May 25
Have You Ever Been?

Here is something for you to think about. First you will laugh. After you have laughed, ask yourself if you have ever been that Scotsman. You will see what I mean.

A young man from Scotland was admitted to Oxford University, and he moved into a dormitory there. His mother worried about how he'd get along with all those snobbish Brits in a strange land. She gave him a call. "How do you find the English students, Donald?" she asked.

"Oh, Mother," he said, "they are strange and noisy people. The one in the room on the left side of mine bangs his head against the wall all night and won't stop. The one on the right-side screams and curses until the sun comes up at dawn."

"Oh, Donald," said his mother, "How do you put up with such rude, noisy, people?"

"I ignore them, Mother," said Donald. "I just sit here quietly each night, playing my bagpipes."

May 26
Hearts Changed

I read a story recently about something really unusual that happened at a busy airport in Texas.

On one particular day, several flights had been overbooked and there was a very long line of travelers waiting to buy tickets. The line grew so long and moved so slowly that patience was wearing thin. As you could guess, at the worst possible moment, two boisterous women carrying large suitcases started elbowing their way to the front, demanding to be served next.

A man near the head of the line saw that the two women were pushing and shoving, and he feared that the situation was getting out of control and might even turn violent. Tempers were flaring. Consequently, the man offered them his own position. This response took everyone, including the two women, by surprise.

All at once a great sense of quietness came over the entire scene. The man then picked up his own luggage and walked to the back of the line. When the long line of people saw what the man did, they erupted into applause and began to laugh and speak kindly to one another.

One simple act of kindness had turned something that could have become ugly into something beautiful. There is great power in kindness; it can change hearts.

May 27
One Simple Gesture

Have you ever heard the story of what happened to Jackie Robinson, the first black man to play major league baseball? My younger brother, who loves baseball, told me this story about Robinson's first season with the Brooklyn Dodgers.

According to the story, Robinson faced hatred nearly everywhere he traveled. Pitchers threw fastballs at his head. Runners spiked him on the bases; brutal insults were written on cards and spoken from the opposing dugouts. Even the home crowds in Brooklyn treated him horribly.

During one game in Boston, the taunts and racial slurs seemed to reach a peak. To make matters worse, in that game, Robinson committed an error and stood at second base, humiliated while the fans hurled insults at him. The boos and screaming were deafening. But then something happened that was truly amazing. When the screaming and shouting was at their loudest, another Dodger, a Southern white man by the name Pee Wee Reese, called time-out.

As the insults flew, Reese walked from his position at shortstop toward Robinson at second base, and with the crowds looking on, he put his arm around Robinson's shoulder. The fans grew absolutely quiet. Robinson later said that arm around his shoulder saved his career and maybe even his life.

That is an amazing story. Is there anyone in your life right now who may be going through a terrible time and who needs you to call a time-out, walk to them, and to put an arm of encouragement around their shoulder? Can you image the good you could do with one simple gesture of kindness and support?

May 28
What Might You Hear?

Most folks are not aware of how much they need quiet time. I think this is one of the reasons that in chapter 6 of Mark's Gospel, Jesus takes his disciples, who had been surrounded by chaos, to an out of the way place to find some quiet.

When I think of how important quiet time can be for each of us, I remember something I read concerning what a fifth-grade teacher did with her students. She decided that she would use quiet time to teach a listening process with her children. Every morning for five minutes she asked them to be totally quiet. That's hard for any of us to do, much less a fifth grader.

At first, her students complained that it was too hard to be still and quiet for a whole five minutes. After about a week, the students started to get the hang of it and even said they liked being quiet. The teacher herself discovered that a great deal of good came from the experience of silence.

After one of these quiet sessions she asked the students if they had listened to their hearts during the quiet and if they did, had they heard anything. One boy said, "Yes, I heard something say that I should be more obedient to my parents." Another said, "I heard something say that you should always be fair. When you are tagged and nobody sees it, you're still out." One boy said, "It might sound strange, but I heard someone say, 'you're a good boy.'"

If you took the time to be quiet on a regular basis, what do you suppose you might hear during your quiet time?

May 29
Find a Fig Tree

I have been spending some time in prayer thinking about the apostle Nathaniel. He was one of the first people to express belief in Jesus Christ as the Son of God. He was also the one who was most skeptical about Jesus. When Nathaniel was told that Jesus was from Nazareth, he is the one who said, "Can anything good come from Nazareth?"

After his initial skepticism however, Nathaniel does go with Phillip to meet Jesus. When he sees Nathaniel coming toward him, Jesus says, "Here is a true Israelite in whom there is no deceit." Nathaniel is amazed that Jesus seems to already know him. He even asks Jesus how he knows him. Jesus tells him "Before Phillip called you, I saw you under the fig tree." The term "under the fig tree" is a Jewish figure of speech referring to spending much time absorbed in the Torah. It basically meant that Jesus saw him as a prayerful, holy man who spends time with God.

Some biblical scholars explain it by describing a fig tree. They say a fig tree is about fifteen feet tall and its branches spread out about 25 feet like an umbrella, creating a space that is almost like a private room. If someone wanted to get away from the chaos of life and worry and strife, he or she would sit under the fig tree. They would sit there to read scripture or to reflect, think, and talk with God. Sitting under a fig tree was a sign of seeking God's living presence. So when Jesus says, "I saw you under the fig tree," he is saying he knows that Nathaniel loves and is very close to God.

If you find yourself overwhelmed by the chaos life can sometimes bring, or if you are worried about someone or find yourself heavily burdened, perhaps Nathaniel can be a good guide for you. The next time you settle down to pray, invite Nathaniel to join you. I bet he will want to take you to Jesus by inviting you to sit with him under the fig tree. That is exactly what was happening with me in my prayer this past week: I found myself sitting under a fig tree with good old Nathaniel. It was some of the richest and deepest prayer I have had for quite some time.

If you need a break from life, go find a fig tree with Nathaniel!

May 30
Letting Them Know

Everyone who ever knew President Harry Truman knew one thing about him, and that was that Harry deeply loved his wife Bess. One of the signs of that love was all of the letters that he wrote to her over the course of a half-century. Truman had a lifelong rule of writing to his wife every day they were apart. He followed this rule whenever he was away on official business or whenever Bess left Washington to visit her family at home.

Many people marvel about the simple fact that the President of the United States, the busiest and most powerful man on earth, took time out from dealing with the world's most powerful leaders to sit down and write a letter to his wife. Bess Truman was the love of Harry's life and he made sure she knew it.

Who are the people in your life that you really love? Do they know how much you love them? When was the last time you took time out of your own busy or hectic schedule to let them know you are thinking about them?

May 31
A Muddled Mind

In my reading this morning I came across a quote from Henry Ford that I found very interesting. Ford complained that one of his weaknesses was that his mind raced through ideas so quickly he often could not keep up with them. He tried many different ways to confront that "weakness," as he called it.

This is what he said that I found so interesting: "A weakness of all human beings is trying to do too many things at once. That scatters effort and destroys direction. It makes for haste, and haste makes waste. So, we do things all the wrong ways possible before we come to the right one. Then we think it is the best way because it works, and it was the only way left that we could see. Every now and then I wake up in the morning headed toward that finality, with a dozen things I want to do. I know I can't do them all at once."

I think many people today find that, just like Henry Ford, their racing minds are too full and their thinking so distracted that they are often bewildered about what to do. Have you ever been bewildered in that way? Jesus taught his disciples that the best thing to do when we are overwhelmed or bewildered is to "Come away to a deserted place and pray." Jesus invited his own to find a place of quiet and let the dust settle so that the truth would become apparent.

As I read about Henry Ford, I began to wonder if he ever did something to let the confusion in his mind settle. I wondered if he ever prayed. Then I came across something he said that made me think that perhaps Ford had his own way of praying without knowing it was a form of prayer. When asked what he did about his spinning thoughts, Ford replied, "I go out and trot around the house. While I'm running off the excess energy that wants to do too much, my mind clears and there is a peaceful calm and a bit of clearing, and then I see what can be done and should be done first."

What do you do when your mind is muddled and you feel bewildered?

June

June 1
Laughing with Good Friends

I love the story of two buddies who met for dinner in a restaurant. Both loved fish so the both ordered filet of sole, and after a few minutes the waiter came back with their order. Two pieces of fish, a large and a small, were on the same platter. One of the men proceeded to serve his friend. Placing the small piece on a plate, he handed it across the table.

"Well, you certainly do have nerve!" exclaimed his friend.

"What's the matter with you?" asked the other.

"Look what you've done," his friend answered. "You've given me the little piece and kept the big one for yourself."

"Well, how would you have done it?" the man asked.

His friend replied, "If I were serving, I would have given you the big piece."

"Well," replied the man, "I have the bigger piece, don't I? So what's the problem?"

At this, they both laughed.

Aren't good friends fun? What a blessing it is for friends to spend time together laughing and just enjoying the depths of their friendship. When is the last time you thanked God for your friends? When is the last time you let your friends know how much you appreciate them?

June 2
Satan's Sowing Seeds

Have you noticed how much really bad news is reported in every news broadcast these days? And have you also noticed how many of the reporters seem to enjoy telling people all of that bad news? So what are we to do about all of this bad news? Well, as I was bringing all of this to prayer this morning, a story came to mind.

According to an old legend, a man once stumbled upon a great red barn after wandering in in a forest for days, seeking refuge from the howling winds of a storm. He entered the barn and slowly, his eyes grew accustomed to the dark. To his astonishment, he discovered that this was not just any old barn; he was in the barn where the devil kept his storehouse of seeds. These were the seeds that were sown in the hearts of men and women of all nations and lands.

The man became curious and lit a match. He began exploring the piles and bins of seeds around him. He couldn't help but notice that the majority of them said, "Seeds of Discouragement."

About that time one of the Santa's helpers arrived to pick up a load of seeds. The man asked him, "Why the abundance of discouragement seeds?" The little devil laughed and replied, "Because they are so effective, and they take root so quickly." "Do they grow everywhere?" the man asked.

At that moment the devil's helper became very quiet and sullen. With eyes full of hatred, he glared at the man and in disgust said, "No. They never seem to grow in the heart of a grateful person."

June 3
Through the Foggy Days

Back in the early 1900s, Winston Churchill received an invitation from George Bernard Shaw to the opening night of one of his plays.

The note read, "Enclosed are two tickets to the performance of a play of mine. Bring a friend -- if you have one."

Churchill sent back this reply: "Dear GBS, I thank you very much for the invitation and tickets. Unfortunately, I am engaged on that night, but could I have tickets for the second night -- if there is one?"

Winston Churchill had many gifts. One of those gifts that both friends and even his enemies admired was his sense of humor. A close friend of Churchill's said that in the darkest and most difficult days, his ability to make a joke, to turn a phrase to get people to laugh, and even to poke fun at himself was very often what got the nation through foggy days.

If you were to stop to think about your own friends, how many of them, through their ability to get you to laugh, have gotten you through your "foggy days?" Is there anyone among your friends who need you to do the same for them?

June 4
Upping Your Game

Have you ever had what might be called a "blue period?" A time when all of your zest for life and the joy of living seems to be gone? I think this happens to lots of people. But I think it can happen to institutions too. Have you ever noticed that some groups of people, however well-intentioned or well-meaning, seem to fall into a kind of slump and lose their enthusiasm?

Many years ago, Richard Cardinal Cushing wrote about the church's need for courage and renewal. He said: "If all the sleeping folks will wake up, and all the lukewarm folks will fire up, and all the disgruntled folks will sweeten up, and all the discouraged folks will cheer up, and all the depressed folks will look up, and all the estranged folks will make up, and all the gossiping folks will shut up, and all the dry bones will shake up, and all the true soldiers will stand up, and all the church members will pray up, and if the Savior of all will be lifted up in praise and thanksgiving ... then we can have the greatest renewal this world has ever known."

What Cardinal Cushing said about the Catholic Church could also be said about every one of us. What "ups" do you need to do to breathe new enthusiasm and excitement into your life?

June 5
The Years of Our Lives

An elderly man in my parish was eager to show me what his grandson sent him for his birthday. He said it tickled him so much that his grandson would make such a thing for him. The gift was a framed bit of calligraphy that his grandson had actually done himself. Beautifully done in several colors, it was very impressive to look at even from a distance. The title at the top of the piece was, "What Happens When We Grow Old." Beneath that title was a quote from one of Grimm's fairy tales.

"God originally determined 30 years as the ideal span of life for all animals, including mankind. The donkey, the dog, and the monkey considered it much too long, however, and begged God to reduce their years by 18, 12, and 10. Being healthy, vigorous, and somewhat greedy, the man asked to be given those extra years. God agreed, so man's years totaled 70."

"The first 30 years are his own and they pass quickly. The next 18 are the 'donkey years,' during which he has to carry countless burdens on his back. Then come the 'dog years,' 12 years when he can do little but growl and drag himself along. This is followed by the 'monkey years, his closing 10, when he grows rather strange and does things that make children laugh at him."

June 6
A Waste of Time?

Leonardo da Vinci was at work in Milan on his famous painting of the Last Supper when the abbot came and complained that the artist was spending too much time doing nothing. He was wasting time, and time was not to be wasted. The abbot said he would not pay Da Vinci if he wasn't working all of the time he was there.

Da Vinci explained that he spent many hours meditating in the chapel of the monastery where he was working in order to be filled with God's creative graces. The monks resented these idle periods and accused the artist of stealing valuable time. But da Vinci defended these periods of reflection by saying, "When I pause the longest, I make the most telling strokes with my brush, and Jesus appears on the wall before me. Is that not what you monks are supposed to be doing when you pray? If you are not doing that, then which of us is wasting or stealing valuable time?"

When you spend periods of time reflecting or meditating, do you feel that you are being filled with God's creative graces? Or do you feel, like da Vinci's monks, that your periods of reflections are just idle times, wasted times?

June 7
Would You Be Open Enough?

Have you ever been so deeply immersed in your prayer that you became completely unaware of what's going on right around you? When I was living as a hermit in the desert in Israel, one of the monks I would occasionally speak with reminded me to be sure to pray in a safe place. When I asked him what he meant, he simply said, "Sometime God may pull you into such deep prayer that you may not know where you are, and you may fall into a river or in a pit because you did not take care where you were praying."

Then he told me about something that happened to the famous poet Dante Alighieri. He said that the poet was in church one Sunday, praying at Mass, when all at once, God pulled him into deep, deep prayer. Being so deeply immersed in that prayer during the Mass, Dante failed to kneel at the appropriate moment. His enemies hurried to the bishop and demanded that Dante be punished for his sacrilege.

The bishop demanded an explanation from the poet. Dante defended himself by saying, "If those who accuse me had had their eyes and minds on God, as I had, they too would have failed to notice events around them, and they most certainly would not have noticed what I was doing."

That monk friend of mind concluded his story by telling me that if he saw me fail to kneel at the appropriate times during Mass, he would kindly assume God had pulled me into deep prayer!

Has God ever pulled you into a deep prayer that made you completely unaware of what was going on around you? Would you be open to such an experience if God offered it to you?

June 8
For Each Other

One of my favorite stories, said to be from the writings of Aesop, is the story of the blind man and the lame man. According to that story, it happened one day that a blind man and a lame man both came to a very dangerous stretch of road. The blind man begged the lame man to guide him along the road so that he didn't come to some terrible harm.

"How could I ever do that," said the lame man, "since I can scarcely drag myself along the road with these bad legs?"

The blind man got an idea and said, "I believe that if I were to carry you, you could warn me about what I might stumble over on the road. Your eyes would be my eyes and my feet would be your feet.

If we would provide for each other's lack, we will get where we are headed safely."

In your life right now, who provides for your lack? Is there anyone in your life right now who needs you to provide for their lack?

June 9
A Contented and Peaceful Fellow

The desert fathers used to tell the story of an angel who met a man carrying a very heavy sack. The angel asked the man what was in the sack, and the man replied, "This sack is filled to the top with all of my worries."

"Would you let me see them?" the angel asked.

When the sack was opened it was empty. When the man saw that the sack was empty, he just couldn't believe it. "Why, I had filled this sack with two great worries, one was of yesterday, which I now see is past; the other worry was of tomorrow, which I see has not arrived yet."

The angel then advised the man that he needed no sack, and the man threw it away immediately. He went on a very contented and peaceful fellow.

June 10
A Good Person

I attended a seminar recently where one of the presenters was talking about how important it is to be a person who always tells the truth. To illustrate his point, he told a story of how he almost got fired from his job at a bank just two days after he had been hired. He was young and new, and just learning the business.

On this particular day his boss told him, "If Mr. Thomas calls for me, tell him I'm out."

The new worker replied, "Oh, are you planning to go somewhere?"

"No, I just don't want to speak to him, so tell him I'm out."

"Let me make sure I understand: do you want me to lie for you?

Now at this, his boss blew up at him, was outraged and angered. His face became almost purple. The new worker prayed that somehow God would help him keep his job.

To his astonishment, God gave him a flash of insight. He turned to his boss and said, "You should be happy, because if I won't lie *for* you, isn't it safe to assume that I won't lie *to* you?" In the end, the guy kept his job.

The speaker concluded his talk with saying that by refusing to tell lies he showed he was a person of integrity. "Integrity," he said, "is allowing others to see the heart of your soul. Only truly good people do that."

Are you a person of integrity?

June 11
The Truth

There is a Yiddish proverb that young students in Hebrew school are taught to memorize, then write an essay on what the proverb means for their lives. The proverb is made up of just seven words, but it is a very powerful teaching. Here it is: "A half-truth is a whole lie."

Once, when a teacher introduced that famous proverb to his students, one of those students asked if the teacher could provide an example that would illustrate the truth of that proverb. The teacher, a former British diplomat who had served in Russia, said he could give an example from his own life. He said that one time, while drinking with a Russian diplomat in a bar in Moscow, he and the diplomat discussed how governments sometimes don't tell the whole truth.

The Russian diplomat said, "Let me show you how my government often shades the truth. Suppose you and I had a race, and you came in first. In England, your newspaper would report that the Russian and British diplomats had a race and the British diplomat won. In my country, the government would report the same event differently. They would report that a race took place between the Russian diplomat and a British diplomat. The Russian diplomat came in second and the British diplomat finished only just in front of the last man."

The teacher concluded his story by saying, "The proverb is, 'A half-truth is a whole lie.' Be sure you never tell a half-truth."

June 12
A Deep Love

At one of our parish retreats, a women's weekend, an older woman gave a witness on how much God had been a part of her marriage. She told the folks at the retreat that she was not a very religious person when she met her husband, but he was.

The woman went on to say that her husband never really preached at her about God, he simply showed her how God makes a man godly and how that godly man made her into a godly woman. She said her marriage was strong because of two factors. The first factor was that the love she and her husband shared was very deep. The second factor was that God was always in the center of this deep love.

That wonderful old woman concluded her witness by using an illustration. She said, "A braid appears to contain only two strands of hair. But if you know anything about braiding, you know it is impossible to create a braid with only two strands. If the two could be put together at all, they would quickly unravel. Herein lies the mystery: what looks like two strands require a third. The third strand, though not immediately evident, keeps the strands tightly woven. In a godly marriage, God's presence, like the third strand in a braid, holds both husband and wife together."

When she finished her talk, everyone in the room was in awe of her kind, thoughtful way of speaking. She looked around and said, "We all need to be braided into God! It will give you a deep love and make you truly happy!"

June 13
A Gentle Nudge

Nathaniel Hawthorne wrote to a friend about an event in his life that gave him the courage and the will to do what he needed to do. He said that if it had not been for the love of his wife and her encouragement, his life would have been entirely different.

Hawthorne said that in 1849, he had been diligently working at his government job in a customs house when, without warning, he was dismissed. He told his friend that he was at the point of suicide and walked home in deep and dark despair. His wife listened to his tale of woe, set pen and ink on the table, lit the fire in the fireplace, put her arms around his shoulders and said, "Now you will be able to write your novel." Her kindness and encouraging words enabled Nathaniel Hawthorne to put pen to paper, and he soon produced his famous work, "The Scarlet Letter."

Has anyone ever changed your life with a loving embrace, a few kind, encouraging words, and a gentle nudge into the future? Is there anyone who needs you to do that for them?

June 14
The Heat of Fear and Anxiety

We are living with a lot of uncertainty in the world right now that creates a lot of anxiety and fear. In these past few weeks, I have been listening to lots of people talk about how much time they are spending being worried and afraid. As I have listened to them, I keep hearing Jesus saying those very consoling words, "Know that I am with you always." One of the things that gives fear its power is that it tends to isolate us. If we try to face fear alone, we will most likely find that it overwhelms us. How do we keep that from happening?

Well, there's an old story that comes out of the U.S. Army. A certain sergeant in a parachute regiment was accompanying some trainees on a nighttime jump. He found himself seated next to a lieutenant fresh out of jump school.

The lieutenant looked a bit pale and sat staring off into space. The sergeant leaned over and touched his arm. "Scared, lieutenant?"

"No, certainly not," said the young officer, "just a bit apprehensive."

"What's the difference?"

The lieutenant turned to him and answered, "The difference is, I'm scared with a university education."

I laughed when I first heard that story, but there is something in it that is important to know when you try to face fear, worry, or anxiety. The Bible teaches about this. If you can name your fear, you are half-way to overcoming it. It doesn't matter what word you use to describe it; fear has great power over us if we let it stay vague and in the dark, whispering or even screaming at us. Once you can name your fear, then you can begin to bring it down to size and know how to cope with it.

The idea of coping with fear reminds me of another story: In the days of the westward expansion, many people traveled out West. Along the way, folks would become terrified when they saw a prairie fire coming. There was no way for them to outrun the fire or guess the safe route out. So, the pioneers would take a match to the grass in a designated area around them, then stand in the burned area and be safe from the threatening prairie fire.

As the roar of the flames approached, they were not afraid. Even as the waves of fire surged around them, they could stop being afraid, because fire had already passed over the place where they stood. They believed they were safe there because Jesus had promised to be with them. They could feel his presence and were no longer afraid.

June 15
In Your Mind and Heart

Picture a scene in your imagination from the life of Jesus and his apostles. Picture Jesus out working, speaking and healing folks, teaching his disciples. Suddenly, out of nowhere come messengers with the tragic news that John the Baptist was dead. The news was devastating to all who knew and loved John.

Imagine Jesus receiving this news; what does he do? A simple and very undramatic thing: he calmly turns to his apostles, perhaps with a heavy sigh, and says softly, "Come apart with me to a quiet place, and let us rest awhile." That was all, just this. And together they went off to rest, gather their thoughts, and pray. In the midst of difficult news, in the midst of chaos and confusion, Jesus takes them aside to calm their hearts and minds.

This is what Jesus invites us to do when life brings us bad news, chaos, storms of any kind, fear, or anxiety. He simply asks us to not fall apart, but rather to come apart with him to gather strength for going on in peace, serenity, and calm.

Jesus does not promise to calm every storm in your life. But Jesus does promise to calm *you* in every storm of life. Try to keep this in your mind and heart.

June 16
When Changes Come

Here is something to spend some time thinking about. A daughter was talking with her mother, who had just celebrated her 88th birthday. She was trying to convince her mother to come live with her. The daughter said, "Now, Mom, I know it is difficult for you now that Dad has gone, and I think it's not good for you to live alone. Why don't you move in with me and my family?"

Her mother looked at her and said, "A thousand times, no! I've always heard from friends how much stress there is when an old bird like me moves into their children's home. It brings too many problems, too much tension. I think that such a change would be too much for me to bear."

The daughter took a few minutes to gather her thoughts, then said, "Mom, I know that's true in some families, but you are different!" To which her mother replied, "Yes, I know I am different ... but you are not!"

A conversation like the one above will probably happen in every family at some time in the future. The question that conversation raises for each of us is, "How well do I adjust to the natural changes life brings with it?" If you were to evaluate your own attitude towards change, would you say you handle change well or not so well? When the changes that everyday life brings come your way, how well will you do?

June 17
Pain and Beauty

Years ago, I read something about the famous artist Auguste Renoir that I have never forgotten. In fact, I often think of it whenever I visit with a parishioner who is sick, in pain, and confined to bed.

In the last twenty years of Renoir's life he was afflicted with terribly painful arthritis. His hands were twisted and gnarled, and the disease in his spine made the slightest movement excruciatingly painful. He needed assistance to move from one position to another. On some days his paint brushes had to be tied to his hands because he could not hold them like he once could. The pain he suffered while painting caused great beads of sweat to roll down his face.

On one occasion, one of his students, the artist Henri Matisse, asked him, "Why do you torture yourself this way and continue painting when it obviously causes you such great pain?" Renoir looked at Matisse and said, "You will learn as you age that pain passes but beauty remains. The beauty is worth the pain."

In your experience, does pain pass and beauty remain? Is beauty truly worth the pain?

June 18
The Best Medicine

One of the things that Abraham Lincoln was famous for was his sense of humor. Old Abe loved a good joke more than most folks. His contemporaries often remarked about how they would find him laughing at jokes, especially jokes that made him the butt of the joke. Here is one that he loved to tell on himself.

Lincoln said that one day, naturally enough, he was much surprised when a man of rather forbidding countenance drew a revolver and thrust the weapon almost into his face. In this circumstance Abe at once concluded that any attempt at debate or argument was a waste of time and words. "What seems to be the matter?" inquired Lincoln, with all the calmness and self-possession he could muster.

"Well," replied the stranger, who did not appear at all excited, "some years ago I swore an oath on the Bible that if I ever came across an uglier man than myself, I'd shoot him on the spot." A feeling of relief took possession of Lincoln at these words, as the expression on his face lost all suggestion of anxiety. "Shoot me, then" Lincoln said to the stranger, "for if I am an uglier man than you, I don't want to live."

When asked why he told so many jokes and spent so much time laughing at other folk's jokes, Lincoln replied that a good sense of humor can cure a lot of deep wounds, lift one out of the darkness that our world can plunge us into, and break the strain of heavy burdens.

Do you have a good sense of humor?

June 19
Do You Need a Holy Man?

Here is an interesting story that comes from the wisdom stories of a branch of Islam. It always makes we laugh whenever I read it. The purpose of the story is to teach us how to solve problems in clever ways. According to the story, there was once a small boy who banged on a drum all day and sometimes far into the night as well. This became a major problem for the villagers because no matter what anyone else said, he would not stop. Various experts and other "wise" people were called in by neighbors and asked to do something about the child.

Since the experts seemed helpless, one by one, townsfolk came to warn the boy about his eardrums, while others tried to tell him that drums were only for sacred ceremonies. Other folks gave him a book and meditation lessons, hoping to calm him down. They even gave neighbors earplugs. Nothing worked.
Eventually, a Sufi holy man came along. At once, he sized up the situation and knew just what to do. Handing the boy a hammer, he said, "I wonder what's *inside* that drum?" Problem solved!

June 20
A Litmus Test

I was talking with a good friend one day when I was having a difficult time making a decision about an assignment that the bishop wanted me to consider taking. My friend said, "Are you looking for a kind of litmus test to help you make the decision?" I told him that I supposed I was. Then he said, "Read some Thomas Merton." I told him I would do that, but I didn't know what part of Merton's vast writings I was supposed to read.

A few days later my friend sent me a note with this information. Thomas Merton once said that whenever he found himself struggling to identify what God wanted him to do in a given situation, he always resolved the problem by asking himself one simple question. That one simple question was: "What is best for the folks around me?"

Merton said that simple question was how he found his way through tough questions. At the bottom of the note he had sent me, my friend wrote, "Mark, I think Merton's question is the litmus test you were looking for the other day."

Have you ever been unsure of your future or not certain about what you think God might want you to do? Perhaps you too can find your litmus test in Merton's question: "What is best for the folks around me?"

June 21
Something to Deepen Your Prayer

Years ago, while studying Zen, I went to a seminar on Zen meditation. One of the things the speaker said at that seminar has stayed with me all these years.

The speaker went around the room asking each person what they were looking for in learning Zen meditation. When everyone had given their reasons for coming and explained what they were looking to learn, he said, "Please listen to me. You all seem to be carrying heavy loads of some kind. I can see it in your faces, and I can hear it your words. You all are like the old man riding down the road on a donkey while he carried a 200-pound sack of wheat on his shoulder. Someone asked him why he didn't take the weight off his shoulders and strap it to the donkey. 'Oh, no!' he protested. 'I couldn't ask the donkey to carry all that weight.' If you are to get anywhere in your Zen practice, you must put down the burdens you carried in here."

Ever since that day so many years ago, whenever I take time to pray, the first thing I do is ask myself what burdens I'm carrying into my prayer. If I am to hear God's voice clearly, I must put the burdens down first.

Here is a gift for your practice of prayer. Do this and you will be freer to hear God's voice. Before you settle down to pray today, ask yourself, "What burdens have I carried in here with me?"

June 22
Caring and Truthful and Kind

This story will give you pause to consider what the desert fathers called the "law of the echo."

There once was a farmer who had planted his fields with a crop of melons. When the crop was near harvesting, he noticed that some of his crop was disappearing fast from his field. Thieves were continually stealing the melons under the cover of night's darkness.

The farmer was quite angry that he was the victim of such thieves, so he vowed to get even with them. The problem was that he was unable to catch them. The farmer finally became desperate and, in an attempt to save his crop from the vandals he decided to put up a sign. The sign had on it a skull and crossbones, and it read: "One of these melons is poisoned"—only the farmer knew that it was not true.

Sure enough, for two nights not a melon was missing. The farmer was thrilled that he had stopped the thieves. He congratulated himself and thought that the problem was solved. But after the third night, the farmer noticed that his sign had been altered. Someone had scratched out the word "one" and replaced it with another word so that the sign now read: "Two of these melons are poisoned."

Thinking to save his whole crop through deception, he lost it all, which goes to illustrate what the desert fathers taught their disciples. They called it the "law of the echo" -- what you send out will always come back to you. With that, the fathers warned their disciples to be caring and truthful and kind.

June 23
Do You Agree?

Here is something to think about. There was a poll on the Internet that asked a series of questions. The first question was, "Which member of your family is the best-looking?"

If you had to answer that question, what would you say? Would you like to guess how respondents answered? The top-rated answer in the poll was, "me." A majority of the respondents listed themselves as the best-looking member of their family.

The next question the survey asked was, "Which member of your family is the smartest?" Now, how would you answer that question? Guess what? "Myself" or "me" were the highest-ranked answers.

The next question was, "Which family member is most likely to tell a lie?" How would you answer that one? The responses to that question were different from the previous ones. "Myself" or "me" only ranked ninth out of ten possible answers.

The researchers who wrote the survey came to one conclusion: most of us think that we are better-looking, smarter, and more honest than the rest of our family. Do you agree?

June 24
Can You Imagine?

I read about an event that happened to the famous abolitionist, Frederick Douglass. Abraham Lincoln had invited him to his second inaugural ball. On the evening of the ball, Douglass approached the front door of the White House, where the event was being held. Just as Douglass was about to knock on the door, two policemen seized him, immediately barring the black man's entrance. Douglass, a large, powerful man, pushed the officers aside and stepped into the White House foyer. Once inside, two military officers grabbed who they thought was an uninvited guest, all the while uttering racial slurs.

As Douglass was being dragged from the hall, he cried to a nearby patron, "Just tell Mr. Lincoln that Fred Douglass is at the door!" Confusion ensued. Then suddenly the officers received orders to usher Douglass into the East Room. In that beautiful room, the great abolitionist stood in the presence of the President. The place quieted as the President approached his newly arrived guest, with his hand outstretched in greeting, smiling and speaking in a voice loud enough so none could mistake his intent: "Here comes my good friend Douglass."

Can you imagine what Frederick Douglass felt when Lincoln welcomed him in that way? What a powerful act of kindness. As I think about that scene, I am reminded that one day, each one of us will be at the door of heaven, hoping to be let in. Can you imagine what it would feel like to have Jesus walk toward you with hand outstretched, smiling and saying, "Here comes my good friend!"?

June 25
Anyone You Know?

I read about a man who was a very successful producer of Broadway plays and other stage productions. Over time, in the course of his very busy work schedule, he began to notice little things about himself and became convinced he was either losing his hearing or losing his mind.

Preferring not to think he was losing his mind, he decided to consult with a hearing specialist, who gave him a thorough checkup. At the conclusion of the examination, the doctor turned to his patient and said, "Let me do just one more test to satisfy my own mind about my conclusions."

The doctor pulled out a gold pocket watch and asked, "Can you hear this thing ticking?" The man said, "Of course I can hear it, clear as a bell." The specialist walked to the door and held up the watch again. "Now can you hear it?" The man concentrated hard and said, "Yes, I can, very clearly." Finally, the doctor walked out the door into the next room and said, "Can you in any way hear this thing now?" Incredibly, the man said, "Yes!"

The doctor said, "Well then, I am now certain of my conclusions. I am certain that there is nothing wrong with your hearing. You are just one of those thickheaded, self-absorbed folks who can hear quite well. You just don't listen."

Do you know anyone like that?

June 26
Looking Down Deep

There are many stories told about the great artist, Michelangelo. One story is about the day when he found that he had attracted a large crowd of spectators as he was carving a statue. There was one little girl in particular who was fascinated by the sight of the marble chips flying and the sound of the mallet on the chisel as the master shaped a large block of white marble.

Unable to contain her curiosity, the little girl shouted, "What are you making?" Pausing, he replied, "You see, there is an angel deep down inside of this block and I must set it free." With eyes as big as saucers, the little girl asked, "Do you mean that an artist can look deep inside a big block of stone and see what's really in there?"

Michelangelo laughed and said, "Why, of course I can!" Then he added, "God also gives some people the ability to look deep into other people's hearts and souls and see what is down real deep in them too." Wide-eyed again, the little girl asked, "Can you look into my heart and soul to see what is down deep in there?" The artist looked right into her eyes and said softly, "Yes, and I can see that there is an angel in your heart!"

Do you have something in common with the great Michelangelo? Can you look into the heart and soul of each of your family members, or into the hearts of each of your friends, and see the goodness that is truly there down deep at the center? Have you ever tried to look for it?

June 27
Truly Faithful

I was in a shopping mall when some college students approached me and asked me if I ever went to church. I assured them that I did go to church, but that was not enough for them. They were from a local megachurch and they were out looking to recruit new members.

When I said I was happy with the church I was attending, they asked me just how faithful I was to it. I said as faithful as I can be. They smiled very warmly at me and said, "We want you to have this picture of Jesus and we would just ask you to read the back side of the picture when you get some quiet time." I agreed to do so, and I stuck the picture in my pocket and went about my business.

As I was getting ready for my night prayer time, I found the picture of Jesus. I turned it over and this is what I read:

How faithful are you to church and to God? Before you answer, consider these levels of faithfulness: If your car started one out of three times, would you consider it faithful? If the paperboy skipped Monday and Thursdays, would you consider the paperboy faithful? If you didn't show up at work two or three times a month, would your boss call you faithful? If your refrigerator quit a day now and then, would you excuse it and say, "Oh, well, it works most of the time." If your water heater greets you with cold water one or two mornings a week while you are in the shower, would it be faithful in your eyes? If you miss a couple of mortgage payments in a year's time, would your mortgage holder say, "Oh, well, ten out of twelve isn't bad"? If you miss worship and attend meetings only often enough to show you are interested but not often enough to get involved, are you faithful?

Having read the above, are you truly faithful to God?

June 28
Miracles

People often ask me if I have ever seen a miracle. I always tell folks that I have seen many in my forty years as a priest. Some of those miracles are right out there in the open; others are ordinary things that, when closely examined, are found to be truly miraculous but hidden. One example of an everyday miracle is the amazing gift of sight.

The way we see is truly a miracle. Let me explain. The nerve cells of the eyes are divided into two separate systems: a set of cones that detect color and operate in good light, and a set of rods that see only monochromatically and come into play in poor light. The momentary blindness we experience when moving from darkness to bright light or vice versa lasts for the time it takes the eye to switch from one system to the other.

The rods tend to be scattered around the edge of the retina, away from the center—which is why it is easier to see things in the dark when one is not looking directly at them. These receptors are astonishingly sensitive; in total darkness, the human eye can detect the light of a solitary candle positioned five miles away. Isn't that amazing? Some would call it miraculous.

Would you call the gift of sight a miracle? Why or why not?

June 29
A Good Lesson

I read something rather interesting about what happened when Apollo 12 took off for the moon. Just moments after take-off the spacecraft was hit by lightning. The entire console began to glow with orange and red trouble lights.

At first, the astronauts were paralyzed with fear. There was a temptation to "do something!" But the pilots asked themselves, "Is this thing still flying in the right direction?" The answer was yes, it was headed for the moon. They let the lights glow as they addressed each of the individual problems, and watched orange and red lights blink out, one by one. Everything was back to normal.

What those astronauts did in the face of a great crisis can be a lesson for us when we face unexpected crises. This is something to think about in any pressure situation. If your "spacecraft" is still flying, don't panic. Think first, and then act.

June 30
Make the World a Better Place

I recently attended a talk given by a very elderly man. He told us that he was going to share some wisdom he had learned over the years about how we ought to think before we ever consider talking about each other. He said that in his experience of life, the world would be a better place if we would all just THINK before we spoke. Then he used the word "think" as an anagram.

T Is it true?
H Is it helpful?
I Is it inspiring?
N Is it necessary?
K Is it kind?

He concluded by saying, "Just say to yourself, 'If what I am about to say does not pass those tests, I will keep my mouth shut!' If you do that you will be doing your part to make the world a better place." Pretty good advice, don't you think?

July

July 1
Changing the World

Here is something to consider before you start your day: How would you go about changing the world for the better? Who, in the story below, has changed the world for the better by their actions?

A few months after moving to a small town a woman was quite unhappy. She complained to one of her new neighbors about the poor service at the local drugstore, hoping that the neighbor would repeat her complaint to the owner.

Next time she went to the drugstore, the druggist greeted her with a big smile and told her how happy he was to see her again. He said he hoped she liked their town and to please let him know if there was anything, he could do to help her and her husband get settled. He then filled her order promptly and efficiently.

Later, the woman reported what she thought was a miraculous change to her neighbor. "I guess you told the druggist how poor I thought the service was?" she asked.

"Well, no," her neighbor said. "In fact -- and I hope you don't mind -- I told him you were amazed at the way he had built up this small-town drugstore, and that you thought it was one of the best run drugstores you'd ever seen."

So, ask yourself again, "How would I go about changing the world for the better?"

July 2
An Instrument of Peace

One day, when Vice-President Calvin Coolidge was presiding over the Senate, one Senator angrily told another to go "straight to hell." The offended Senator, a man who took himself 'way too seriously, immediately complained to Coolidge as presiding officer. With a twinkle in his eye, Coolidge looked up from the book he had been leafing through while listening to the debate. "I've been looking through the rule book," he said. "You don't have to go."

With that remark, the entire Senate broke out in a roar of laughter. In fact, even the offended senator was laughing.

When I first read that story, I was really impressed by how Coolidge could take a potentially disastrous situation and with a bit of humor defuse the rancor, calm the tensions in the room, and get the members of the Senate to not take themselves so seriously. In a very unassuming way, he was truly a peacemaker that day. I like this story because it reminds me that, at any moment, in very ordinary situations, I could be called on to be the same kind of peacemaker.

You too could be called on at any moment today to step into a potentially disastrous situation, and with a simple sentence or calming attitude be an instrument of peace. Cal Coolidge was alert enough, and even kind enough, to do that very thing on the floor of the U. S. Senate.

July 3
What Principle do you Follow?

William B. McKinley, who was President of the United States from 1897 to 1901, was a man who believed in and lived by a principle from a an ancient Roman man by the name of Publilius Syrus.

McKinley himself practiced that same principle during one of his campaigns. There was a reporter from an opposition newspaper who followed him constantly and just as persistently misrepresented McKinley's views and spread half-truths about him to make him look bad. He was a real nuisance for McKinley.

At one point during this campaign, the weather became extremely cold, and even though the reporter didn't have sufficiently warm clothing, he still followed McKinley. One bitter evening, the president-to-be was riding in his closed carriage, and the young reporter sat shivering on the driver's seat outside. McKinley had noticed how the reporter was dressed so he stopped the carriage and invited the reporter to put on his coat and ride with him inside the warm carriage.

The young man, astonished, protested that McKinley knew that he was opposition and that he wasn't going to stop opposing McKinley during the campaign. McKinley knew that, but he wasn't out to seek revenge. In the remaining days of the campaign, the reporter continued to oppose McKinley, but never again did he write anything unfair or biased about the future president.

What was the principle that McKinley learned from that ancient Roman Publilius Sysrus? Simply this: "You can accomplish much more by kindness than you could ever accomplish by force."

July 4
Freedom

Today is Independence Day in the United States of America. It is a day to celebrate the gift and meaning of freedom, a time to consider what freedom means for each of us as individuals and as a nation.

I have been thinking about a quote that someone gave me a few months ago from a well-known apostle of freedom. He is not known for being a founding father of the United States, but he is a founding father of freedom for the whole world. The person I am talking about is Nelson Mandela. When he was asked what it means to be free, this is what he said: "For to be free is not merely to cast off one's chains, but to live in a way that respects and enhances the freedom of others."

On this Independence Day, why not take some time to consider your own independence. What have you done with the freedoms you enjoy? Have you kept those freedoms for yourself, or do you look for ways for others to share in those freedoms? What does freedom mean to you?

July 5
What Can?

What is your attitude when it comes to money? Do you spend a lot of your time and energy thinking about it? Is having a lot of money an important goal for you in life? Do you derive your own sense of self-worth based on how much money you earn? And finally, one more question: Do you own your money or does your money own you?

The ancient Greeks thought about money and they made some interesting observations about it. For instance, they said that money can buy you a bed, but it can't buy you a good night's sleep. It can buy you books, but not intelligence. It can buy you food, but not an appetite. It is important to know that money can buy you a house, but not a home. It can buy medicine, but it can't buy health. It can buy all kinds of amusements, but it can't buy happiness. Money can even buy a great dog, but money won't make the dog wag its tail.

So, what is your attitude towards money? Can it really give you what you need most? What is it that gives meaning to your life? Can money or any kind of material wealth ever make you truly happy? If money cannot do all the things listed above, what can?

July 6
In Their Hands

On a recent off day, I decided to spend the morning at a local art museum. It turned out to be a wonderful morning because I was able to tag along as a university art teacher was teaching his students about the art of sculpture. What I remember most about that tour was a story the professor told. He was telling his students that artists have a great gift to help us all see the world with new eyes. Then he said the people who most need affirmation in this world are the artists themselves because they work so hard, yet few ever notice how much of themselves they put into their work. Here is the story that he told:

In Florence, Italy, a young, timid artist labored long and hard over a marble statue of an angel. When finished, he was so proud of what he had done that he asked Michelangelo to examine it. The young artist stood alongside as Michelangelo examined his work. No master looked over the work more carefully. It was perfect in every detail.

The young artist waited, but his heart broke when Michelangelo said, "It lacks only one thing," then walked away. For days the artist could neither eat nor sleep. He called on Michelangelo at his studio and asked, "What is this one thing my work lacks? Please, tell me, I must know!" Michelangelo responded, "It is perfect in every detail. Your work is magnificent. It only lacks one thing: life itself!" Now the master could not pay any artist a finer compliment, but the young man thought he had failed.

A few days later Michelangelo found the young artist and explained that the statue of the angel was truly magnificent, but it could never match the life in that young artist's hands. Michelangelo said that the statue had no life of its own, but it reflected the life and love of the one who created it. The young artist then went away truly happy.

The professor concluded his story by saying to each of the artists in his class, "Never forget what life and love is in each of your hands when you set out to create new works of art!"

As I left the museum that day, I began to think of all the people I know who, although they may not be artists, they certainly have life and love in their hands, which they use to change the world. Who in your life can you identify as people with life and love in their hands?

July 7
Freedom

There is a famous story that comes from India about a man who went to a circus. As he got closer to the elephants the man noticed that these huge creatures were being held by only a small rope tied to their front leg. The rope was tied to a wooden peg in the ground: no chains, no cages. It was obvious that the elephants could, at any time, break away from their bonds, but for some reason they did not.

The man saw a trainer nearby and asked why these animals just stood there and made no attempt to get away. "Well," trainer said, "when they are very young babies, we use the same size rope to tie them to a peg. At that age, the elephant is not strong enough to break free of them. As they grow up, they are conditioned to believe they cannot break away. They believe the rope can still hold them, so they no longer even try to break free."

The trainer concluded by saying that the mighty elephants could at any time break free from their bonds, but because they believe they can't they don't.

What we believe can either keep us captive or set us free. Do you have any beliefs that are keeping you captive? Do you have any beliefs that are setting you free?

July 8
Paybacks

Here's a story that you can take to your meditation today. Spend some time thinking about it, then throughout the next few days, think about how you will treat the people God sends your way.

There once was a farmer who regularly sold butter to the local baker. One day, the baker decided to weigh the butter to see if he was getting the exact amount that he asked for. He found out that he wasn't, so he took the farmer to court.

The judge asked the farmer if he used any measure to weigh the butter. The farmer replied, "Your Honor, I'm a simple guy. I don't have a proper measure, but I do have a balance scale."

The judge replied, "Then how do you weigh the butter?"

The farmer replied; "Your Honor, long before the baker started buying butter from me, I have been buying a pound loaf of bread from him. Every day, when the baker brings the bread, I put it on the scale and give him the same weight in butter. If my butter does not weigh a pound, it must be that the baker's bread must not weigh a pound. If anyone is to be blamed, it's the baker."

July 9
According to You

I want to give you a corny little poem to take to your prayer today. It always brings a smile to my face when I read it and recall where I got it. I have kept a copy of it in my bible all these years. I want to tell you the memory I have that goes with it.

When I was in seminary years ago, I had an elderly priest who was a great mentor to me. If I am a good priest today, it is probably due to his kind influence. He was quite old, having been ordained in 1916, and he would often tell me that since he had been around for such a long time that I should be sure to listen to him. I did listen to him and I have never forgotten the wisdom he shared with me.

Today, when I was at prayer I recalled something that old Father Bernard did when he went into a class of fifth graders to teach the something about the Bible. He gave the students a copy of a little poem and asked each student to memorize it. If they could do that in 15 minutes he promised to give each one who did it a quarter. Every kid in that class memorized that poem! And, true to his word, Father Bernard paid each one of them one a quarter. I memorized the poem too, and he even gave me a quarter as well. I still remember that little poem and often think of it when I sit down in the early the morning to pray with the Scriptures.
Here is that "quarter winning" poem:

"You are writing a Gospel, a chapter each day
By the deeds that you do, by the words that you say.
Men read what you write, whether faithless or true,
Now, what is the Gospel according to you?

July 10
Problems

There is a story told about a very practical holy man who many townsfolk would go out to the desert to consult. They loved his down-to-earth advice because they always felt better about themselves and about life whenever they spent time with him.

The story goes that many people who were visiting him complained about the same problems over and over again. So, the next time someone came to him with the same problem they had at the last several visits, the holy man at first would listen very attentively. Then, he would tell the person a joke, and they would roar with laughter.

A few minutes after that, he would tell them the same joke. This time, only a few of the people would smile. Then he told the same joke for a third time. Now, after the third time, no one laughed or smiled.

The wise man would smile and say, "You can't laugh at the same joke over and over. So why are you always crying about the same problems over and over?"

Do you cry about the same problems over and over?

July 11
Worries

At a small university, some very unhappy students came to a wise, old teacher to ask for his advice. They wanted to know how they could ever be free from all of the worry, anxiety, fear, and stress that life seems to bring. They had all talked about how this teacher always seemed to be at peace and never worried about anything.

The teacher wanted to help these young folks but knew they would not listen if he simply talked with them So, he invited them to join him down in the dining hall. When they arrived there, he gave each of the students an empty glass. Then he got a pitcher of water and began to fill each person's glass to the very top. He asked the students to hold the glass of water at arm's length, straight out in front of them, and asked, "How heavy is your glass of water?"

The students started to shout out guesses ranging anywhere from 4 ounces to 6 ounces to 8 ounces.
Then their teacher said, "The absolute weight of this glass isn't what matters while you are holding it. Rather, it's the amount of time that you have to hold onto it that makes an impact. If you hold it for, say, two minutes, it doesn't feel like much of a burden. If you were to hold it for an hour, that would be a different story altogether. Can you image how heavy it would seem if you had to hold it for an entire day? What if you had to hold it for an entire week?"

The whole time the teacher talked, the students continued to hold the glass of water in front of them. Then the wise old teacher said, "The actual weight of the glass will remain the same, no matter how long you hold it. But the longer you hold onto it, the heavier it feels to you and the more burdensome it is to hold. Now, pay attention to what I am about to say to you. The glass of water represents the worries and stresses that you carry around with you every day. If you think about them for a few minutes and then put them aside, it's not a heavy burden to bear. If you think about them for a longer period of time, you will start to feel the impact of the stress. If you carry your worries with you all day and all night, you will become incapacitated, paralyzed, and unable to be happy. You won't be able to enjoy much of anything until you let them go."

"My advice to you all is very simple. Just put down your worries and stress, and don't hold on to them. Don't give them your entire attention or you will discover you are miserable while your life is passing you by."

Are you holding on to some fear or worry that is becoming too heavy to hold onto any longer? Is your life passing you by?

July 12
Listen to the Dogs

There is a woman in my neighborhood who is always out walking her dog. She makes a point of stopping to talk to me when she sees me out walking. The woman brings her dog to me and says, "If you want to be close to God, you have to go to the dogs!" Then she laughs. We usually continue to talk about what's going on in the world and in the neighborhood. When our conversation is over, she always tells me that her dog has taught her everything, especially how to be a good person. It is always a very enjoyable encounter when she and I and her dog meet when we are out for a walk.

The last time we met, my friend was excited to give me something she had discovered. She told me that the author is unknown, but she is certain that it must be an angel sent from God. The little essay is entitled, "If a dog were your teacher." I have to admit, I really like it. See if you do too.

If a dog were your teacher, these are some of the lessons you might learn:
When loved ones come home, always run to greet them.
Never pass up the opportunity to go for a joyride.
Allow the experience of fresh air and the wind in your face to be pure ecstasy.
When it's in your best interest, practice obedience.
Let others know when they've invaded your territory.
Take naps and stretch before rising.
Run, romp, and play daily.
Thrive on attention and let people touch you.
Avoid biting when a simple growl will do.
On warm days stop to lie on your back on the grass.
On hot days drink lots of water and lay under a shady tree.
When you're happy, dance around and wag your entire body.
No matter how often you're scolded, don't buy into the guilt thing and pout:
run right back and make friends.
Delight in the simple joy of a long walk.
Eat with gusto and enthusiasm.
Stop when you have had enough.
Be loyal.
Never pretend to be something you're not.
If what you want lies buried, dig until you find it.
When someone is having a bad day, be silent and stay close by.

July 13
Shining Light

Here is an interesting story from my college days, when I majored in history. When we studied European history, our professor went on and on about how much of that history is filled with one war after another. Then he said, "The amazing thing is that in the midst of the darkest times, there are always wonderful people who are shining lights. They endure terrible things, but somehow, they produce goodness in themselves and in the people around them. They are shining lights! I encourage you to look for them as you study history."

Our professor than gave us an example of a church pastor who was just such a burning light. In 1636, amid the darkness of the Thirty Years' War, Martin Rinkart, a German pastor, is said to have buried five thousand of his parishioners in one year -- an average of fifteen a day. His parish was ravaged by war, death, and economic disaster. In the heart of that darkness, with the cries of fear outside his own window, he sat down and wrote this table grace for his children. You may recognize the words:

Now thank we all our God
With heart and hands and voices;
Who wondrous things had done,
In whom his world rejoices.
Who, from our mother's arms
Hath led us on our way
With countless gifts of love
And still is ours today.

Pastor Martin Rinkart was a shining light in a very dark time. He was a man who knew thanksgiving comes from love of God, not from outward circumstance.

July 14
The Love of Money

Take a moment to ask yourself this question: How important is money to me? Saint Francis of Assisi would ask his followers, "Do you own your money, or does your money, and your need for it, own you?"
These are important questions because one's attitude when it comes to wealth can make or break your soul. Here is a story to illustrate that point. It comes from a Jewish sage.

One day a certain old, extremely rich man of miserable disposition visited his rabbi, who took the rich man by the hand and led him to a window. "Look out there," he said. The wealthy man looked into the street. "What do you see?" asked the rabbi. "I see men, women, and children," answered the rich man. Again, the rabbi took the man by the hand and this time led him to a mirror. "Now, what do you see?" "Now I just see myself," the rich man replied.

Then the rabbi said, "Now let me teach you what God would tell you. Behold, in the window there is glass, and in the mirror, there is glass. But the glass of the mirror is covered with a little silver, and no sooner is the silver added than you cease to be able to see others, so you see only yourself. This is what happens when money is everything to you. This is how money becomes silver on the window of your life."

So consider: How important is money to you?

July 15
What Could Be

Here is a story that I have been using in my meditation this week. It helps me to see the world around me and the people around me in an entirely new way. Spend some time with this story and see if that happens to you, too.

Once there was a man on a train that was going across the desert in Arizona. He was the only person in the car who had not pulled down the window shades to keep out the glare of the hot sun on the parched earth. In contrast to the other passengers, he kept looking out his window and seemed actually to enjoy the hot, barren, and forsaken scene.

After a while, a curious man seated across the aisle asked, "Sir, what are you seeing out there in that wasteland that makes you smile so much?"

"Oh," he replied, "I'm in the irrigation business, and I was thinking that if we could only get water to this land the desert would become a thriving, beautiful garden. When you look out there, you see what's there now, a wasteland. I look and see what could be there, and that makes me smile."

July 16
When the Night Ends

When all of the protests and riots were breaking out in the United States during the spring of 2020, I began thinking about a wise rabbi who taught over two thousand years ago. The wisdom he shared all those years ago is something we must all take to heart.

That wise rabbi once asked his disciples how they could tell when the night had ended, and the day had begun. "Could it be," asked one student, "when you can see an animal in the distance and tell whether it's a sheep or a dog?" "No," answered the rabbi.

Another asked, "Is it when you can look at a tree in the distance and tell whether it's a fig tree or a peach tree?" "No," answered the rabbi.

"Then when is it?" the pupils demanded. "It is when you can look on the face of any person and see that it is your sister and brother. Because if you cannot see this, it is still night."

July 17
From Different Directions

A man was driving in the country one day when he saw an old man sitting on a fence rail watching the cars go by. Stopping to take a break, the traveler said, "I never could stand living out here. You don't see anything, and I'm sure you don't travel like I do. You just seem to be wasting time. I'm on the go all the time."

The old man looked down at the stranger and drawled, "I can't see much difference in what I'm doing and what you're doing. I sit on the fence and watch the cars go by, and you sit in your car and watch the fences go by. It's just the way you look at things. Neither one of us is doing much but watching. We both are watching our lives pass by from different directions. We both need to be doing much more with the lives we have been given."

July 18
Strong Headwinds

I was reading a novel recently in which the author was describing something I found rather interesting. It is that sailors in the northern oceans say they often see icebergs moving along in one direction even though strong winds are blowing in the opposite direction. They can see icebergs actually moving against the winds.

So how do such large icebergs move against the winds? The explanation is that the icebergs, with almost 90 percent of their bulk under the surface of the water, get caught in the grip of strong underwater currents that move them in a certain direction, no matter which way the winds are blowing.

When I read about those moving icebergs, it was as if the Lord was telling me directly that no matter how strong the winds are blowing around us, we must get our direction from something much deeper and stronger than any head wind. We must get our direction and our movement from the depths of our love for God, and most especially, from the depths of God's love for us. There is certainly nothing stronger than the depths of God's love for us, and it is from this deep love that we know who we are and in what direction we are headed.

July 19
Forget It!

Perhaps one of the greatest spiritual gifts that God could ever give to any of us is the power to forget.
The ability to forgive another person is certainly one of God's greatest gifts as well, but I do think that the ability to forget may even surpass the ability to forgive.

One of the best examples of this is Clara Barton, the famous pioneering nurse. Anyone who knew and loved Clara Barton recognized that she was never known to hold resentment against anyone. One time a friend recalled a cruel thing that had happened to Barton some years previously, but she seemed not to remember the incident. "Don't you remember the wrong that was done you?" the friend asked Barton. She answered calmly, "No, I distinctly remember forgetting that."

Do you have the ability to forget?

July 20
Integrity

So much has been said and written about Abraham Lincoln. But there is one thing Lincoln said that I have always admired.

Although he is a much admired and loved person today, during his lifetime that was certainly not the case. Throughout his administration he was always a man under fire, especially during the scarring years of the Civil War. And though he knew he would make mistakes and errors of judgment, he was determined to never compromise his integrity.

So strong was this desire to be truthful and a man of good moral principle that he once said, "I desire so to conduct the affairs of my personal life and of this administration that if at the end, when I come to lay down the reins of power, I have lost every other friend on earth, I shall at least have one friend left, and that friend shall be down inside of me who remained true and honest."

One thing that Abraham Lincoln knew was how important it is to be a person who never loses that friend down deep inside. As you look back over your life, have you maintained a deep friendship with that person down deep inside you?

July 21
Burdens

A wise old pastor began to notice how downcast his parishioners were. They seemed worn-out, and many seemed completely disheartened. So, on the next Sunday morning before he began to celebrate the Mass, he stood up and said, "My people, I am very worried about you. You all seem so overwhelmed and heavenly burdened. I, too, have felt the weight of all of hardships our world is enduring. Now listen to me!"

The people sat up at attention and the old priest went on, "We are like the old man riding down the road on a donkey while he carried a 200-pound sack of wheat on his shoulder. Someone asked him why he didn't take the weight off of his shoulders and strap it to the donkey. "Oh, no!" he protested. "I couldn't ask the donkey to carry all that weight."

There was complete quiet in the church, then one man stood up and said, "Father, what does that mean?" Then in a quiet but firm voice the pastor said, "Many of us are carrying burdens today that we do not have to carry. Perhaps it's our lack of faith, trust, and confidence that God really is alive and cares for us and is truly able to relieve us of our burdens keeps us in bondage. But, trust me on this, God will carry our burdens. We just have to put them down."

Are you carrying any burdens that you need to put down? God really is alive and cares for you and is able to carry any burden. Why not put yours down?

July 22
Regaining Your Inner Calm

I read about an interesting event in the life of the famous artist, Leonardo da Vinci. The story is told that when he was in the process of painting "The Last Supper," he became violently angry with one of his workers and lashed out at him. He threatened to hurt or even kill him. The man was deeply hurt, and also quite frightened, so he ran for his life.

After a short time, Leonardo da Vinci went back to his fresco and tried to paint the face of Jesus. He couldn't, for there was too much evil stirring inside him. The lack of peace forced him to put down his brushes, go find the man, and ask his forgiveness. Only then did he have the inner calm needed to do the face of Jesus.

Ask yourself, is there anyone in your life who you have hurt or wounded in some way? Is there anything in your life that you need to "put down" so you can go and ask to be forgiven, and the inner calm you need to get on with your life can be returned to you?

July 23
How Does God Talk to You?

Recently I was having lunch with a friend. In the course of our meal, he asked me what I was going to do that afternoon. I told him that I was going to see an older woman in hospice who wanted to talk to me about what it will be like when she dies. He asked, "So what are you going to tell her?" I said, "I have no idea. I'll wait to see what kinds of questions she has or what she wants to talk about. I find that in those kinds of conversations, God always seems to provide me with the right words at the right time. I'll just wait until I get there. I try not to worry about that before I am even there."

My friend just looked at me and said, "Can I write something down for you to give her?" I said I would be sure to give her whatever he wanted me to give her. Then he said, "I know these lines by heart. They were helpful to me when my dad died." He quickly took a napkin and wrote down these lines:

What must it be like to step on shore, and find it—heaven;
To take hold of a hand, and find it—God's;
To breathe a new air, and find it—celestial;
To feel invigorated, and find it—immortality;
To rise from the care, the loneliness, and turmoil of earth
Into one unbroken calm;
To wake up and find it—glory?

I did take that napkin with me when I went to hospice that afternoon. When I gave it to the woman, she burst into tears. She said, "How did you know that this is exactly what I have been worried about? God must talk directly to you!"

I just smiled and said, "He does in a kind of roundabout way."

July 24
What Would You Do?

As a passenger boarded the Los Angeles-to-New York plane, he told the flight attendant to wake him and make sure he got off in Dallas. That passenger awoke just as the plane was landing in New York. When he realized he was in New York, he became furious, called the flight attendant over, cussed him out, and demanded an explanation. The poor flight attendant withered under all of the yelling and mumbled an apology.

Not satisfied, the passenger continued his raging and stomped off the plane. "Boy, was he ever mad!" another crew member observed to her errant colleague. The embarrassed flight attendant swallowed hard and said, "If you think he was mad, I bet the guy I put off the plane in Dallas is a lot madder!"

What did you think when you read that story? For whom did you feel the most sympathy? If you were the errant flight attendant, how do you think you would have reacted to the raging and cussing passenger? If you were that passenger who ended up in New York, how would you have reacted to that situation? And finally, if you were the poor guy who mistakenly got put off the plane back in Dallas, how would you act?

I am sure we all hope we would act in a way that respects the fact that anyone can make a mistake, but would we? What do you think you would do?

July 25
Better Off?

One of the desert fathers would teach his students that they were given a mission to make the wonder of God's creation even more wonderful. He told them they were to do that by being truly good people, and that their goodness would change the people they encountered.

The desert father would conclude his teaching by saying, "Jesus accepted people just the way they were, but he never left people just the way they were because he loved them. Jesus always made them better. The question for you, then, is this: Will the people you spend time with be better because they have known you and been loved by you?"

July 26
The World We Live In

I want to tell you about a philosopher by the name of Epictetus who lived about 2000 years ago. He said something that is very important to remember as you make your way through your daily life. He said, "Men are disturbed not by the things that happen but by their opinion of those things that happen." In other words, our understanding of events tells us who we really are.

I think what Epictetus was trying to tell us is simply this: A person who loves will live in a loving world. But a person who is hostile will live in a world that is hostile. A person who is sincere will see most everyone else's actions as sincere, while the person who is a hypocrite will be certain to see hypocrisy even in the sincerest of people.

The question for us, then, is this: What kind of world do you live in?

July 27
Blessed!

Former president Jimmy Carter spoke about an incident that occurred after he left the White House. He said that a reporter came to Plains, Georgia, to interview his mother for an article about Carter and his family. His mother really didn't want to be interviewed but was being gracious, and when the reporter knocked at her door, Mrs. Carter invited her in. The reporter asked some hard questions and actually was quite rude.

"I want to ask you a question," the reporter said. "Your son ran for the presidency on the premise that he would always tell the truth. Has he ever lied?" Lillian Carter said, "I think he's truthful; I think you can depend on his word."

The reporter again asked, "So you are telling me he never lied in his entire life?" His mother said, "Well, I guess maybe he's told a little white lie."

"Ah, I knew he had to have lied some time," the reporter exclaimed. "He's lied! If he told a white lie, he has lied."

But the reporter was still not satisfied and asked, "What is a white lie?" And then Lillian Carter said, "Let me give you an example: It's like a moment ago when you knocked on the door and I opened the door and said I was glad to see you."

Jimmy Carter concluded the story by saying how easy it is to throw darts at people and find faults or flaws, then feel superior. He told his audience that he has always found it much more rewarding to look for the best in people, and then feel blessed to know them.

When you look at the people in your family, or when you look at your neighbors and friends, do you feel blessed to know them with both their good qualities and their flaws?

July 28
Readily Available Power

While traveling the backroads of the hills in central Missouri, a man ran out of gas and went to the nearest farmhouse. Imagine his surprise to find that there was no phone service to the house. Furthermore, even though there were electrical lines leading to the house, the owner of the farm was busy trimming the wicks of his kerosene lanterns.

"Did you blow a fuse?" the visitor asked. "Is that why you're lighting the lamps?"

"Oh, no," the farmer replied. "We have electricity hooked up, but we haven't had to use it yet because we've never run out of kerosene."

What was your first reaction when you read the story above? Are you are acting like the farmer in some area of your life right now? Is there power that could make your life better that you are not using, even though it is readily available to you?

God's help is readily available to you. Are you connecting to that power?

July 29
Haunted

People often send me stories. Recently a young girl sent me a story that she said has really haunted her. She said it reminded her to not take people or their gifts for granted. When she had said that, I was really intrigued and wanted to read her story right away. When I had read it, I was haunted by it, too. See if you are haunted by it as well.

There once was a blind woman who hated herself purely because she could not see. The only person she loved was her boyfriend, as he was always there for her. She said that if she could only see the world, then she would marry him.

One day, someone donated a pair of eyes to her. Now she could see everything, including her boyfriend. Her loving boyfriend asked her, "Now that you can see the world, will you marry me?" The woman was shocked when she saw that her boyfriend was blind, too and refused to marry him.

Her boyfriend walked away in tears and wrote a short note to her, saying: "Just take care of my eyes, dear."

July 30
See Where It Takes You

When I was living as a hermit in the desert in Israel, I would spend some time writing out answers to spiritual questions. One day, a monk came to visit with me as I was sitting under a tree writing an answer to one of those questions. He said, "What lofty spiritual question are you trying to answer this afternoon?" I told him that the prior of the monastery nearby gave me a simple question to think about: "Why are you here?"

The monk laughed at me and said it was a silly question and a profound question at one and the same time. He said, "Let me give you a story my spiritual master gave me when he told me to meditate on that very same question."

A soldier asked his soldier friend, "Why did you join the army?" "I had no wife and I loved war, so here I am. What about you?" The first soldier then said, "My case is the exact opposite. I had a wife, and I loved peace. So here I am."

I laughed at the story and then asked, "What does that have to do with the question, "Why are you here?" The monk replied, "First, you must not take yourself too seriously, and second, the reason you originally came here may have very little to do with why God has you here today. Ask yourself why God might have you here, not why you chose to come here."

That monk had given me a great insight that I would not have come to on my own. Now ask yourself the question, "Why am I here?" See where it takes you.

July 31
A Complaining Tourist

I always find it interesting how some people deal with difficult people. Someone told me that they had a great story for me about a very feisty, complaining lady.

As the story goes, a guide at Blarney Castle in Ireland was explaining to some visitors that his job was not always as pleasant as it seemed. He went on to tell them about a group of disgruntled American tourists he had taken to the castle earlier in the week. He explained, "These people had nothing but criticisms about everything. They didn't like the weather, the food, their hotel accommodations, the prices, everything. Then to top it off, when we arrived at the castle, we found that the area around the Blarney Stone was roped off. Workmen were doing some kind of repairs."

"This is the last straw!" exclaimed one lady, who seemed to be the chief faultfinder in the group. "I've come all this way, and now I can't even kiss the Blarney Stone."

"Well, you know," the guide said, "according to legend, if you kiss someone who has kissed the stone, it's the same as kissing the stone itself." "And I suppose you've kissed the stone," said the exasperated lady. "Better than that," replied the guide. "I've sat on it."

Isn't that a great story? I asked the person who gave me the story how the critical woman handled what the guide at Blarney Castle had said to her. "She just loved that tour guide and laughed her head off at his comment. Truth be told, she got his not so subtle message that her complaining was both rude and unnecessary. She eventually apologized and stopped complaining."

If you were in that tour guide's shoes, how would you have dealt with that complaining tourist? Have you ever been a "complaining tourist" even when you are at home or at work?

August

August 1
The Little Sins

There is an old story told by Jewish sages of a rabbi who sat one day, toward the end of the Jewish new year celebration, with three of his disciples. To help them, he asked each one individually, "What were your sins this past year?"

The first disciple thought for a brief moment and said, "Rabbi, I committed one very serious sin this year and I am very much ashamed." "You must go out from here and find a very large stone and bring it back to me in atonement for your grievous sin," the rabbi instructed.

Next, the second disciple said, "Rabbi, I sinned several times this past year and I am truly aggrieved by my actions." The rabbi told the second disciple, "You must go and find several large stones and bring them back to me in atonement for your several sins."

Finally, the third disciple approached the rabbi and said, "Sir, I have sinned many, many small times. Nothing too serious, but I did sin many times this past year." "You must go, then, and find me many small stones and bring them back here in atonement for your many small sins," the rabbi said.

All three disciples left and went in search of their stones, just as the rabbi had instructed them. When all three had returned with the stones they had collected, the rabbi spoke to them and said, "Now, you must go back to the exact spot where you found each stone and put them back just as you found them."

The three disciples immediately ran out to do what they had been instructed to do. It wasn't too long before the first two disciples returned to the rabbi, having done their tasks. The third disciple did not return until just after sundown. He was very upset and cried out to the rabbi, "Oh, I am worn out, rabbi. I searched and searched all day to find the exact spot for each of my many stones. It was impossible for me to remember where I had found every one of them. I cannot put back what I took!"

The rabbi gathered all three disciples to himself and began to teach them. "So it is with sins. The large sins are easy to remember and rectify. But one can never remember all of the little and seemingly inconsequential sins. These must be corrected at once when they happen, or you will be left with a thousand little burdens that will weigh you down and keep you from all the good deeds in your heart. The smallest of sins have great power to sap your strength so that you end up doing very little good for anyone."

August 2
Green Memories

There is a story written by Charles Dickens called "The Haunted Man," which I found really interesting when I was in college. I remember our English professor warning us that Dickens' story could turn us into "haunted" people.

The story tells of a chemist who is very unhappy with his life and with all of his unhappy memories. One night, as he sat before a fire depressed over his unhappy life, a ghost appears to him and offers him the chance to have his memory destroyed. The haunted man jumps at the chance and takes up the ghost's offer. Immediately, the man is left without his memory. Not only that, but the man discovers that he has a new and very dread power to strip others of their memory, too!

For a while that haunted man was happy, but it wasn't too long before he wanted the ghost to take back what he had given him. The haunted man's misery was great, and even more terrible was the unhappiness and misery that he had inflicted on others. He pleaded with the ghost to restore his memory and take away the dreaded power to steal other folks' memories, too.

At the end of the story the haunted man is restored, and he offers a prayer of gratitude to God. At the end of his prayer he says, "Lord, keep my memory green."

August 3
The Joy of Singing

There is an old story about a very wealthy man who lived in a grand house in the middle of town. There he spent his days counting his gold. Beside the man's house was a poor cobbler who spent his days singing as he repaired people's shoes.

The joyful singing irritated the rich man, and one day he decided to give some gold coins to the cobbler. Now at first the cobbler was overjoyed, and he took the coins and hid them. But it wasn't too long before he became worried about the coins, and he would go back to check if the coins were still there. Then he would be worried in case someone had seen him, and he would move the coins and hide them in another place.

During all this, he ceased to sing. One day he realized that he had ceased to sing, and he knew that it was because of the gold coins. So he took the gold coins back to the rich man and said, "Take back your coins and give me back my songs."

Is there anything in your life right now that has the power to steal your songs from you? If there is, perhaps today is the day you should let go of whatever is stealing your song.

August 4
Holes in the Darkness

Years ago, a young boy was looking out the front window of his home one dark, winter evening. As he looked, he saw a man coming down the street with a flame on the end of a long stick. One by one, the man was lighting the gas lights that were used to illuminate the streets in those days.

The boy was fascinated by the way the man could light up the whole street with that little flame on a stick. When the boy's mother came to see what her son was looking at, he said to her, "Look, mom, that man is poking holes in the darkness!"

Is there anyone in your life who pokes holes in the darkness for you? Is there someone in your life right now who needs you to poke holes in the darkness of their life?

August 5
Feeling Weak

Have you ever read something that you know immediately is true? I remember having that experience one day when I came across a passage from Lao Tzu, a Chinese philosopher who is known as the founder of Taoism. Here is what he said: "There is nothing softer and weaker than water. And yet there is nothing better for attacking hard and strong things. For this reason, there is no substitute for it. From this all the world knows that the weak eventually overcomes the strong, and the soft overcomes the hard. But, alas, there are few who practice it."

Lao Tzu taught his disciples that many people give up because what is before them seems too strong and they feel so weak. Others give up because what they face is hard. What they need to do is observe water.

Is there anything that you face in life right now that seems too strong and too hard for you? If there is, think of water, as Lao Tzu suggests. You might also think of Saint Paul writing to the Corinthians and describing all of the hardships he was facing. In the end he concludes by saying, "It is when I am weak, that I am strong!"

August 6
Forget It!

I've been thinking lately about freedom, and as I do, I realize there is one freedom most folks do not even know exists. If they did know of it, they would be so much happier in life. I became aware of this freedom when I read an interview in a news magazine.

In the interview, a sportswriter was asking an Olympic runner the secret of his success. The runner's answer has much to teach us: "The only way to win a race is to forget all previous victories, which would give you false pride, and all former failures, which would give you false fears. Each race is a new beginning. Pressing on to the finish tape is all that's important!"

Near the end of the interview, the runner was asked if there was anything he wanted to add. He said, "I think the most important gift a runner can have is the freedom to forget. I just ask God to give me the freedom to forget past achievements and failures so that I can press ahead to the goal."

Do you enjoy the freedom to forget?

August 7
Your Motto in Life

William B. McKinley, president of the United States from 1897 to 1901, was a man with many talents who was known to be highly intelligent. Those who knew him said there was one thing everyone appreciated about him: that he was a very kind man.

That fact was illustrated on one particular occasion a few months before he was elected to the White House. During one of his campaign trips, a reporter from an opposition newspaper followed him constantly and just as persistently misrepresented McKinley's views. Most of McKinley's campaign workers hated that reporter.

During the course of the campaign, the weather became extremely cold. Even though the reporter didn't have sufficiently warm clothing, he still followed McKinley wherever he went, causing controversy along the way.

One bitterly cold evening, the president-to-be was riding in his closed carriage, while the young reporter sat shivering on the driver's seat outside in the sub-freezing weather. McKinley stopped the carriage and invited the reporter to take his own coat, put it on, and ride with him inside the warm carriage. The young man was astonished at such kindness. He protested that McKinley knew he was the opposition and that he wasn't going to stop opposing McKinley during the campaign.

McKinley replied that he knew this but told the reporter that, just because he opposed him, it didn't mean McKinley should stop being the man he had always been. The President-to-be simply added one more sentence: "It never hurts to be a little kind."

In the remaining days of the campaign, the reporter continued to oppose McKinley, but never again did he write anything unfair or biased about the future president. The reporter said, "Mr. McKinley is a genuine human being."

What would happen if President McKinley's words, "It never hurts to be kind," became your motto in life?

August 8
What Is Your Purpose?

Here is an interesting story. A Texas rancher had spent his whole adult life raising prime beef. As he realized he was slowing down, he decided to turn his ranch over to his two sons. He wanted them to have the same enthusiasm and dedication for the ranch as he did, so he thought about a way to get his message across to his two boys. He decided the best way to do that was to change the name of the ranch. So the rancher had a new sign made and hung it over the main entrance to the ranch. He renamed the ranch "Focus."

The rancher asked his two sons if they had any idea why he had chosen that name. The sons thought about it for a few moments and then said, "We assume it means that you want us to continue to focus on raising quality prime beef, just like you did, and not just worry about making money."

Their father was very happy with their answer. Then he told his sons that they were only partially right and went on to explain what the word "focus" meant. He said, "Focus is where the sun's rays meet."

Now the two boys were very confused. Their dad laughed and said, "Let me really spell it out to you:
I named the ranch Focus because it's 'where the sons raise meat!' I just wanted to remind you what the ranch's purpose really is."

August 9
Could It Happen to You?

History can be a great teacher. Studying the lives of history's great men and women can be a big help to us as we try make our way through life. For example, Alexander the Great was one of the most powerful men in history. He was known for his many virtues and few flaws. Those who knew him well said that he was energetic, versatile, and intelligent. Although hatred was not generally part of his nature, several times in his life he was tragically defeated by a rare display of rage.

One of the most famous stories told about Alexander's rage is when a very close friend of his, a general in his army, became intoxicated and began to ridicule the emperor in front of his men. Blinded by anger and quick as lightning, Alexander snatched a spear from the hand of a soldier and hurled it at his friend. Although he had only intended to scare the drunken general, his aim was true and the spear took the life of his childhood friend.

Deep remorse and intense grief followed his anger. Completely overcome with guilt, Alexander attempted to take his own life with the same spear, but he was stopped by his men. For days he lay sick, calling for his friend and chiding himself as a murderer.

Historians and commentators have said that Alexander the Great conquered many cities and vanquished many countries, but his failure to control his own spirit of rage cost him dearly. Could that ever happen to you?

August 10
If You Were Near Death

A very old letter, dating back to the third century, was discovered by historians. The letter was written by a man who was anticipating death within days, and he wrote these last words to a friend: "It's a bad world, an incredibly bad world. But I have discovered in the midst of it a quiet and holy people who have learned a great secret. They have found a joy which is a thousand times better than any pleasure of our sinful life. They are despised and persecuted, but they care not. They are masters of their souls. They have overcome the world. These people are the Christians and I have become one of them. I have never felt such comfort."

How are you affected by reading these heartfelt words? If you were near death and were going to send a note to your family or friends, what would you want them to know?

August 11
Christy's Great-Grandmother

One of my parishioners, a young woman in her mid-twenties named Christy, stopped me after church one morning and asked to speak with me. She wanted to tell me that she had just been released from the hospital after a suicide attempt. She said, "I am really embarrassed by all of the fuss I caused. I had broken up with the guy I've been with for four years. I could see no reason to go one because I felt like a loser. I felt complete rejection."

As I listened to her, I noticed that she seemed very peaceful and not at all distressed. "You seem so calm to me. " I said.

She replied, "You know, I really am calm. I've done a lot of talking with counselors and even with a psychiatrist. That helped some, but it was my great-grandmother who helped me most. She talked so kindly to me and so forcefully that I just found myself healing!"

"What did your great grandmother say to you?" I asked.

"At first, she didn't say anything. She just listened. Then, when I had poured out my heart, she looked me in the eye, and with tears running down her face, she said, 'Christy, men are bums!'"

I said, "I bet that helped you a lot when you heard her say that, didn't it?"

She said, "Absolutely! I mean, how many 93-year-old ladies would say that to you? I laughed for a full ten minutes. She is such a kind lady. Just being with her made me feel whole again. A few days after our meeting, she sent me something which I think was really sweet."

The young woman reached for her purse and pulled out an envelope and a little note card. Here is what her great grandmother wrote to her: Two little teardrops were floating down the river of life. One teardrop asked the other, "Who are you?" "I am a teardrop from a girl who loved a man and lost him. But who are *you?*" The first teardrop replied, "I am a teardrop from the girl who got him." Christy, just remember this: Life is like that. We cry over the things we can't have, but we might cry twice as hard if we had been forced to keep them."

I think Christy's great-grandmother is a very wise woman, don't you?

August 12
No "Ifs"

Someone sent me a beautiful greeting card with this little note attached: "What the piano player said reminds me of something you would say. Take this as a compliment!"

On the front of the greeting card were these words: Famed pianist Artur Rubinstein, celebrating his 84th birthday, said: "As long as we have what we have inside, the capacity to love, to work, to hear music, to see a flower, to look at the world as it is, nothing can stop us from being happy. But one thing you must take seriously. You must get rid of the "ifs" of life. Many people tell you, "I would be happy if I had a certain job, or if I were better looking, or if a certain person would marry me." There isn't any such thing. You must live your life unconditionally, without the "ifs."

I love the piano player's words! I do take what he said as a great compliment, too.

August 13
A Peaceful Pause

A woman came up to me one afternoon and handed me a little note card with these four letters printed on the front: ASAP. Just about everyone knows that those letters stand for the phrase, "As Soon As Possible." The woman saw me looking at the front of the note card, so she turned to me and whispered, "Open the card and read what it says."

This note was written inside the card: "Maybe if we think of this abbreviation in a different manner, we'll begin to find a new way to deal with those rough days we seem to be having When there's work to do and deadlines to meet, and you've just got no time to spare, remember the letters ASAP. They do not have to mean, "As Soon As Possible;" they can also mean, "Always Say a Prayer."

As I read the little note, I was reminded of how often I have been in a hectic time of chaos when a brief pause for a peaceful breath of air, making me aware of God's presence, has brought me almost instant serenity.

I thanked the woman for that note card. That simple, kind gesture changed how I now see the letters ASAP as a call for a peaceful pause that leads me to God.

August 14
Looking

All of the world's religious teachers will tell you that one of the greatest teachers anyone can have is nature itself. I remember listening to a biologist speak about how all of nature is in harmony, and that each creature plays an important role in creation. No creature is unimportant.

The same professor of biology then said to us, "Every creature in the universe sees only what it is looking for." Then, by way of example, he told us that both the hummingbird and the vulture fly over our deserts. All the vultures see is rotting meat, because that is what they look for. They thrive on that diet. Hummingbirds, on the other hand, ignore the rotten flesh of dead animals. Instead, they look for the colorful blossoms of desert plants.

The vultures live on what was. They live on the past. They fill themselves with what is dead and gone. But hummingbirds live on what is. They seek new life. They fill themselves with freshness and life. Each bird finds what it is looking for. So do we.

August 15
Your List

I would like to ask you to do something. Take a few minutes right now to write down a list of 25 blessings that God has given you. Carefully look over the list and be aware of how blessed you are.

Now say a personal prayer of thanksgiving to God for all of your blessings. Finally, read this story about creation.

An ancient legend tells us that when the Great Lord of all created all things -- animals, birds, mountains, seas, and human beings -- when he finished his work, there was only silence. No sound was anywhere. The angels, having examined creation, reported to the Great Creator that, to be complete, it needed the sound of the Creator's quiet, loving voice. So the Lord God put a song in the throats of birds, gave a murmur to running brooks, gave the wind a voice to whisper as it moved among the trees, and put a melody in the heart of human beings.

Now, look back at your list of blessings and see if you included the sounds of nature there. Look to see if you included God's quiet, loving voice among your blessings.

August 16
Like Tea

There is an ancient story about a young Christian monk who sought out one of the well-known desert hermits. He asked the hermit, who was said to be God's good friend, what he needed to do to experience true conversion of heart and soul.

The hermit told the young man that if he truly wanted to experience conversion, he had to spend time with the holy scriptures, and he needed to spend time in the presence of the living God. Then the hermit made the young man a cup of tea. When he handed the monk the cup of tea, the hermit said, "I will give you your first lesson in becoming God's good friend." The hermit then went on to say:

"Consider the difference between a strong and a weak cup of tea. The same ingredients—water and tea—are used for both.
The difference is that the strong cup of tea results from the tea leaves' immersion in the water longer, allowing the water more

time to get into the tea and the tea into the water. The longer the steeping process, the stronger the cup of tea."

"In the same way, the length of time we spend in God's Word determines how deeply we get into it and it gets into us. Just like the tea, the longer we are in the Word, the 'stronger' we become. The longer you stay steeped in the holy presence of the loving God, the stronger your friendship with him and he with you."

August 17
A Deadly Temptation

One of the deadliest of all temptations is greed. In the many years that I have been a priest and have worked to help people overcome their temptations, it has always amazed me how greed can ruin friendships, destroy marriages, and condemn people to a deadly isolation. Whenever I am asked to preach about greed, I often refer my parishioners to a famous story.

The story is one of Geoffrey Chaucer's *Canterbury Tales*, called "Pardoner's Tale." Three men decide to seek out and destroy death himself. On their way they discover a pot of gold. The youngest is sent to get wine, food, and water to celebrate their discovery. He thinks to himself how the gold could be his alone if he didn't have the two partners. To that end he poisons the wine.

His two colleagues have similar thoughts and when the youngest returns they kill him, thinking they would divide the gold between the two of them. To celebrate they ate the food brought by the young man and drank the poisonous wine. The three men wanted to destroy death, but their greed distracted them. They all, however, did meet death.

August 18
Deep Peace and a Restful Sleep

I spoke with an older man one day who said that one of his greatest blessings in this life is that at the end of every day, after he has prayed his favorite night prayer, God has always given him a deep peace that allows him to fall immediately into a deep and restful sleep. The prayer had been given to him by his favorite uncle, whom he knew was one of God's closest friends. "That prayer," he said, "has been a doorway to God that has given me peace at the close of every day since I first started saying it."

When I asked him what prayer he said each night, he said it was a prayer written a century ago by John Henry Newman. The man wrote the prayer down for me and here it is:

"Support me, O Lord, all the long day of this troubled life until the shadows lengthen, and the evening comes, when the busy fever of life is hushed, and my work is done. Then in thy mercy grant me a safe lodging, a holy rest, and peace at the last, through Jesus Christ our Lord. Amen."

In the days following the conversation with that older man, I have quietly prayed that prayer before I have gone to bed. It brings a deep peace and, as the man who gave it to me said, and a very restful sleep. Perhaps you will find it does the same for you.

August 19
The Choices We Make

I majored in history when I was in college and it began a lifelong fascination with the people who have influenced civilization. Some of those people have made the world a better place to live, others have brought ruin and havoc to the world. Each of these folks can serve as a warning to remind us what can happen if we are not careful with the choices we make.

One of the people I had to write a paper on was Julius Caesar. There is a story about him that I have never forgotten. It happened in the early part of his political career, when feelings against him ran so high that he thought it best to leave Rome. He sailed for the Aegean island of Rhodes, but on route the ship was attacked by pirates and Caesar was captured.

The pirates demanded a ransom of 12,000 gold pieces, and Caesar's guards were sent back to arrange the payment. Caesar spent almost 40 days with his captors, jokingly telling the pirates on several occasions that he would someday capture and crucify them to a man. The kidnappers were greatly amused, but when the ransom was paid and Caesar was freed, the first thing he did was gather a fleet and pursue the pirates. They were captured.

It wasn't long before those pirates realized that Caesar's resentment over having been held for ransom was no joke. During those 40 days of captivity, Julius Caesar nursed a grudge that lead to a very deep anger, then to resentment, and finally rage. He had those pirates lined up and one by one they were crucified -- to a man! Caesar himself is said to have remarked that he was surprised how quickly a minor grudge could turn into a rage that led to a desire to kill.

August 20
Angels Swearing

How do you deal with criticism? Some people find that criticism shuts them down and keeps them from producing much good fruit. Others say that criticism makes them angry but also helps them grow and become better as people. Whatever your own response to criticism might be, just about everyone finds criticism difficult to handle.

There is probably no one in history who was as criticized and ridiculed as President Abraham Lincoln. If you were to research the things that were said about Lincoln by his contemporaries -- the insults, the caricatures, the unjust criticisms, and even outright lies -

- you would discover that his opponents never let up. They railed against him up to the very day he was assassinated.

So how did Abraham Lincoln deal with the hurtful things that were said about him? Well, he was a keenly insightful person. He wanted to do good for others and he knew if he got caught up in worry about what others said about him, he might give in and quit doing good. He was determined to persevere through any criticism.

This is what he wrote about it: "If I were to try to read, much less answer, all the attacks made on me, this shop might as well be closed for any other business. I do the very best I know how, and I mean to keep doing so until the end. If the end brings me out all right, what is said against me won't amount to anything. If the end brings me out wrong, then angels swearing I was right would make no difference."

August 21
What Are You Doing?

One of the most beautiful buildings in all of London is St. Paul's Cathedral. The story is told that when the famous English architect Sir Christopher Wren was supervising the construction of that magnificent cathedral, a journalist thought it would be interesting to interview some of the workers.

The journalist chose three and asked each of them this question: "What are you doing?" The first replied, "I'm cutting stone for 10 shillings a day." The next answered, "I'm putting in 10 hours a day on this job." But the third said, "I'm helping Sir Christopher Wren construct one of London's greatest masterpieces."

If you were asked that same question about your job, what would you say you are doing?

August 22
What You See

Long before Harry Truman was President of the United States, he served as a county judge. He was not the kind of judge who presides over a court of law; rather, he was an official who supervised the building of county roads.

It has been said that he often told the following story to people who worked for him. The story took place back in the day when gas stations provided what they called "full service," which meant that an attendant would come out to your car, fill the gas tank with fuel, check the car's oil, and wash the windshield.

According to Truman's story, a man and his wife, who were on a long trip, stopped at a full-service gas station. After the station attendant had washed the car's windshield, the man in the car said to the station attendant, "It's still dirty. Wash it again."

The station attendant complied. After washing it again, the man in the car angrily said, "It's still dirty. Don't you know how to wash a windshield?" Just then the man's wife reached over, removed her husband's glasses from his face, and cleaned them with a tissue. Then he put them back on and behold—the windshield was clean!

Harry Truman would conclude his story by saying, "Our mental attitude has a great deal to do with how we look at things. The whole world can appear pretty bleak if we have a depressed mental outlook. Yet how bright the world can appear if we have a joyful and decent attitude of hope."

If you were to take a look at your daily attitudes, do you think you need someone to clean your glasses?

August 23
Things Are Really Good

When people come to me and tell me that they are unsettled because everyone else's life seems better than theirs, I often tell them this story:

A man became envious of his friends because they had larger and more luxurious homes. It made him feel very unsettled and unsatisfied with life. He began to wonder where he had gone wrong. So, he listed his house with a real estate firm, planning to sell it and purchase a more impressive home.

Shortly afterward, as he was reading the classified section of the newspaper, he saw an ad for a house that seemed just right. He promptly called the realtor and said, "A house described in today's paper is exactly what I'm looking for. I would like to go through it as soon as possible!" The agent asked him several questions about it and then replied, "But sir, that's your house you're describing."

Sometimes we don't realize that we already have everything we really wanted. Sometimes it takes getting a fresh look to find out that things are really good.

August 24
Words

If history teaches us anything, it is this: words have power. When Demosthenes, the famed Greek orator, first spoke in public, he was hissed off the platform. That experience crushed Demosthenes. He had hoped to be a man who could inspire others and move them to do great things. He fell into great despair because he realized that if truth be told, his voice was harsh and weak and his appearance unimpressive.

Demosthenes was determined that if he worked at it, his fellow citizens would yet appreciate his words. He practiced day and night.

In order to make time to practice, he shaved half his head so no one would want to invite him to social events. In order to overcome his stammer, he recited with pebbles in his mouth and yelled against the roaring of the Aegean Sea so his voice would get louder. He stood beneath a suspended sword to train himself not to favor a shoulder that kept hitching. He practiced facial expressions in front of a mirror.

After all that effort, Demosthenes was a different man. So, when Greece was threatened by an impending war, he and another speaker were invited to address a huge crowd. Both men hoped to move the nation to action.

The other speaker spoke first, and the crowd seemed to be impressed. When the first man concluded his speech, the crowd said, "What marvelous oratory! What a great speech!"

Demosthenes stood and waited for silence. He began slowly in a whispering voice, and as he continued, he spoke louder and louder. The people listened in silence and stared at him intently. But when Demosthenes finished, they cried with one voice, "To war! To war! Let us go and fight our enemy, Philip!"

Words have great power.

August 25
A Truth

One of the unwritten truths of the universe is that small things can make a big difference. An article I read recently got me thinking about that truth.

According to the article, a man from New York City decided to raise money for a firefighter who had been very badly injured in a major fire. The firefighter's recovery was a long and quite difficult ordeal. In addition, his medical expenses were astronomical. The New Yorker decided he would be in solidarity with the firefighter by walking from New York all the way across the United States to San Francisco to help raise money to pay for the firefighter's recovery.

Imagine all the obstacles a person might have to overcome if he were to walk from New York City to San Francisco. The man met every hardship thrown at him and eventually accomplished this rare achievement.

In an interview after the long walk, he was asked to tell of his biggest hurdle. He said that the toughest part of the trip wasn't traversing the steep slopes of the mountains or crossing hot, dry, barren stretches of desert. Instead, he said, "The thing that came the closest to defeating me was that awful day I got sand in my shoes." He was not brought to the point of quitting by some huge obstacle; it was just a pinch or two of sand in his shoes that almost destroyed his efforts.

If you stop to think about it, isn't that often the case for each of us? All too often it's a very small and seemingly insignificant thing that can bring us to our knees.

August 26
What Happened to Grandma when she died?

I want to tell you about a grandpa who likes to take his grandkids on walks with him. He said it is a wonderful thing to take the time to go on a walk with each one separately so that he can get to know each one of his grandchildren. On one of those walks, his youngest granddaughter, Maddie, asked if she could ask him a very important and serious question. He told her that she could ask him anything. She said, "Grandpa, what do you think it was like for grandma when she died? Was she scared or upset? Did she have a lot of pain?"

This is how he answered Maddie's question. He said, when I was young, my mama died and I was scared for her. So, as soon as I could, I asked my grandma about what had happened to my mama. She told me not to worry about my mom because God took good care of her and even walked her into heaven!

Then she went on to tell me the story of an old man who everyday would take long walks with God. On these walks, he and the Lord God would talk about all kinds of things, about the important times in the old man's life: when he met his wife, the birth of his children, special Christmases, happy times and sad times too. Then one day while they were out walking for an especially long time, the Lord looked at the old man and said: "You know, we are closer to my house than we are to yours. Why don't you just come home with me?" That is just what he did! He went home with God to heaven.

After grandma had told that story, she told me that when my mama died, God took her by the hand and walked her right in to the Lord's own home. "

When grandpa finished telling that story to Maddie, he said, "What my grandma told me happened to my mama, is exactly what happened to your grandma!"

August 27
Where God Dwells

Centuries ago, a Hasidic rabbi was asked an important question — "Where does God dwell?" -- by one of the smartest members of his congregation. The holy man thought for a moment and said, "Some would say God dwells in the great beauty and majesty of nature. Others might say God dwells in the glories of human progress. Still others might say God dwells in that spark of divinity that is in every living human being. And there are some who simply say, 'God is everywhere.'"

The smartest man in the congregation looked intently at the old rabbi and asked, "I know about all of those other folk's opinions of where God dwells, but where do you say God dwells?"

The rabbi bowed low and said, "After years of searching and in years and years of study, now I know where God dwells. The truth of the matter is that God dwells wherever a person lets God in."

There was a period of quiet. Then, the rabbi spoke to the man and asked, "So, does God dwell in *your* heart?"

August 28
Disappointment

Singer Ray Charles once told an audience at a concert that he remembered well something that changed his life. He said that when he was first starting out in the music business, he was excited to try out to be a part of Lucky Miller's band. At the end of his tryout, however, he heard four terrible words: "Ain't good enough, kid."

Ray Charles said that all at once a great, big, dark cloud of disappointment settled down on him. He said he brooded under that dark cloud for a long time, becoming more and more bitter and angry. He felt very sorry for himself for a while, and then decided he had had enough of the gloom. He said, "I found that there was only one way to pierce that cloud of doom. I went back home and started practicing so much that nobody would or could ever say that to me again."

When a cloud of disappointment settles over you, what do you do to pierce it?

August 29
Shining Through You

Have you ever wondered if you make a difference in this world? Probably everyone has asked themselves that question at some point in their life, and there are probably many people who think they have never made a difference to anybody. As I think about that, I am reminded of something I read about Rudyard Kipling.

In his autobiography, Kipling describes something he experienced soon after his marriage in 1892. He and his new wife had built a house and settled into it. The house overlooked a very wide valley in one of the loneliest places in all of New England. They lived there throughout the winter and when spring finally came, he and his wife decided to make the trip all the way across that vast valley. When they finally arrived at the far side, they were met by a very elderly lady with a haggard and worn face.

She looked at them and said, "You must be the new lights that shone across our valley last winter." Kipling and his wife told her they certainly were new to the area. Then she turned to them with a big smile and said, "You have no idea what a great comfort your new light was for me all through the dark grey days and nights of this past winter. Please promise me you will never shade your lights!"

Kipling said that as long as he and his wife lived at that homestead, they never once shaded their lights during the winter. He said the memory of meeting that lonely old woman would always come to mind whenever either of them went to light their lamps.

If you ever wonder whether or not your life makes a difference, just remember that your life may be a light to someone you do not know, who gains great comfort and assurance from the light that shines through you.

August 30
Hidden Gifts

When the famous Polish pianist, Jan Paderewski, was just beginning his career, he was scheduled to leave his native Poland to play his first recital in London. As a beginner, he was very nervous, so he asked an influential compatriot to give him a letter of introduction to a leading figure in Britain's musical world. He thought that if he had such a letter perhaps things would go much better for him in England.

The influential Polish musician did write a letter, which he handed to Paderewski in a sealed envelope. He hoped that everything would proceed smoothly, and he would not have to use it. In the end, Paderewski did not have to use the letter and the concert went well.

When Paderewski returned to Poland and unpacked his suitcase, he found the sealed letter and put it in his desk drawer. Ten years later the letter was still in his desk drawer. By that time Paderewski had become a very well-known and respected artist.

Paderewski decided to read the letter and barked out a loud laugh as he read it. The letter was short and to the point: "This will introduce Jan Paderewski, who plays the piano, for which he demonstrates no conspicuous talent that I can see."

How's that for a letter of introduction? It was certainly a good thing no one in England ever saw that letter. Had the letter been opened, Jan Paderewski's career would have ended even before it ever began, and the world would have been deprived of enjoying a great talent.

That anecdote from Paderewski's life can serve as a great reminder to each of us to be careful about what we say about each other. If we say something negative, we may end up depriving the world of some hidden gifts.

August 31
Do You Know Anyone Like That?

I read a story that is attributed to Daniel Boone. He told this story whenever young folks were around because he wanted to impress them with how important it is to admit when you make a mistake or are wrong. Boone would tell the young folks that, back in "the good old days," he had a cousin who was a young know-it-all who could never admit his mistakes.

One day, that cousin walked into the village blacksmith shop shortly after the blacksmith had thrown a horseshoe on the ground to cool. Seeing it there, the young man reached down, picked it up, and instantly threw it back down because it burned his fingers.

"That damned thing is hotter than hell, isn't it, son?" said the blacksmith.

"No, not hot," said Boone's cousin. "It just doesn't take me long to look at a horseshoe!"

Daniel Boone would conclude that story by saying, "And so it is; some people never can admit that they make mistakes."

Do you know anyone like that?

September

September 1
What We Need

Have you ever felt that what you really need is a bit of peace and quiet so that you can rest? Most of us, I think, long for a little bit of peace and quiet in our hectic days. This past week, on a particularly busy day, someone stopped to tell me about what her two young boys had given her for her birthday.

The woman told me that she has a son who is 5 years old and another son who is 6 years old. The two brothers had gone shopping with their dad to find a good birthday present for their mom, and they ended up in a flower shop. The little guys came home and presented Mom with a house plant. They told her they had put their allowances together to buy the plant and they were beaming as they told her all about it.

Their mom told them how much she loved the plant and both boys laughed. The older boy then told her, "There was a big bunch of flowers that we wanted to give you at the flower shop. It was real pretty, but it cost too much. It had a ribbon on it that said, 'Rest in Peace,' and we thought it would be just perfect since you are always asking for a little peace and quiet so that you can rest."

September 2
Faces to the Coal

I am often struck by how many people tell me that they could endure all of the hardships they are experiencing if only they knew it was making a difference. That always reminds me of something I read about Winston Churchill.

During World War II, England needed to increase its production of coal. Yet everyone said that it was impossible for the miners to produce any more coal. So Winston Churchill called together the leaders of the miners to enlist their support. At the end of his presentation, he asked them to picture a parade that would be held in Picadilly Circus after the war.

First would come the sailors, said Churchill, who had kept the vital sea lanes open. Then would come the soldiers, who had come home from Dunkirk and then gone on to defeat Rommel in Africa. Then would come the pilots, who had driven the Luftwaffe from the sky in the Battle of Britain.

Last of all, he said, would come a long line of sweat-stained, soot-streaked men in miner's caps. Someone would cry from the crowd, "And where were you during the critical days of our struggle during the war?" And from 10,000 throats would come the answer, "We were deep in the earth with our faces to the coal, so you didn't freeze to death in the winter nor be without light when darkness came."

Then Churchill told those miners, "Not all the jobs in a war are prominent and glamorous and filled with glory. But it is often the people with their 'faces to the coal' who help the most to accomplish the things that most benefit others."

Are you someone who, in the midst of a great or even a minor crisis, has your face to the coal?

September 3
Man Overboard!

Here is something to think about. A mail boat was returning from the West Indies. Now among the passengers on that boat was a man and his dog. A bored, small child began playing with the man's dog. The child tossed a stick onto the deck and the dog immediately went and retrieved it.

The boy and the dog continued playing together until one toss went too far and ended up in the sea. At once the dog jumped in after the stick. In great fear, the owner of the dog went to the captain and begged him to turn the boat around to go and rescue the dog.

"Stop the mails for a stupid dog? I can't do that!" screamed the captain.

"Then you shall stop the boat for a man!" screamed the dog's owner and jumped overboard.

The captain would, of course, stop the mail boat for a man. He did turn the boat around and rescued both man and dog.

Now ask yourself, if that were your dog, would you have jumped into the sea to save it? That story can bring up other questions as well. Is there anyone in your life right now who is "overboard," flailing around in dangerous waters, needing someone to jump in to save them? Would you be willing to turn the boat of your life around to rescue someone in dire need?

September 4
Each One

In 1979 Mother Teresa of Calcutta was awarded the Nobel Peace Prize. Before she went into the ceremony in which she would receive the award, a reporter spoke with her and said, "Mother, I have done some research about your work. If one would tally up the numbers, we find that 7,500 children have been educated in your schools, 960,000 people have been cared for in your dispensaries, 47,000 lepers looked after in 54 clinics, some 1,600 orphans brought up in some 20 different homes, and far too many dying people to count who have been cared for in 23 homes. These are amazing numbers."

Mother Teresa's response was, "Those aren't numbers you are talking about; those are people, whom Jesus loves and so do we."

The reporter replied, "Well, these numbers are important for people to know."

Mother Teresa smiled at him and said, "The only important number for me and for each of my sisters is the number one. It is the *one* person with whom I am working at a time. One suffering person at a time. Each one important. You must always remember that God will give you a person to care for, one at a time. Each one is important."

September 5
Real Power

Back in my college days, I took a philosophy course. One day the professor gave each of the students a particular quote from a famous person. We were to read that quote every day for two weeks and then write a paper explaining the impact that the quote had on us.

The citation I was assigned was from Emerson. Here it is: "A man is what he thinks about all day long. The way we think determines how we live. A single thought in the morning may fill our whole day with joy and sunshine, or gloom and depression. Our life is what our inner thoughts make it. The highest possible stage in moral culture is when we recognize that we ought to control our thoughts."

I have never forgotten that quote and have found it helpful not only in my own life, but in helping other folks deal with the difficulties they encounter in their lives as well. I often recommend that troubled folks or even truly happy folks do with Emerson's words what my college philosophy professor asked me to do all those years ago. If you read those words every day for two weeks, I am sure that you will soon discover the real power contained in them.

September 6
Before It's Too Late

I was at a parish retreat some years ago where a woman, a lawyer, spoke about a conversation she had with her dad. She told of how her career had really taken off, and she kept getting more and more promotions. With those promotion came some transfers, and she ended up living 500 miles away from her parents and extended family. She had not seen nor spoken to her elderly parents in quite a few months when she received a very unexpected phone call from her father.

The woman said, "Before I could even say hello, my dad bellowed into the phone, 'When are you coming home for a visit? I miss you.'"

Startled that he was yelling, she immediately tried to calm him down and began to explain to him about all of the demands on her time, her court schedule, the many meetings she was required to attend, and all the other obligations she had to tend to. There was a pause on the other end of the phone. Then, in a very calm voice her father said, "I have been wondering something for quite some time now. You must tell me. When I die, do you intend to come to the funeral?"

Shaken by the question, his daughter replied, "Dad, I can't believe you even have to ask that question. Of course, I would drop everything and come to your funeral!"

Before she could say anything else, her father said, "Good, let's make a deal. You can skip my funeral. I need to be with you now much more than I will need you at my funeral!" She was on a flight home the next morning.

The woman concluded by saying, "My dad's call that day was truly a wake-up call in every sense of the word. What I want you to know is what I have learned from my dad; that time spent with a loved one is the most precious gift we have to give. I am glad his call came before it was too late."

September 7
On Purpose

Years ago, I was in a particular parish and found it a very difficult place to be. After a year or so, I went to a very elderly priest who was known for his practical advice and uncommon wisdom. I told him that I was considering asking for a transfer because ministry in the parish I was assigned to seemed so difficult and the people so unappreciative.

The old priest looked me in the eye and said, "Mark, every good priest I know has been in the same situation that you are in now." He didn't say anything more for about 10 minutes. We both sat in silence. Then I asked, "Did any of them ask for a transfer?"

"Well, just about all of them wanted to ask for a transfer. Then they talked to me and I told them about old Bishop Nathan Soderblom of Sweden. Once they heard about him, each one went back to his parish and worked there until their term of office was up. Not one of them transferred. Not one of them was disappointed. In fact, each of them found their assignment to be really right where they belonged."

"Tell me about old Bishop Soderblom," I said.

The old priest said, "The story is that after working for a long time in his diocese in Sweden, Bishop Soderblom went to the King of Sweden one day and said, "Your Majesty, I have discovered a little island off the coast of Spain. It has one little church, only one main street, and only a few hundred people live on that beautiful island. I want you, Your Majesty, to release me from my present assignment as bishop here, so that I can go and be a simple parish priest for the congregation on that tiny island. Life would be much better there."

The king looked at Bishop Soderblom and said very kindly, "Ah yes, I know that little Island. It is so very lovely. The people there need a postman to bring in the mail and to pick up the mail just twice a week. Each day the postman walks through the little village delivering letters to the lovely people. Now bishop, I would love to be that postman. But, alas, God didn't put me on earth to be a postman to those lovely people. He has made me king here."

The bishop said, "Your Majesty, I don't know what to say."

The king replied, "Bishop, it is my belief that God has made you bishop here on purpose, for a purpose. He has made me king here on purpose, for a purpose too. You and I must admit that God knows what he is doing, and if he made me king here, and you bishop here, perhaps he has seen something we have not. So, let us leave this in his hands. If some day he wishes to change his mind and transfer us to that island, so be it. But, since he has us where we are, I propose we both stay where he has put us."

After listening to the story of Bishop Soderblom, I went back to my parish. I did not ask for a transfer, and just like all the other men who had talked to that old priest about transferring, I found the parish to be a great place to discover God at work and met some of the finest people ever.

If you are questioning where you are right now and the work you are doing, perhaps it's time to think about old Bishop Soderblom. Maybe God has you where you are on purpose, for a purpose.

September 8
What Are You Doing with Your Gifts?

Life itself has a way of teaching us some spiritual truths. I have been thinking about this because I was reading a novel about China that described how many Chinese farmers could not support themselves or their communities. That is because years ago, Chinese farmers ran their farms on the idea that they should eat all of their large potatoes and keep the small ones to use as seeds for future crops.

They practiced farming in this way for decades until finally, one of the wisest of the farmers realized that each year, more and more of the crop turned out to be very small potatoes. He began to use the biggest potatoes for seeds and used the smaller ones for food. Within a few years, the other farmers discovered that what the wise farmer did was to save the future.

Is there a truth here for each of us when it comes to what we do with the good things God gives us?

September 9
Are You Ready?

Leo Tolstoy is famous for many of the characters in his books. One of my favorites is Martin the cobbler. Martin was a very happy man until both his wife and his son died. He became bitter and angry and could not cope very well with his grief.

One day, a visitor secretly left a copy of the New Testament in Martin's shop. Eventually Martin found the book and began to carefully read it. The book changed his outlook on life. Then one night, as he was preparing for bed, Martin actually heard Jesus speaking to him. The Lord spoke very softly to him saying, "Martin, tomorrow I shall come to visit you."

When the morning came, Martin was excited like he had not been in quite a long time. As the day wore on, Martin was a bit disappointed because he had no special visitors. Only these people came to his shop: an old soldier who was half-frozen from the bitter winter day; Martin settled the man by the fire and fed him some hot soup. Then a young woman and her child who didn't have coats; Martin gave her one of his wife's old coats, and the child he gave the coat his son used to wear. Finally, there was an old woman, and a young boy who had stolen apples from her orchard storehouse; Martin helped them to work out their problems.

As Martin got ready for bed that night, he prayed, "Lord, you promised to come visit me today. Were you too busy to come?" There was a period of quiet during which the only sound Martin heard was the clock ticking. Then came a very quiet voice that said, "But Martin, I did visit you. Then out of the shadows stepped the old soldier, the woman and her child, and the young boy and the old woman.

Martin had been ready to welcome the Lord. He did welcome the Lord in welcoming each of his visitors that day. Then, at the end of the day, he welcomed the Lord in his nightly prayer.

Are you ready to welcome the Lord each day?

September 10
The Power to Rebound

Recently, I came across a quotation from a movie director named Michael Todd that really impressed me. In an interview, he was asked about the times in his career when he had lost everything. His response to that question was fascinating. He said, "Many times I have been broke, but I have never been poor."

Todd went on to explain that whenever misfortune took over his life, he could always draw upon the true treasure of his life -- the Jewish faith and heritage that had been instilled in him from a very early age. He said that looking back to Moses and to all that God had done in and for his own people had given him great strength to rebound from any crisis. Todd said that he had discovered that God never abandons us.

What is your source of strength in times of crisis? What gives you the power to rebound?

September 11
Are You Intelligent?

In ancient Rome a famous philosophy teacher gathered his students together to help them with their moral life. He told his students that the best thing they could all do to improve the moral life of the city of Rome was to be people of intelligence.

When he was asked by his students what "intelligence" is, the teacher paused to compose himself, then said: "The word 'intelligence' is derived from two other words: 'inter' and 'legere.' One word means 'to choose' and the other means 'between.' So an intelligent person is the person who has learned to choose between good and evil, and who knows that trust is better than fear, that love is better than hate, that gentleness is much better than cruelty, that forbearance better than tolerance, that humility is better than arrogance, and that being truthful is better than being a liar."

Having read that philosophy teacher's definition of "intelligence," do you qualify as a person of intelligence?

September 12
If Only

Over 2,000 years ago, a rabbi known to be a great sage began to take stock of his life. He concluded his thinking by saying, "I wish I had lived differently. From where I stand now, I know I could have done better. When I was young and full of idealism, I set out to reform all of humankind. After that, I realized that I should first try to reform my country. Shortly after that I realized that I needed to reform my province. Next, I turned to my city, then I turned on my family."

"Now, when I am certain that my death is nearly at hand, I realize that I should have begun by reforming myself. If I had done that first, then I could have gone on to change my family, my city, my province, and maybe the world too. If only I had begun with me. Now I know that true reform begins only with oneself."

September 13
Just Like Bart

A doctor went to visit one of his patients, who was also a close friend. As soon as the doctor entered his friend's room, the patient spoke in a very shaky voice, "We've been good friends for many years, so I want you to be honest with me. I feel like I am very close to death. Is it true, am I near death?" The physician was silent, not knowing what to say. So, he just nodded and whispered, "I don't think it will be long now."

His friend said, "I am so scared. I don't want to die. I believe in Jesus, but I can't know what to expect. Please, can you help me?"

Just then a whining and scratching was heard at the door. When the doctor opened it, in bounded his big, beautiful dog, who often went with him as he made house calls. The dog was glad to see his master. Sensing an opportunity to comfort his troubled patient, the doctor said, "My dog, Bart, has never been in your room before, so he didn't know what it was like in here. But he knew I was in here, and that was enough."

"I know you are scared about going to the other side. I would be too. I also want to tell you something. I'm looking forward to heaven. I don't know much about it, but I know my Savior, Jesus, is there behind the door waiting for me. And that's all I need to know! So, when your time comes, you will be just like Bart here -- when the door to heaven is opened, you will find your master happy to see you, and you will be happy to see him!"

September 14
Overcoming Terror

I read something very interesting about the famous scientist Louis Pasteur. According to those who knew him well, Pasteur was terrified of dogs. Even a distant bark would almost paralyze him with fear. In his mind he could still see a wolf, mad with rabies, that had raged through his boyhood village bringing agony and death to many of his neighbors. "I have always been haunted by the cries of those victims," he said time and again.

Yet in 1882, still fearful of dogs, Pasteur gave up all his other studies in an intense search for a cure for rabies. For three long years, in spite of his deep-seated personal terrors, he risked his life living with mad dogs. At last he came through with a vaccine to cure the victims of rabies.

On a July night in 1885, he tried the first injection on a little boy whose life seemed doomed. The boy lived. Those haunting old memories from childhood and the agony of his past neighbors spurred Louis Pasteur to find a cure for this dread disease. By harnessing his fear, he set many people free.

September 15
Afraid of the Dark?

President John F. Kennedy often closed his speeches with the story of Colonel Davenport, who many years prior had been the Speaker of the Connecticut House of Representatives. As Kennedy told the story, on May 19, 1780, the sky of Hartford darkened ominously. There were great flashes of lightning and howling winds. Some of the representatives, glancing out the windows, were terrified that the end of the world was at hand.

The Speaker tried to calm them all down as there began a clamor for immediate adjournment. Davenport rose and said, "The Day of Judgment is either approaching or it is not. If it is not, there is no cause for adjournment. If it is, I choose to be found doing my duty. Therefore, I wish that candles be brought. Rather than cowering here, fearing what is to come, we ought to be faithful until Jesus Christ returns. Instead of being afraid of the dark, we ought to be lights as we watch and wait for him."

When difficult times come, do you find yourself cowering in fear of the dark, or do you choose to be a light as you watch and wait for Jesus to come?

September 16
Worthwhile

A young, newly ordained priest, serving in his first parish and preparing his first homily, sought out the advice of a very elderly priest. The young priest said to the old pastor, "Father, I was wondering if you could tell me something."

"What is it you want to know?" the old priest replied.

The newly ordained man said, "If you knew you were giving your very last sermon, what would you want to tell our parishioners?"

After a long pause, the old pastor spoke very softly and said, "I would tell them that there is one thing that God wants his people to do."

The young priest eagerly jumped right in and said, "So, father, what is it that you think God wants us all to do?"

There was another long pause, after which the retired priest said, "I would tell them that God really wants each of his people to go out and get themselves some worthwhile memories."

As you get older and begin to look back over your life, what are your most important, worthwhile memories?

September 17
Swift and Slow

One of the philosophers and thinkers from ancient Rome, Epictetus by name, used to begin each of his classes by telling his students, "Our Mother Nature has given each of us one tongue, but also two ears. By this she is teaching us that we must always listen twice as much as we speak, lest the world find out how truly ignorant we really are."

Epictetus has given us something to ponder. Are you a person who speaks before they listen, or one who listens before they speak? The Apostle James advised those who wish to follow in the steps of Jesus to "Be swift to listen, and slow to speak." So, are you someone who is swift to listen or swift to speak?

September 18
Pay Attention

A friend of mine went on vacation to England. While touring Chester Cathedral, she came upon an inscription engraved on a huge grandfather clock. She quickly jotted down the inscription on a postcard and sent it to me. My friend added a little note at the bottom of the card that read, "You must know, I hope, that the work you do bringing an awareness of God's presence to others is truly important, because time is surely way too short. Thank you for the work you do."

Here is that inscription:
Pay attention to time:
When, as a child, I laughed and wept, Time crept.
When, as a youth, I dreamed and talked, Time walked.
When I became a full-grown man, Time ran.
And later, as I older grew, Time flew.
Soon I shall find, while traveling on, Time gone.
Will Christ have saved my soul by then?

September 19
What We Let In

I read something rather interesting about John Pulitzer, the man for whom journalism's most important prize is named. It is said he had a peculiar quirk that made him unable to think or work if there was any kind of noise going on around him. In fact, he made sure that his New York office was completely soundproofed so he could get a decent day's work done.

Pulitzer found that the city was far too noisy for him, so he bought a cottage 'way out in the countryside of Connecticut. It wasn't long after he moved there that he contracted to have a soundproof room installed, so he could sleep and get work done at home.

When Pulitzer's neighbor noticed all of the construction going on, he visited to see what his neighbor was up to. Pulitzer explained that he had to do something about the incessant noise that disturbed him every day. His neighbor was baffled because he found that part of Connecticut to be one of the quietest places he had ever been. He said, "Mr. Pulitzer, what noise are you talking about?"

The reply came, "It's your rooster crowing that is driving me mad!"

"Surely my rooster cannot be disturbing you to this extreme," the neighbor said, "He only crows at most three times a day! In fact, my rooster has crowed so often that I no longer hear it."

"True," said Pulitzer, "but if only you knew what I suffer just waiting for him to disturb me!"

Have you ever let something like Pulitzer's rooster get inside your head? Something like that can happen to any of us, if we let it. The problem is that once we let something inside to frustrate and worry us, we lose all sense of peace and a lot of time gets wasted. Poor John Pulitzer! If only he had concentrated on the long periods of silence between the rooster's crowing, he would have had such peace.

September 20
Your Heart's Desire

Have you ever been angry with God because he doesn't seem to answer your prayers? I've been thinking and praying about this recently because something I had been praying for didn't work out the way I thought it should. I was disappointed and wondered what God was up to. I asked God to show me what I needed to learn from the situation, but for a while, no answer seemed to come.

Then one morning, during my prayer time, I read something from a talk given by Ruth Graham, the wife of Billy Graham. It came to me like a bolt from the blue. She had been talking to an audience of young women in Minneapolis, and her topic was, "What to Do When God Doesn't Answer Your Prayers!" Her talk was the answer to my prayers. Perhaps it can be an answer for you too.

Here is the one sentence that made me both laugh and gave me peace. Graham said, "God has not always answered my heart's desire. If he had, I would have married the wrong man -- several times!"

September 21
What Jesus Would Do

Someone gave me a book called *The Little Minister*. It was written by a man named James Barry, and it is the story of a very young minister who is assigned to be the pastor of a church in a small town in Scotland. He is to take the place of a very elderly and wise old preacher who had been pastoring that church for over fifty years.

Hoping to say something kind and complimentary to the old man, the little minister introduces himself and says, "Reverend, I appreciate what you have done. Now, I will begin where you left off." The old preacher thought for a few minutes, then wisely said, "No, my son, you must begin where I began."

When the little minister looked puzzled, the old man simply said, "You must begin to get to know and love these folks. It's what Jesus would do."

September 22
Hide and Seek

Whenever someone tells me that they are so busy with life that they have no time for prayer, I often think of a famous Hasidic story. It's about a young boy who is playing hide-and-seek with his friends. They stopped playing while he was hiding and since they didn't come to find him, he began to cry. His old grandfather, a rabbi, tried to comfort him.

"Do not cry because your own friends did not come to find you," the old man said. The boy looked up at his grandpa with big eyes, trying not to cry. Then his grandpa continued: "There is something important for you to learn from this big disappointment in your friends. Just like you, God waits every day to be found by his friends, but like your friends, many of them have gone off in search of other things."

Did you know that God is waiting to be found by you? The question is, what other things have you been seeking?

September 23
Can You Imagine?

Johannes Brahms was once asked how he went about composing the beautiful music he produced. Here is what he said: "I always contemplate my oneness with the Creator before commencing to compose. I immediately feel vibrations that thrill my whole being …. I then see clearly what is obscure in my ordinary moods ….

Straightaway the idea flows in upon me. Then, measure by measure, the finished product is revealed."

What do you suppose would happen to you if you took some time each day to contemplate your oneness with the Creator? What gifts for the world do you think would be produced by you if you invited the Creator into your daily life? Can you imagine what God could do in and with you if you opened up to his presence?

September 24
True Treasures

Biographers of the famous Catholic theologian and philosopher, St. Thomas Aquinas, often tell about a conversation that took place between the saint and the pope. According to the story, the pope and Aquinas met just a few months before the saint died in 1274. After the meeting, the pope showed Aquinas all of the art and many of the gold and silver treasures of the Vatican.

When the two men had finished their tour, the pope said to Aquinas, "Well, as you can see, the Church can no longer say what St. Peter said in Acts 3 to the paralyzed man, 'Neither silver nor gold do I have.'" Then the pope, smiling broadly, said, "The Church has done quite well for herself. Look at all of her treasures."

Aquinas was very quick in saying, "Yes, Your Holiness, the Church can no longer say that it has neither silver nor gold like St. Peter did. But you must also realize that the Church can also no longer say, like St. Peter did to that paralyzed man in Acts 3, 'In the name of Jesus of Nazareth, rise and walk!'"

I do not know what reaction the pope had to Aquinas' words, but it is obvious that the pope and St. Thomas Aquinas had very different ideas about what the true treasures of the Church really are.

September 25
What Owns You

An Amish man and his wife and family stopped to watch their new neighbors move into the house down the road. The Amish folks were fascinated by all of the things that were being unloaded from the moving van. Many of the things they observed being carted into their neighbor's house were unfamiliar to them, but they remained fascinated, nonetheless.

The next day, the Amish man and his wife visited their new neighbors and brought them a gift of homemade muffins and jam. They had a wonderful visit, and the two families became quick friends.
As they got ready to leave, the Amish man said, "If all those appliances and machines that you just moved into your house should break down and need repairing, don't hesitate to call me."

"Well, thank you so much, that is great of you to offer your help. I didn't realize that you Amish folks knew enough about modern appliances to know how to repair them," said the new neighbor.

"To tell you the truth," the Amish farmer said, "I don't know a thing about how to fix those things. What I can do for you, my friend, is to teach you to live without them."

If you were to take a look at all of the things you own, how many of them could you very happily do without? Are you able to let them go? Are there any possessions that you know you definitely cannot do without? What makes them so important that you just cannot do without them?

It was St. Francis of Assisi who told us that things should never own us. We may own them, but they should never own us. Is there anything in your life right now that you think might be actually owning you?

September 26
Miners

I read something recently that became a part of my morning prayer the day after I read it. It had been written by a college student named Susan, who had an assignment to write about the teacher in her life who had the biggest impact on her.

Susan wrote about her high school chemistry teacher who had to flunk her because she did so poorly in her class. When she got her report card and discovered that she had indeed gotten an "F" in chemistry, Susan was not surprised and admitted that she was completely baffled by science in general and chemistry in particular.

What Susan wrote next is what caught my attention. She wrote that her teacher had done something extraordinary that made all the difference. The teacher had put a star next to the "F," and at the bottom of the report card, next to another star, had written, "We can't all be good chemists, but we all would like to be as good a person as Susan."

Susan had concluded her college assignment by saying that her chemistry teacher was her heroine not because she wrote something nice on her report card, rather, because she always recognized and made the students aware of their best qualities. She was like a miner who searched for the gold in each person.

The day after I read her comments, I spent time meditating on her words. I looked back at my own life for the "miners" who found good in others and made them aware of it. I know I had quite a few teachers who did that for me.

Can you recall any "miners" in your life who helped you discover the gold within you? Those folks may or may not have been teachers, but I bet there are more than a few people in your life who helped you discover the good in you. Perhaps today would be a good day to look back in your life for those "miners," then pause to give thanks to God for each one of them.

September 27
When the Future Is Done

The famous mechanical and electrical genius, Charles Kettering, was always thinking about new ways of seeing things and of making things. Even far into his 80s, he was still inventing. When he would go to work, he would constantly talk to the younger men and women there about the future.

One day, as Kettering was talking about what he wanted to do in the next six months with regard to a project he was proposing, a younger colleague interrupted him and said, "Sir, why are you always talking about the future? Why is someone as old as you so interested in the future?"

Kettering threw his head back, laughed, and said, "Why am I interested in the future? Well, it's really quite simple. I am interested in the future because that is where I have to spend all of the rest of my life! I also think about what will happen to me when my future on earth is done."

How much time do you spend thinking about the future? Have you ever spent time thinking about what will be in store for you when your future on earth is done?

September 28
At Peace in the Storm

I've been thinking about hurricanes. I started thinking about those storms because of a conversation I had with a woman who knew that she would probably die within a few days. When I asked her if she was scared, she said, "Only a little bit on the outside, but not on the inside." When I asked her what she meant by that, she replied, "When I see my husband and my kids so upset, I get frightened for them. But down in my heart of hearts, I know that Jesus is with me and I am perfectly calm. I guess I am like a hurricane!"

When she said that I remembered that a hurricane is a storm with winds over 74 m.p.h. Tremendous amounts of rain, thunder, and lightning usually accompany the winds. Hurricanes are storms with relentless pounding winds that continue hour after hour. Of course, the fascinating thing about a hurricane is its "eye" — a place of perfect calm in its center. Though the winds blow and rage all around it, there are none in the eye.

Even though my parishioner was facing death, she had her own "eye" in the center of her heart and soul -- a place of perfect calm. She told me that she felt God in her heart, and that with the Lord at the center of one's life, there is calm and peace even in the darkest of life's storms.

September 29
Back Home

There is an old Jewish legend that describes what happened when God created the human race. The legend says that God asked some of the angels who stood near him as he created human beings what they thought.

There was an angel who was much concerned about justice, who said, "Do not create human beings, for they will commit all kinds of wickedness against each other and will be hard and cruel and dishonest and unrighteous."

Next to that angel stood an angel who was quite concerned about truth, who said, "Lord, please do not create humans, for they will be false and deceitful to one another and even to you!"

And next to that angel stood an angel who was most concerned about holiness, who said, "Oh Lord, do not create human beings because they will do many wicked things in your sight, and dishonor you to your face."

Then an angel stepped forward who was full of much mercy, who said, "My Lord, do create the human race, for when people sin and turn from the path of right and truth and holiness, I will take each one tenderly by the hand, speak your loving words to them, and then lead them back to you."

If you look back over your life, did God ever send that angel of mercy to you to lead you back home?

September 30
Where Would You Go?

I read a biography of President Harry Truman in which the author describes a meeting Truman had with one of his friends, Sam Rayburn, the day after President Roosevelt died.

Harry Truman was feeling very overwhelmed by being suddenly thrust into the presidency, and Rayburn gave him some fatherly advice: "Harry, from here on out, you're going to have lots of people around you. They'll try to put a wall around you and cut you off from any ideas but theirs. They'll tell you what a great man you are, Harry. But you and I both know you ain't."

Harry Truman said that it was the best advice he received as he began his work as president. He also said that his friend Sam Rayburn did something else that he never forgot.

One day, Rayburn came to Truman to tell him that he was going to make an important announcement to the House of Representatives that day, and he wanted Truman to observe from the gallery. Truman agreed to do so. Later that day, Rayburn told the members of the House that his doctors had discovered that he was quite ill. He told his colleagues in the House that he was going home for more tests. Some wondered why he did not stay in Washington, where there were excellent medical facilities. He supplied the answer when he told the Congressmen, "Bonham, my hometown, is a place where people know it when you're sick, and where they really care when you die."

Rayburn did go home. His sickness grew worse, but caring people surrounded him and took good care of him. When he died people wept for the loss of a good man. What he had told his colleagues in Washington turned out to be true -- the people of his hometown knew he was sick, reached out to care for him, and yes, they cared deeply when he died.

If you found yourself seriously ill or in some kind of need, where would you go to find people who know when you are sick and would care deeply if you died?

October

October 1
Reaching Across the Distance

I read something interesting about the famous Norwegian explorer Ronald Amundsen. He was the first person to discover the magnetic meridian of the North Pole and then to discover the South Pole.

What I found interesting about Amundsen is that he was extraordinarily close to his wife. His explorations to such faraway places was a heavy burden on the couple. Long separations without contact made for difficult and fearful times. Mrs. Amundsen said that she often longed for some kind of word from him that he was alive and well.

Because he knew how his wife felt, on one of his long trips, Amundsen took a homing pigeon with him. When he had finally reached the top of the world, he opened the bird's cage and sent it home with a love note attached to its foot. Imagine the delight of Amundsen's wife, back in Norway, when she looked up from the doorway of her home and saw the pigeon circling in the sky above. She is said to have exclaimed, "He's alive! My husband is still alive! In his love, Ronald has found a way to cross the great distance between us!"

Is there a relationship in your life right now that might need a "homing pigeon" to reach across the great distance between the two of you?

October 2
Hard Times

The next time you hear any part of Handel's *Messiah*, consider what was happening in Handel's life when he wrote his most famous work. On hearing it you probably would think that the musician who wrote it was at the top of his game. You might think that, but you would be wrong.

In fact, the *Messiah* was written after Handel had suffered a very debilitating stroke. As he was trying to deal with the harsh realities and terrible effects of such a devastating stroke, Handel lived in poverty amid bleak surroundings. He had suffered through what he described as a particularly deep night of gloom and despair over his sense that he was a failure as a musician.

One particular night he was in the deepest depression, very close to ending it all. But the next morning he unleashed his creative genius in a musical score that continues to inspire millions of people.

Isn't it amazing that something so beautiful and inspiring could be born out of such misery? There is a message in this for all of us. None of us escapes hard times. It is part of the human condition. It is not what happens to us that matters, it is what we do with what happens to us. We might ask ourselves a simple question, then: What can I do to bring good fruit out of hard times?

October 3
Finding the Way

There is a famous story about Supreme Court Justice Oliver Wendell Holmes, who once found himself on a train but couldn't locate his ticket. While the conductor watched, smiling, the somewhat confused eighty-year-old Justice Holmes searched through all his pockets without success.

Of course, the conductor recognized the distinguished man, so he said, "Mr. Holmes, don't worry. If we can't trust you, who can we trust? You don't need your ticket. You'll probably find it when you get off the train and I'm sure the Pennsylvania Railroad will trust you to mail it back later."

Holmes looked up with some irritation and said, "My dear man, that is not the problem at all. The problem is, where am I going? I was hoping the ticket would tell me where to get off!"

Have you ever felt like Justice Holmes, not quite sure where you are going or even where to "get off the train?" There are many ways to be lost and many ways to be baffled by what life throws at you. But one thing is certain. Jesus said, "I am the Way, the Truth, and the Life." If you are feeling lost, perhaps some time spent with him may help you find the direction in which you need to go.

October 4
What?

One of the greatest poets of the Renaissance, Dante, described how he was exiled from his home in Florence, Italy. Completely overwhelmed and discouraged by this cruel turn of events, he decided to walk from Italy to Paris, so that he could study philosophy, in order to find a clue to the meaning of life. As he traveled, Dante found himself a weary pilgrim, forced to beg along the way and eventually to knock at the door of Santa Croce Monastery to find refuge from the night. A half-asleep, angry brother within was finally aroused. He came to the door, flung it open, and in a gruff voice asked, "What do you want?" Dante answered in a single word, "Peace." And with that very word that came from his own mouth, he came to realize what he was truly looking for in life, peace of mind and heart.

Why not take a moment right now to consider your own life and circumstances? What do you want? What are you looking for in life? Where do you suppose you will find it?

October 5
Something to Consider

One of the ancient Desert Fathers would often warn his disciples about the danger of ignoring the anger that could be welling up in their heart. He taught them that anger that is nurtured in your heart is like an eagle that swooped to the ground catching a weasel in its claws. However, when the great bird flew away clutching its prey in its talons, all at once the bird fell headlong to the ground with a great thud. What made the eagle fall to the earth? When the eagle began to fly into the sky, the weasel bit the bird, which caused it to bleed profusely. The higher the eagle flew, the more blood it lost until it died and fell to the earth. The Desert Father concluded by saying, "If we cling to an attitude of anger or jealousy or spite, it will, like the weasel, sink its teeth into us and drain away all of the strength and life from us."

October 6
Leading

Years ago, when I was a newly appointed pastor of a small, poor parish, I was having lunch with a good friend who was a successful businessman. When I told him that I was going to become pastor of a local parish he was excited and congratulated me. He said, "I will pray for you that when you step into your new position you will be a true leader after God's own heart, and not merely a boss."

When I asked him what he meant by that, the man said, "In a day or two I will send you a note with what I have learned through the years that I have been a leader in business. Your business is to care for people. So, read the note I send you and pay attention to it."

A few days later I received a note from my friend with these words of advice: "Please remember to be a leader and not a boss. Remember this: a boss creates fear; a leader creates confidence. Bossism creates resentment; leadership breeds enthusiasm. A boss says, 'I'; a leader says, 'we.' A boss fixes blame; a leader fixes mistakes. A boss knows how; a leader shows how. Bossism makes work drudgery; leadership makes work interesting. A boss relies on authority; a leader relies on cooperation. A boss drives; a leader leads. Jesus was a true leader. If you want to serve his people as a pastor, be a leader like him."

I thought that was great advice. I have tried to follow it. In the work that you do or in the way you live your life, are you a boss or a leader?

October 7
Stuck in the Shadows

One of my parishioners recently asked to see me. When he met with me, he told me that he felt he had to do something pretty soon or he would end up taking his own life. I asked him what the issue was, and he just said, "I am stuck in a 'going nowhere' job. I go to a bar every night after work and sit and listen to my friends talk about how unhappy they are until the bar closes. I go home and fall asleep only to wake up the next day feeling depressed. I go to work, I end up at the bar, I come home. It's always the same. I need something. Tell me what I need."

I thought for a moment about what he said, then told him the following story: There is a fable about a man who lived in the desert. He would wake up every morning and follow his shadow. As the sun moved across the sky from east to west the man essentially walked in a large oval. At sundown he ended up where he had started. This continued for years. The man walked in circles day after day, following his shadow.

One night the man heard the voice of God in a dream while he slept. The voice told him to stop following his shadow. Instead, the voice challenged, "Follow the sun and you will experience life as you have never dreamed it could be."

The man thought for many days about his vision of God while he continued to walk around in circles in the desert. But one day he mustered up enough courage to break away from his shadow. Little by little, step-by-step, the man began to follow the sun. And he discovered a kingdom that was, heretofore, way beyond his wildest dreams and imagination. Ultimately, he became friends with the sun.

When I finished telling him that story, the man looked at me with wide eyes, saying, "My girlfriend told me if I came to you, you would convince me to stop drinking! So, are you telling me that my 'shadow' is my drinking?"

I didn't say anything; I just smiled at him.

The man then smiled back at me and said, "I promised my girlfriend that if you told me to stop drinking, I would go to the AA meetings she wants me to attend with her. I guess I am going to stop following my shadow. I guess I am going to those meetings!"

After a short pause, the man asked, "What do you think?"

I said, "I think you are a wise man, and you have an even wiser girlfriend."

October 8
What Is Your Life About?

I have read many books about Abraham Lincoln throughout the years. The more I learn about him the more impressed I am by the man's humility, humor, and wisdom. There are so many stories about him that I find it hard to choose only one favorite story, but there is one that I often share with people. Here it is:

Abraham Lincoln was once hired by a man to sue someone else because they owed him $2.50. Now, two dollars and fifty cents is not a lot of money to us today, but in the 1860s it certainly was. Lincoln didn't want to take the case but his client, a good friend, insisted. So, Abe asked for a $10.00 retainer fee up front. His client and friend gladly handed him the $10. Lincoln then gave the man who owed $2.50 half of the ten. The man was so impressed with Lincoln's generosity that he promptly paid his debt. The result was that everyone went home happy.

Lincoln is said to have remarked that he preferred finding ways of sending folks home happy rather than helping people fight each other. His life turned out to be about just that. What is your life about?

October 9
When the Music Stops

I read something about the famous composer Johannes Brahms that I found very interesting. It happened when he was in the later stages of his life. Brahms said that there was one very frightening point at which he just could not seem to compose anything. He would start working on something and by the time he got into it, he could not seem to finish. He felt completely powerless. He feared he lost his ear for music, and even more frightening, he thought he had lost music itself. He concluded that age had crept up on him and he was used up.

Brahms thought, "I am much too old. I have worked long and diligently, and I suppose I have achieved enough. I now have before me a carefree old age. I suppose I can now enjoy my years in peace. I will compose no more. The music has stopped in my life and in my soul."

You would think that this would have ended the man's career. That was not the case. The remarkable thing was that his decision to stop composing cleared his mind and relaxed his faculties so much that he was able to feel the music again. It wasn't long before he was able to pick up his composing without difficulty.

There is much to learn from Johannes Brahms. Many, many people are a bundle of anxieties. Anxiety steals their peace, and that is why they accomplish so little. Perhaps by giving up our worry and fear we may not have to give up that which makes our souls so full. Don't let the music in your life be stopped by fear.

October 10
Progress

Here is something to think about. In 1879, a child was born to a poor Jewish merchant. The young boy suffered a haunting sense of inferiority from an early age because of the anti-Semitic feelings he encountered every day. He became very shy and introspective. In fact, that shyness led the boy to be so slow in learning that his parents had him examined by specialists to see if he was normal. They worried that he might be feeble-minded. The specialists declared him normal but somewhat dull-witted.

The boy became a young man who worked hard as he struggled in school. Then in 1895, he decided to go to college. Unfortunately, he failed his entrance examinations at the Polytechnicum in Zurich, Switzerland. His parents worried that he would end up a beggar, yet a year later he tried again and succeeded. Later he received a doctorate from the University of Zurich, yet at first, he obtained only an obscure job as a patent examiner in the Berne patent office.

Who was he? The man who formulated the theory of relativity, Albert Einstein, one of the greatest geniuses who ever lived.

At so many points in Einstein's life it looked as though he was an utter failure who would never amount to anything. When asked about those failure points in his life, he simply said, "I was a work in progress."

How do you look at the failure points in your life? Are they a final verdict, or are they simply signs that you are a work in progress?

October 11
Reassurance

Robert Louis Stevenson told a story of a storm that threatened to send a ship to the bottom of the sea. The ship was caught off a rocky coast which likely meant death to all on board should it crash along the shore. Most of the people were terrified that it would not be long before they would all be lost.

When the terror among the people on board was at its worst, one man, more daring than the rest, struggled to make his way to the pilot house to see just how bad things were. As the man walked into the pilot house, he saw the pilot lashed to his post with his hands firmly on the wheel, turning the ship little by little into the open sea. When the pilot saw the ghastly white, terror-stricken face of the man, he smiled and said, "It's only a storm."

When the man saw the smile and heard the words, he rushed to the deck below, shouting: "I have seen the face of the pilot, and he smiled. All is well." The sight of that pilot's smiling face calmed the panic and transformed despair into hope.

When you are going through the terrible storms that life sometimes brings, to whom to you look for that smile and reassuring words?

October 12
What Do You Think?

Here is a situation to consider. Imagine what you would do in such a situation. At a wedding ceremony, the pastor came to the point in the service in which he asked if anyone had anything to say concerning the union of the bride and groom. It was their time to stand up and talk, or forever hold their peace.

All at once the moment of utter silence was broken by a beautiful young woman carrying a baby. To everyone's surprise, she started slowly walking toward the pastor. Everything quickly turned to chaos. The bride turned and slapped the groom. The groom's mother fainted. The groomsmen started giving each other looks and wondered how best to help save the situation.

Before any more chaos broke out, the pastor asked the woman, "Can you tell us why you came forward? What do you have to say?"

Looking around at all the people staring at her, the woman replied, "We can't hear in the back."

I have always loved that story. A good friend of mine, who was a real mentor to me, used to tell that story to remind folks that things are not always what they appear to be. He would always laugh and say that we should never jump to judgement about anyone or anything until we know we have the whole story and the whole truth.

I have always thought that was very sound advice. What do you think?

October 13
Knowing God's Peace

Back in my college days, I majored in world history. I remember one of my professors reading from the diaries of Joseph Goebbels, the infamous Nazi propaganda minister. In those diaries there are two or three references to Mahatma Gandhi. Goebbels believed that Gandhi was a fool and a fanatic. He made fun of him and said that he was half-witted and sub-human. If Gandhi had the sense to organize militarily, Goebbels thought, he might hope to win the freedom of India. He was certain that Gandhi couldn't succeed following a path of nonviolence and peaceful revolution.

When my professor finished reading those passages from Goebbels' writings, he looked around at us and said, "You must always remember how things played out over time. India peacefully won her independence while the Nazi military machine was utterly and completely destroyed. What Goebbels regarded as weakness actually turned out to be strength. What he thought of as strength turned out to be weakness. There is, in history, nothing stronger than God's peace. Mahatma Gandhi knew God's peace; Joseph Goebbels did not."

October 14
A Sermon Walking

I would like to tell you a true story to keep with you throughout today. Perhaps it will give you something to think about.

Back in 1953, a man arrived at the Chicago railroad station to receive the Nobel Peace Prize. He stepped off the train, a tall man with bushy hair and a big mustache. As the cameras flashed and city officials approached with hands outstretched to meet him, he thanked them politely.

The man looked beyond the welcoming committee and began to look concerned. Then he asked to be excused for a minute. He walked through the crowd to an elderly black woman struggling with two large suitcases. He picked them up, smiled, escorted her to the bus, helped her get on, wished her a safe journey, and waved to the woman as the bus departed. When the bus turned into traffic, Albert Schweitzer turned to the crowd and apologized for keeping them waiting. It is reported that one member of the reception committee told a reporter, "That's the first time I ever saw a sermon walking."

I would ask you to think of this story throughout your day today. As you go through your day, keep your eyes open and see if you can find a "sermon walking" among the people you meet today.

October 15
Feeling Like Grandpa

Recently I read the story of a young boy who approached his slightly older sister with a question about God. "Annie, can anybody ever really see God?" "Of course not, silly," came the response. "God is so far up in heaven that no one can see God."

Sometime later the boy approached his mother with the same nagging question, "Mom, can anybody really see God?" More gently, his mother answered, "No, not really. God is a spirit and dwells in our hearts, but we can never really see God." His mother's answer was somewhat more satisfying, but still the boy wondered. Not long afterwards, the boy's grandfather took him on a fishing trip, and the two had a great day together

As the day was winding down, the sun began to set with unusual splendor. The grandfather was just looking intently at all of the beauty, and the grandson was aware of a deep peace and contentment on his grandpa's face. "Grandpa," the boy began, a bit hesitatingly, "I wasn't going to ask anyone else, but I wonder if you can tell me the answer to something I've been wondering about for a long time. Can anybody ever really see God?"

Grandpa sat in thought for a few moments, then said simply, "You know what, it's getting so I can't see anything else."

Have you ever felt like Grandpa?

October 16
Keep It Simple

The history of the human race is full of discoveries. New ideas, new lands, new theories, new ways of doing things are all a part of the many discoveries that have marked the development of human beings. Among the discoveries in our history is the discovery of people with a great talent for thinking and for insight. Some people can see and think in such clarity that it can take your breath away.

I recently read about a math teacher who made the discovery of a young boy with a remarkable mind. Here is how it happened.

One day a class of noisy boys in a German primary school was being punished by their teacher. Since their teacher was a math teacher, he punished those boys by making them solve the problem of adding together all the numbers from 1 to 100.

The boys settled down, scribbling busily on their slates: all but one. This boy looked off into space for a few moments, then wrote something on his slate and turned it in. His was the only right answer.

When the amazed teacher asked how he did it, the boy replied, "I thought there might be some short cut, and I found one: 100 plus 1 is 101; 99 plus 2 is 101; 98 plus 3 is 101, and, if I continued the series all the way to 51 plus 50, I have 101 50 times, which is 5,050."

After this episode, the young scholar received special tutoring from his teacher. The boy was Karl Friedrich Gauss, who is considered one of the great mathematicians of the 19th century.

Gauss said that he knew there had to be a simpler way to solve the problem. He said he just got his brain to think of how to make what seemed like a complicated problem simple. As you look at the problems you face right now, is there a way to make what seems complicated, simple?

October 17
It Is About Service

I read something interesting about King George III of England, who was king during the American Revolutionary War. It was well-known that the king felt terrible about the loss of the colonies. In fact, it was said that for the rest of his life, he could not say the word "independence" without tripping over it. George III was very much shaken by the loss of the colonies and was afraid of what might happen next.

When the fighting in America stopped, King George and all his royal cronies in Europe were sure that George Washington would have himself crowned emperor of the New World. That's what they would have done themselves, so they thought it wouldn't be too long before Washington would proclaim himself a king too.

When George III was told that, on the contrary, Washington planned to surrender his military commission and return to farming at Mount Vernon, the king said, "Well, if he does that, he will be the greatest man in the world." Then he added, "There is power in giving up power when your work is done." For Washington, what he did when the fighting was done was most important. The kings of Europe were surprised by Washington's character and his goodness.

Why was George Washington able to give up power when he was at the peak of his career? Simply put, Washington saw leadership as an exercise in service to others rather than power over them. He could freely give up power to those who would take the nation to the next stage of its growth.

What is your attitude about service to others?

October 18
Experience

Think for a moment about some of the decisions you have made in your life. Which decision turned out to be the best decision you ever made? Which of your decisions would you like to be able to take back? A story I came across this past week has had me looking back at some of my past decisions. See if this story gets you thinking about your own life "experience."

One morning the young, new president of a bank made an appointment with his predecessor, first to make a courtesy call and then to get some advice. He began, "Sir, as you well know, I have been appointed to your position at the bank, and you well know that I lack a great deal of the qualifications you already have for this job. You have been very successful as president of this bank, and I wondered if you would be kind enough to share with me some of the things you have learned from your years here that have been the keys to your success."

The older man looked at him with a stare and replied: "Young man, two words: good decisions."

The young man responded, "Thank you very much, sir, but how does one come to know which is the good decision?"

"One word, young man: experience."

"But how does one get experience?"

"Two words, young man: bad decisions.""

So, as you finished that story, what were you thinking about the decisions you have made throughout your life? Have you had a lot of "experience?"

October 19
Get Ready

I was reading about Moses and came to the part of the story in which Moses was camped with his people in the valley at the base of Mount Sinai. As he is resting, God came to him there and said, "Be ready in the morning, for tomorrow I want you to come up into the mountain."

When morning came Moses made himself ready, and he went up on Mount Sinai. There God met him face to face. And through that meeting the whole world has been blessed with God's Law.

The important thing to realize from this story is that Moses was not the first nor the last person to hear a call from God to go up the mountain. Every so often it is good for each of us to remember that in whatever valleys we are, God is there, inviting us to meet him somewhere on his mountain.

Today you and I can accept his invitation. From wherever we are right now, we are invited to meet God in an intimate setting that he will call you to experience. It is indeed by invitation that we come to his mountain. All that God asks of us is to "be ready." So, why not set about getting ready right now so that when the invitation comes, and it will come, you will be ready?

October 20
All Shall Be Well

I recently was visiting a young woman, a parishioner of mine, who was hospitalized because she was at a critical stage in a high-risk pregnancy. I had seen her a few days earlier and she was very much afraid that she might lose the baby and maybe even her own life. We had prayed together, and after our time came to a close, I reassured her that I would be back to check on her in a day or two. When I left her, she was still quite agitated and unsettled. She begged me to keep praying for her, and as I left, she called out, "Please come back tomorrow morning, would you?"

I told her I'd be back first thing in the morning. When I arrived that next morning, I expected to find her as I had left her, frightened and unsure about the future, but that was not how I found her. I walked into her room, and she was sitting up in a chair eating her breakfast and smiling at me. I told her she looked so much better than the last time I saw her.

She said, "I am so much better because God sent me someone in the middle of the night who talked with me and gave me a way to deal with the fear and the uncertainty that had me scared to death. It was the night nurse. She saw how frightened I was and told me that she was going to give me some words to say over and over again when I get scared. She told me she learned them when she had a child suffering from cancer. The words were from a mystic who was very close to God."

I asked her, "Who was the mystic and what are the words that have helped you so much?" The woman replied, "I had never heard of the mystic, but her name is Julian of Norwich. That nurse told me that God had given Julian the words in a vision and that they always gave her peace."

My young parishioner then looked at me and said, "Fr. Mark, those words really do work! I have been saying them all night long, and once the sun came up this morning, I have felt this great peace. I know now that whatever happens, God will be with me! In fact, now I know that he has already been with me!"

I knew who Julian was, and I was also aware of her famous words, so I said, "Let's say them together right now." We did and that young woman glowed as we spoke them. In the end, she eventually delivered a healthy baby girl, and both she and her daughter are doing quite well.

What were the words that brought her such comfort and peace? Here they are: All shall be well, and all shall be well, and all manner of thing shall be well.

October 21
Discovering Compassion

Here's a story from the Desert Fathers that has long been a part of their tradition. According to the story, there was a brother who had been caught in a grave sin. The sinful monk was called before the holy council of monks. The council invited the revered and most holy Abba Moses to join, but Abba Moses refused. He wanted no part of judging another monk. Finally, the council sent someone to get him, and he agreed to come.

Abba Moses took a leaking jug, filled it with water, and carried it with him to the council. The monks of the whole community saw him coming with the jug leaving a trail of water, and asked, "What's this?" Abba Moses said, "My sins run out behind me and I do not see them, and today you are asking me to judge the sins of another? If you are not able to see your own sins, how can you choose to see a brother's sins and then to judge him harshly? Please, my brothers, be people of compassion and not judgement!"

When the council heard these words, they forgave the brother and went away quietly to consider their own failings and thus discover how to be compassionate.

October 22
The Gifts Our Fathers Have Left Us

I recently came across something I read years ago. It was a list of sayings that came from a college class assignment in which the students were to bring in things they remembered hearing their dad say. The list was quite long, and I remember enjoying reading through it. I wrote down just six of those sayings and put them in a file folder because I thought they were fun things to remember. When I came across the list, I immediately thought of things my dad used to say. It brought a smile to my face.

Here are those six bits of "fatherly wisdom":
1. Honesty is like a trail through the wilderness: once you leave it, you are lost.
2. Wherever you are in life, always make friends with the cook.
3. Never buy anything that eats!
4. In most cases, if it's to be, it's up to me.
5. The one who quits last, wins.
6. If everyone else is doing it, it's probably wrong.

Can you remember any bits of fatherly wisdom your dad passed on to you? It's fun to recall the wisdom our dads passed on to us over the years. Recalling that wisdom may be one of the best ways to celebrate the gift our fathers have been to us.

October 23
Being True to Your Soul

There is an ancient story about what it means to be a good person that I love no matter how many times I hear it. I like the story because it reminds me of the importance of being true to your soul. Here is the story:

A holy man was engaged in his morning meditation under a tree whose roots stretched out over the riverbank. During his meditation he noticed that the river was rising, and a scorpion caught in the roots was about to drown. He crawled out on the roots and reached down to free the scorpion, but every time he did so, the scorpion struck back at him.

An observer came along and said to the holy man, "Don't you know that's a scorpion, and it's in the nature of a scorpion to want to sting?" To which the holy man replied, "That may well be, but it is my nature to save, and I will not choose to change my nature because the scorpion does not change his, even if it causes me pain to remain true to who I am."

October 24
In the End

When I talk with students about what we will do with the life we have been given, one of my favorite stories to tell is of Alfred Nobel.

Nobel made lots of money as the result of the invention of dynamite. He lived a very comfortable life as a result of his great wealth. One morning, however, Nobel saw something that shook him to his soul. On that fateful day, he awoke to read his own obituary in the paper.

Alfred Nobel's brother had died, but a careless reporter had published the obituary of the wrong Nobel. Instead of his deceased brother, the reporter had written about Alfred. The obituary described him as "the dynamite king, the industrialist who became rich from destruction." It made Alfred Nobel sound like nothing more than an evil merchant of death.

Nobel was horrified by what he saw. He could not believe how his life was being summed up. Not only was the wrong person being remembered, but the horrible portrait it painted was beyond anything he had ever felt about himself.

Alfred Nobel resolved that from that day forward he would spend his life striving to do something positive for society. He wanted a new legacy, to rewrite his obituary by living an entirely different life.

He left his entire fortune to be awarded to individuals who have done the most to benefit humanity, and to bring peace to the world.

In the end, he did change his obituary. When Alfred Nobel died, he was no longer remembered as "the dynamite king," but as the founder of the Nobel Peace Prize.

October 25
Bringing Out Your Best

I recently read a funny story about the FBI that took place when that agency was run by the famous J. Edgar Hoover. According to the story, everyone knew that Hoover ran a tight ship at the FBI, so everyone who worked there was always on their best behavior, hoping to impress "the boss" with their job performance. As a result, almost all of his subordinates were on the lookout for ways to get in Hoover's good graces.

Thus, when a young FBI man was put in charge of the FBI's supply department, he decided to cut some costs and thereby impress his boss. As part of that plan, the young man reduced the size of the office memo paper. It wasn't long before one of the new memo sheets ended up on Hoover's desk. Hoover took one look at it, determined he didn't like the size of the margins on the paper, and quickly scribbled on the memo, "Watch the borders!"

That memo was passed on through the office, and every officer and agent took notice. The result was that for the next six weeks, it was extremely difficult to enter the United States by road from either Mexico or Canada. The FBI was watching the borders.

Now, why was the FBI watching the borders? They thought they had received an order from their chief. But they hadn't. The need to keep the boss happy turned a comment on the size of the margins of a memo into an order about national defense!

That story reminds us of how the need to impress someone can lead to unintended consequences. Our efforts at "people pleasing" seldom end up producing good fruit. Doing things well because it is the right thing to do is admirable. Doing things to curry favor in an attempt to get ahead rarely brings out the best in us.

October 26
A Better Place

There are many stories about Abraham Lincoln that illustrate what a wise man he was. One of my favorites is about an incident between President Lincoln and his secretary of war, Edwin Stanton. Stanton had told Lincoln about how angry he was with one of the army officers who wasn't doing his job. So, Lincoln suggested that Stanton write the officer a sharp letter.

Stanton spent a great deal of time writing a very nasty letter and when he had finished it, he showed it to the president.

"What are you going to do with it?" Lincoln inquired. Surprised, Stanton replied, "Send it." Lincoln shook his head. "You don't want to send that letter," he said. "Put it in the stove. That's what I do when I have written a letter while I am angry. It's a good letter and you had a good time writing it, and you feel better. Now burn it and write a better letter that will bring out the best in the man you are writing to."

President Lincoln had learned from years of experience that letting anger rule your heart only leads to more anger and much bitterness. He urged those who knew him to make the world a better place and work to get rid of all bitterness.

October 27
Morning Prayer

A kindergarten teacher began her day with prayer. She first thanked God for the new day, then she asked God to teach her something new that day. She finished her prayer by adding, "and most importantly, Lord, give me the chance and the ability to be patient."

By the end of the day that teacher had her prayers answered. She had enjoyed her day with the children in her class and had just finished putting the last pair of galoshes on her young students — twenty pairs in all. The last little girl said, "You know what? These aren't my galoshes."

The teacher removed them from the girl's feet. The teacher began to panic because if these were not this little one's boots, who was wearing hers? Then the little girl continued, "They are my sister's, and she let me wear them." The teacher quietly put them back on the little girl's feet. Then the teacher realized that God had answered her morning prayer by giving her a chance to be very patient!

October 28
Truly Precious

It may sound rather morbid, but one of my favorite things to do is walk through cemeteries looking at all of the various grave markers. Each one tells a story that fascinates me.

On a recent trip to one of the largest of our local cemeteries, I noticed a whole section of graves of young men who died in the Civil War. Each gravestone told of a young life cut down in one of the cruelest wars in history. Young men so full of life and excitement and enthusiasm for the future were lost at such an early age.

As I stopped at each grave, I became aware of just how short life really is and how quickly it passes. I began to pray, and as my prayer came to an end, I noticed a grave marker for a young man who died in that horrible war at the age of 17. At the top of that gravestone were two Latin words carved beneath a laurel wreath. Those words were *carpe diem*, ancient words that are translated, "seize the day."

In the context of that young man buried in that grave, they remind us that life is precious, life is short, and it is important to grab on to it and make it count before it slips through your fingers. Even though you may think you have a lot of time left in your life, be aware that your life is a precious gift to you, not to be wasted.

The next time you are in a cemetery, take time to read some of the stories etched on the tombstones. If you take the time to ponder the lives of those buried there, and if you listen intently enough, you may hear the voices of the dead whispering those words, *"Carpe diem,"* "Seize the day," for each day is truly precious.

October 29
What's to Come

Here's a thought with which to either start or end your day. Two caterpillars were crawling across the grass when a butterfly flew over them. They looked up, and one nudged the other and said, "You couldn't get me up in one of those things for a million dollars."

That always brings a smile to my face, and yet it also brings home an important spiritual truth. Those two caterpillars had no idea what they would eventually become in God's plan for their lives. We, like those two lowly larvae, have no clue as to the glory that God has in store for them. If God can do such wonders in the lives of an insect, imagine what God can do in you!

October 30
Changing People

As a priest, I have spent countless hours listening to folks who are troubled and discouraged. Very often these folks are disturbed because they have been trying to change someone they love. They are frustrated by the fact that no matter how many times they have tried and no matter how many different plans they have devised, nothing seems to work in their effort to change their spouse, their child, or their friend. They tell me that they are at their wit's end and beg me to help them.

My response to folks who are so troubled by their inability to change other people is to give them a quote from a very famous man who was able to change the world. Most of these folks expect that I am going to cite something Jesus said, and you can see them brace themselves for some pious saying that I might give them. They are always surprised when I don't quote Jesus. They are often shocked when I tell them I want to share a quotation from a very humble and holy Hindu.

I tell them that in all of my years of experience, what Mahatma Gandhi said about changing the world is still one of the best pieces of advice that I have heard on the subject. He said that if you want to change the world, "You must *be* the change you wish to see in others." Only by being an inspiration to others by being what you want others to be, will you ever make a difference.

Have you ever tried to change someone? How did that work out for you? The only way any of us can change someone else or the world, for that matter, is to change ourselves.

October 31
Making a Difference

Here is a question for you to consider. What did you want to be when you were growing up? Have you become what you wanted to be all of those years ago? What did you dream about becoming?

When I was in college, one of my favorite authors was Chaim Potok. His novels were fascinating because in them he opened up the world of Judaism to me. Many years after college I read an article about Potok that made me appreciate his writing even more than I had when I was a lot younger.

In the article Potok was described as an intensely religious man, a Jew who explored the dimensions of faith in ways that helped non-

Jews understand how faith can be lived. I had found that very thing to be true for me when I read Potok's works.

But what I really enjoyed learning from that article was that from an early age, Potok knew he wanted to be a writer. His mother wasn't so sure, however. When he went away to college she said, "Son, now I know you want to be a writer. But I want you to think about being a doctor. I want you to be a brain surgeon. You'll keep a lot of people from dying. And you'll make a lot of money." To which Chaim Potok responded, "No, Mama, I want to be a writer."

His mother did not want to hear her son say no. So, every vacation break for four years she would repeat her comments about his becoming a brain surgeon and keeping people from dying and making a lot of money, and always his response was the same. Finally, Potok had enough, and when his mother began the same speech, he cut off his mother with exasperation, and with great passion he told her, "Mama, I don't want to keep people from dying. I want to show them how to live." When his mother heard her son put it that way, she finally understood why he wanted to be a writer.

What was it you wanted to be when you were younger? Have you made that happen? Have you become someone who has made a difference in other people's lives?

November

November 1
What We All Need to Hear

This past week, I took an old book from the bottom of a box that had been stored in my garage. When I opened the book, a piece of paper fell out and floated down to the garage floor. When I picked it up, I noticed it was a note I had written to myself years ago. At the top of the page I had written, "Save this for when you need it."

What I had written was this: In the library today, the librarian told me that she had once met Dr. Norman Vincent Peale, the famous Protestant minister who had written many self-help books. She said he told her that he had an experience which he found helped him cope with difficult health issues. Dr. Peale said he had been on a cruise ship that ran into some pretty foul weather. In fact, the foul weather turned out to be a hurricane! Dr. Peale told of spending a whole night in his cabin feeling very seasick.

After a day and a half of rough seas, Dr. Peale found himself at dinner that night at the captain's table. He asked the captain how he was able to remain so calm through rough seas and howling winds.

The captain said he had always lived by a simple philosophy, namely, that if the sea is smooth, it will get rough; and if it is rough, it will get smooth. He added something worth remembering: "But with a good ship and a calm leader at the helm," the captain said, "you can always ride it out."

Dr. Peale added, "When I heard those words, it was as if God was speaking to my soul telling me that we all are on a good ship that is piloted by Jesus. We need not be afraid of anything because Jesus will know how to steer the ship!"

The librarian said Dr. Peale had told her that after his conversation with the ship's captain, he no longer worried about his failing health. When she asked him why not, Dr. Peale simply said, "Because Jesus will steer me through it and get me safely home."

Doesn't that sound like something we all need to hear in our own difficult times?

November 2
When Death Comes for You

In the Catholic Church, this second day of November is called All Souls Day. It is a day to recall all of those who have died and gone ahead of us. I remember something from grade school that one of my teachers told us in religion class about this day. That teacher was a Catholic nun, and she very earnestly told us 8-year-old boys and girls that this is a day for us to remember that one day we will die. Then she said, "On the day you die, Mary, the mother of Jesus, will pick you up in her arms and carry you to heaven to be with her son, Jesus." Obviously, what Sister said made a big impression on us. I remember it like it was yesterday. What she told us that day brought me peace then and it still does today.

As I think about what my third-grade teacher told us so many years ago, I am reminded of a powerful story I came across last week, about a Jewish family during the Second World War. According to the story, the Rosenberg family was arrested together and taken to a concentration camp where prisoners could escape the gas ovens as long as they could continue to work. One of the younger boys in the family was partially disabled from birth and found it terribly difficult to do a full workload. The parents were separated during the day by their separate work responsibilities, so at the end of each of their shifts, they would quickly check on the condition of each family member.

One evening the father's worse fears were realized. He could not spot his disabled boy. Then he saw one of his older sons crying in a corner. The son told the father that his disabled brother was taken to the gas chambers because he could no longer work. The father asked, "But where is your mother?" The older boy told how his little brother was afraid to go and clung to his mother, who said, "Don't cry. I'll go with you and hold you close, and God will take us home to heaven."

This is a good day to remember in prayer all of your family and friends who have died. It might also be a good day to consider your own attitude toward death. It might be good to consider what you believe will happen when death finally comes for you.

November 3
Lincoln Knew

I read something recently that got my attention, especially during this time of year when we have elections. What I read was from the life of Abraham Lincoln. During the second year of his first term as president, someone came to visit him seeking an appointment to a particular federal job. In an attempt to flatter Lincoln, the man said to him, "Mr. President, people say some wonderful things about you. They say that the welfare of our entire nation depends on God and Abraham Lincoln."

Lincoln looked up from behind his desk and simply said, "Well, they are half right."

No one recorded whether that man got the appointment to the job he was seeking. What people remembered from that meeting is what Lincoln said to the man as he was showing him to the door. He said, "As far as me being president of this nation, without heavenly help I cannot succeed. With it, I cannot fail. The welfare of our country is in the hands of the Almighty God. The best thing you can do for me and for the country is to pray for us all."

In this time of elections, with our nation going through various problems and difficulties, I think Abraham Lincoln's advice is just as sound today as it was in his own time. Let us all pray for each other and for our nation! Lincoln knew what he was talking about.

November 4
There May Be More to the Story

Yesterday I gave you a story that always makes me laugh. Today I want to give you another story that makes me laugh. I have heard it told by rabbis, by imams, and by Christian ministers as well, so no one religion has a corner on this.

There once was a Catholic priest who prided himself on being called a philosopher, and he wanted to have a friendly religious debate with the monsignor. They had gone through a long struggle coming up with a date on which the two priests and all of their families and friends could be there to witness their debate. So when the priest came to the monsignor's house on the day and time of the debate and found the door locked, he was highly offended. He had been stood up and he was not at all happy about it.

"How dare he not be home when he knew I was coming!" the priest fumed. He took out a notebook, tore out a piece of paper, scribbled STUPID FOOL! and taped the note to the door. In a fury and muttering unkind words, he went away.

When the monsignor returned in the evening, he saw the note with the words STUPID FOOL! on his door. The embarrassed monsignor immediately realized what had transpired. Without waiting a minute, he went to the learned priest's home.

He knocked on the door and apologized as soon as the door was opened. "My sincere apologies my friend, for forgetting you were coming over for a debate. But I only just realized you had come the moment I saw your signature on my door!"

This very funny yet truly human story can serve to remind us to practice what I like to call purposeful pausing. We purposely pause when we set time aside to pray, but we can also purposely pause when we feel offended. When we take time to pause before we act, we give ourselves time to consider whether we want to react to the offense or respond to it.

We can feel offended and strike out in an even more offensive way by reacting violently to what has happened. Or we may pause long enough to respond in a thoughtful way, taking the time to understand what has happened before we possibly hurt someone who may be innocent of the offence that you feel has been done to you. There may be, and often is, more to the story than we may know.

November 5
Which One Do You Need?

I have a story that I want to share with you, and at the end of it I will ask you a question. There once was a great mystic who awoke one day to find that the king had come to see him. The king had brought a present for him: a beautiful pair of scissors, golden, studded with diamonds. It was very valuable, very rare, something unique. He brought those scissors to the holy man and put them at his feet.

The mystic took them, looked at them, gave them back to the king, and said, "Sir, thank you for the present that you have brought. It is a beautiful thing, but utterly useless for me. It will be better if you can give me a needle. Scissors I don't need: a needle is what I need."

The king said, "I don't understand. If you need a needle, wouldn't you need scissors too?"

The holy man said, "I am talking in metaphors. Scissors I don't need because scissors cut things apart. A needle I need because a needle puts things together. I teach love. My whole teaching is based on love — putting things together, teaching people communion. I need a needle so that I can put people together. The scissors are useless; they cut; they disconnect. Next time when you come, just an ordinary needle will be enough for me."

Now that you have read the story, when it comes to your family or life among your friends, what do you need right now in your life, scissors or a needle?

November 6
Sharing Deep Insights

Have you ever come across something when you are reading that just kind of grabs your attention and then stays with you through the day? I had that very experience just yesterday when I was reading a book about the lives of famous U. S. Presidents. In the course of a description of John Hinckley's assassination attempt on Ronald Reagan, the author of the book cited something that President Reagan's daughter, Patti Davis, had said with regard to almost losing her father that day. Shaken by the events that took place that day, she was horrified as to how close to death her father had actually come. She said, "I wasn't ready to have my dad taken from me."

The Patti Davis quotation that stayed with me, however, was this one: "My dad made a lasting impression on me the day after the assassination attempt of 1982. She went on to explain, "The following day my father said he knew his physical healing was directly dependent on his ability to forgive John Hinckley. By showing me that forgiveness is the key to everything, including physical health and healing, he gave me an example of Christ-like thinking."

Pattie Davis was amazed that her father had such deep spiritual insight into the power of forgiveness. His shared wisdom changed her in some very profound ways.

Is there anyone in your life whose shared spiritual wisdom or insights have changed you in profound ways? Is there a person in your life who has been a really good example of living according to "Christ-like thinking"? Can you name someone who has made living the gospel message of Jesus real to you? Have you ever had the opportunity to model Jesus' way of thinking for someone you love?

November 7
Doing Nothing

A few months ago, I was on retreat at a Trappist monastery near Bardstown, Kentucky. One afternoon, as I was walking through one of the courtyards there, I heard a roar of laughter that made me laugh just hearing such a great belly laugh. When I came around a corner there was an old monk with tears running down his face. When he saw me, he said, "Hey buddy, you have to read this! It just tickles my funny bone because I know several monks in this monastery just like this!"

A young monk, a novice, was loading the larder with flour and oil and, spotting one of the monks under a banyan tree, asked him for help. "Sorry," said the monk, "I'm busy." "But your eyes are shut!" replied the student. "Yes, I'm busy doing nothing. It's much harder than what you're doing. It's what the food is for, it's what the kitchen is for, it's what the chapel is for. All of it is so that I can sit here and do nothing well. Don't interrupt me again with your lardering."

Hours later, with his task complete, the novice spotted the monk slouching on a bench and said, "Can we talk now?" "No," came the reply, "I haven't finished yet."

The laughing monk waited for me to finish reading the story. Then he said, "Do you know anyone who is very good at doing nothing?" I said yes. Then he said, "You know, that story has a major bit of true wisdom in it!" "It does?" I asked.

The monk laughed again and said, "It sure does. The truth of the matter is that those folks who are the closest to God, they know how to do nothing very well. That is because when we are doing nothing we can more clearly hear God's voice. So, my advice to you is to go get good at doing nothing!" Then he laughed again and said,

"I am sitting here doing that very thing, I am practicing doing nothing!"

How good are you at doing nothing?

November 8
Anxious?

Lots of people in recent weeks have called me or texted or sent emails telling me how frightened they are. The situation of the world, with so many unemployed, many not able to go out because of the various levels of lockdowns, as well as worries about loved ones, has raised everyone's anxiety levels.

Did you know that the word "anxiety" comes from the Greek word *ananke*, meaning "throat" or "to press together?" *Ananke* was the name of the Greek god of constraint who presided over slavery. *Ananke* was the word used for the metal rings that were put on the necks of slaves.

The feelings of doubt and fear can make us very much aware fear is a real chain around our necks. Certainly, fear of the future takes us by the throat, and chains us like a slave. There is a German word, "angst," that means a general dread. Are you feeling that in our present situation? That German word is said to come from the Latin word *angere,* which means to choke or strangle. In addition to that, in English the word "angina," which means the tight sensation in the chest that accompanies dread, comes from *angere.*

There are probably as many ways of dealing with fear and anxiety as there are people, but there is one example of how someone copes with their fears that has been part of my meditation this past week. I read about a Lutheran minister who is pastor of a church in the inner city of Detroit. It is a very dangerous neighborhood filled with much violence, drug addiction, and many serious crimes. This pastor said he was always amazed by a certain woman, a member of his church, who seemed to have no fear about coming to meetings and services at the church at night, even though she had no car and would have to walk home through the dark and frightening streets.

According to the minister, one night, after a prayer service at which this woman had been present, the minister was locking up his church, and he happened to see her walking from the church down the street toward her apartment. As she walked, she was holding out her hand, as if some unseen companion were walking with her and holding her hand. As she walked, she was humming a familiar spiritual, "Precious Lord, take my hand, lead me on. Hold my hand, lest I fall. Take my hand, precious Lord, lead me home."

The minister stopped the woman and asked her if she was afraid. "Yes," she said. "It's dark and this is a bad neighborhood. I don't let it steal my peace though." The minister then said, "How do you overcome your fear?"

The woman looked up at him and said, "Well, Reverend, I would be a lot more scared if I had to walk home in the dark alone. But then I realize that I am not walking home alone; the Precious Lord takes my hand and gets me home. That's why I don't allow myself to fall into fear. The Lord has my hand, I shall not fall."

If you are being choked by fear and anxiety, why not let the Precious Lord take your hand?

November 9
Looking for Us

In the Gospel of John, Jesus calls himself the Good Shepherd and tells us that he will seek out the lost sheep. Have you ever wondered how sheep get lost in the first place?

When a shepherd was asked how sheep get lost, he replied, "Sheep don't just run off all at once. The fact of the matter is that they just nibble themselves into being lost. They go from one tuft of grass to another, until at last they have no idea where they are or how to get back to the flock."

After a brief pause, the shepherd softly said, "That's what happens with us too, isn't it? We nibble away at life with little purpose or direction, until it's years later and we have no idea how we got where we are and how to get back home. It's a good thing we all have a Good Shepherd who comes looking for us when we have nibbled ourselves lost."

That shepherd sounds like he knows what he's talking about. Have you nibbled your way into being lost?

November 10
Be Careful with the Facts

I was praying the other day when I remembered something a professor told our class back in graduate school. The professor was teaching a class on Christian morality when he stopped in mid-sentence and said, "As you go about living your life, you will be faced with many decisions that will have great consequences. I want to warn you that you must always be very careful of the facts of life. Facts can either help others or harm others. They can be seeds that do good, or they can be bullets that wound and even kill. Be very careful how you use facts!"

When we all looked a little puzzled, he said, "Let me tell you a little story to illustrate what I mean." Then he told the following story:

Two men worked on a large, ocean-going vessel. One day the mate, who normally did not drink, became intoxicated. The captain, who hated him, entered in the daily log: "Mate drunk today." He knew this was his first offense, but he wanted to get him fired. The mate was aware of his evil intent and begged him to change the record. The captain, however, replied, "It's a fact, and into the log it goes!"

A few days later the mate was keeping the log and he concluded it with: "Captain sober today." Realizing the implications of this statement, the captain asked that it be removed. In reply the mate said, "It's a fact, and in the log, it stays!"

Are you careful with the facts in your life?

November 11
When Panic Makes You Leap

I found it rather interesting during the time of the pandemic how so many people kept listening to the news, only to find themselves full of fear, worry, and panic. I kept looking for a way to calm folks down or at least get them to stop tuning into negative news, because panic can make us do stupid, often useless things.

I was thinking about all of that yesterday when I read a story about a man who prided himself on always being in control of his life, especially his daily schedule. He said what gave him serenity and peace was being exceedingly punctual. The man followed a very precise routine every morning. His alarm went off at 6:30. He rose briskly, shaved, showered, ate his breakfast, brushed his teeth, picked up his briefcase, got into his car, drove to the nearby ferry landing, parked his car, rode the ferry across to the downtown business area, got off the ferry, walked to his building, marched to the elevator, rode to the seventeenth floor, hung up his coat, opened his briefcase, spread his papers out on his desk, and sat down in his chair at precisely 8:00. Not at 8:01, not even 7:59. Always at 8:00 A.M. He followed this same routine without variation for too many years to count. He admitted that he lived a very calm and peaceful life, although others might have said that he lived a very boring, uneventful life.

That was the man's life until one fateful morning. On that unexpected morning, the man's alarm did not go off and he slept fifteen minutes late. When he did awake, he was so panic-stricken that he felt he was having a heart attack. He told himself he had no time for a heart attack and jumped out of bed with a great thud. Quickly, he rushed through his shower, nicked himself when he shaved, gulped down his breakfast, only halfway brushed his teeth, grabbed his briefcase, jumped into his car, sped to the ferry landing, jumped out of his car, and looked for the ferry.

There it was, out in the water a few feet from the dock. He said to himself, "I think I can make it," and ran down the dock toward the ferry at full speed. Reaching the edge of the pier he made an enormous leap out over the water and miraculously landed, with a second loud thud of the day and to his own great surprise, on the deck of the ferry. The mean was thrilled. He made it and he might just make it to work on time even though he could hardly breathe because he was so full of panic.

In the meantime, the captain rushed down to make sure he was all right and said, "Man, that was a tremendous leap, but if you would have just waited another minute, we would have reached the dock, and you could have walked on. We were arriving at the dock, not departing!"

Think about your own life. Have you ever let feelings of panic make you leap into the wrong direction in life?

November 12
Seeing What You Can't See

Have you ever tried to help someone who was afraid and couldn't see their way out of their problems? Or have you ever had the experience of one of your children who have seemed beyond help because they couldn't get out from under their fears? How did you help them?

Whenever someone comes to me with difficult fears or ideas that steal their peace, I often use the following story to get them to see life through another set of eyes. I say I am going to tell them a story to help them see what they are just not able to see right now. Here's the story:

A certain man was troubled with dizzy spells. He went from one doctor to another, and none could tell him what the problem was. He tried everything, it seemed. Finally, it was bothering him so much he started to lose weight and couldn't sleep at night. He became a nervous wreck and his health began to deteriorate. He had lost hope that he would ever recover.

The man decided to prepare for the worst. He made out his will, bought a cemetery plot, and even made arrangements with the local undertaker for what he was convinced was his soon demise. He decided to buy a new set of clothes to be buried in. When he went into the haberdasher's he was measured for everything and picked out shoes, socks, coat, pants — and he asked for a size 15 shirt, as well. The clerk said, "But, sir, you need a size 16½ shirt, not 15." The man insisted he wore a size 15. Finally, in exasperation the clerk said, "But if you wear a size 15, you'll get dizzy spells."

November 13
People with Fortitude

One of my favorite U.S. presidents is Harry Truman. I like him because he always spoke what he knew to be the truth and he didn't mince words when he did so.

One of my favorite quotes is from the day he gave a speech in which he commented on the importance of polls when it came to leadership. He looked at the crowd and said, "I wonder how far Moses would have gone if he'd taken a poll in Egypt? What would Jesus Christ have preached if he'd taken a poll in Israel? Where would the Reformation have gone if Martin Luther had taken a poll? It isn't the polls or public opinion of the moment that counts. It is right and wrong and leadership — people with fortitude, honesty, and a belief in the right — that makes epochs in the history of the world."

With so much emphasis in the news media and political worlds on polls, I think Harry Truman has much to teach us.

November 14
What We Need

I was speaking with a young man who had just come from a courtroom where his divorce became final. He was in tears and said that he never felt such pain and such a sense of bitterness before. After a long period of time when neither I nor he said a word, the young man looked up at me and said, "How do I keep this whole thing from literally killing me?"

At a loss for words, I sat in silence as he sobbed. I said a quick prayer to the Holy Spirit, hoping that I would be inspired to say something profound. Nothing came to me. The young man sitting across from me finally stopped sobbing and whispered, "This is killing me by inches!"

All at once an image flooded into my mind. I saw South African Archbishop Desmond Tutu, and recalled something I heard him say in an interview on television. He said something like, "As I am remembering the hurts of apartheid, I know that only forgiveness draws out the sting in the memory that threatens to poison our entire existence. We need God to remove the sting of past hurts. The stinger of the evil things done to us in the past must be removed or it will poison our soul."

I shared those words with the young man. He asked me what I thought Desmond Tutu meant. I said, "Once the sting of evil is removed, the past is redeemed to help us forgive and to ask for forgiveness."
He replied, "I think that is what I want. I think that is what I need."

November 15
Did You Miss Anything?

Have you ever been eager to do a good job? I am sure we all at one time or other have been eager to do an outstanding job at whatever we have been asked to do. I think this is especially true when we are young and want to prove that we know what we are doing and can be trusted to actually do a good job. The next time you are eager to do a good job, I encourage you to think of the story below and learn to take your time to pay attention to the details of the job you are asked to do. Here's the story:

A young ensign, after nearly completing his first overseas cruise, was given an opportunity to display his capabilities at getting the ship under way. With a stream of commands, he had the decks buzzing with men, and soon the ship was steaming out the channel in route to the states.

His efficiency established a new record for getting a destroyer under way, and he was not surprised when a seaman approached him with a message from the captain. He was a bit surprised, though, to find it a radio message and even more surprised to read: "My personal congratulations upon completing your underway preparation exercise according to the book and with amazing speed. In your haste, however, you have overlooked one of the unwritten rules—make sure the captain is aboard before getting under way."

November 16
When the Critics Hurt You

I woke up this morning laughing because for some reason, I remembered something that happened to me many years ago, when I was a newly ordained parish priest. I was very earnestly trying to do a good job and serve the parishioners well. As hard as I was trying, however, I must not have been doing a good enough job because within weeks of my arrival at the parish, I received several very critical letters from "a concerned parishioner." I became very discouraged.

My pastor, Fr. Kennedy, noticed that I seemed a bit down, so he asked me what was wrong. I showed him the letters and he just laughed. He said letters like this mean you are doing a good job! Take such letters as a compliment, he said. They are just whiners. Then he told me a story:

A salesman went to his barber for a haircut, and he told the barber about his upcoming trip to Rome. The barber had only negative comments to make about the airline the salesman had chosen, the hotel where he was going to stay, about Rome in general, and even about his hope of having an audience with the pope. The barber was so critical that the salesman now dreaded going to Rome because he was worried it would be a miserable experience.

A month later the salesman returned to the barbershop. He said, "I had a wonderful trip. The flight was perfect, and the hotel service was excellent. And I got to meet the pope!" The barber asked, "What did the pope say to you?" The salesman said, "He placed his hand on my head and said, 'My son, where did you get such a lousy haircut?'"

Father Kennedy then looked at me and said, "May such an experience happen to every sourpuss in our parish who is mean to you!"

November 17
Passing on God's Generosity

I have a special place I go to for quiet and to listen for God's voice. I was there in prayer one day when God let me know, "Pay attention to the story you will hear today. You will know it when you hear it." Now that got my attention! As my day began, I wondered how long I would have to wait to hear the story. I didn't have to wait too long, because just before lunch, a young man came into my office. His great-grandmother had passed away, and he was quite shaken by her death. I asked him to tell me about her. Here is a summary of what he said:

"In every way, she was a beautiful woman. Although she died at ninety years old, she never really seemed old. She always seemed so full of life. She has always been extremely generous with everything she had. Even as recently as a month ago, she helped foreign students who want to come to this country to study. She is a person who sends flowers and food to people who have had a distressing time of any kind. She gives frequent dinners and parties in order to be able to introduce people to one another. Often, she sends theater and concert tickets to people she knows would appreciate them but can't afford to buy them. She is always doing something nice for somebody or giving somebody something he or she needs. Everyone loves her because of her selflessness."

The young man said, "See, I talk about her like she is still here! I said to her one day, 'You are so good to everybody.' 'Oh no,' she said, 'It is God who has been good to me. He has given me so much more than I can ever use. The more I give away, the more I have. It is wonderful!'"

I am sure that was the story God wanted me to hear and think about. As our yearly celebration of Thanksgiving is not too far off, it can serve as a good time for us to examine our own approach to what God has done for us. We all have to ask ourselves, "Does our behavior towards others truly reflect God's generosity toward us?" In other words, are we passing on the gifts God has shared with us?

November 18
What Were You Saying?

Have you ever regretted saying something? Have you ever said something that seemed so right and so true at the time that you could not tolerate anyone not accepting or believing what you said? Have you ever done that and then later discovered that what you thought was so absolutely true turned out to be wrong? Well, if you have been there, you are not alone. Let me give you an example.

In the year 1870 the Methodists in Indiana were having their annual conference. At one point, the president of the college where they were meeting said, "I think we live in a very exciting age." The presiding bishop said, "What do you see?" The college president responded, "I believe we are coming into a time of great inventions. I believe, for example, that men will fly through the air like birds."

The bishop said, "This is heresy! The Bible says that flight is reserved for the angels. We will have no such talk here."

After the conference, the bishop, whose name was Wright, went home to his two small sons, Wilbur and Orville. So much for what their father thought and said!

November 19
What Does It Mean?

Spend some time with the following parable. What do you think it means for you in your life right now?

There once was a Chinese boy who wanted to learn about jade, so he went to study with a talented old teacher. The teacher knew jade very well and traded it in the markets around China.

The teacher and jade dealer agreed to teach the boy. This is how he did it. This gentle man put a piece of the precious stone into boy's hand and told him to hold it tight. Then he began to talk of philosophy, men, women, the sun and almost everything under it. After an hour he took back the stone and sent the boy home.

The procedure was repeated for several weeks. The boy became frustrated. He began to lose his enthusiasm. When would he be told about the jade? He was too polite, however, to question his venerable teacher. Then one day, when the old man put a stone into his hands, the boy cried out instinctively, "That's not jade!"

November 20
Holding On

I like to read first person accounts of people who have lived through some remarkable events. I recently read about a man who had served as a Catholic chaplain in the U. S. Army during the Second World War. That chaplain said that one of his favorite experiences from the war was an encounter with a young soldier in the middle of a battle in which the German army was shelling the American position.

During the bombardment a young soldier searching desperately for cover from the exploding artillery shells jumped into a foxhole. Shaking with fear, he immediately did his best to deepen the hole for more protection and was frantically scraping away the dirt with his hands. As he continued to dig, he unearthed something metal. It turned out to be a silver crucifix, probably left by a former resident of the foxhole.

Just at the moment he was looking at the crucifix, another soldier leaped into the foxhole right next to him as the shells screamed overhead. When the soldier got a chance to look at the guy next to him, he saw that his fellow soldier was an army chaplain. Holding out the crucifix, the soldier gasped, "Am I glad to see you, chaplain! Quick, how do you work this thing?"

Have you ever been in a very scary situation in which you knew the only way through it was to get God's help, but realized that you didn't know "how to work this thing?" It always amazes me that it is not until people find themselves in desperate situations that they actually turn to prayer, not exactly knowing how to make this thing work.

Do you know what that army chaplain told that young soldier in the foxhole? He said, "Son, hold on to that thing with all of your strength and then with all of your heart and soul say, 'God help me!' God will take over from there."

If you find yourself in a bad situation, overwhelmed by panic or fear, perhaps you too can hold on with all of your strength and then say, with all of your heart and soul, "God help me!" God will certainly take it from there!

November 21
A Common Whiner

I was recently at a local restaurant waiting with quite a few other customers for a table to come open. As we all sat in the waiting area, one man became very impatient and started to speak out loud about how he did not intend to wait much longer because his time was valuable. It wasn't clear to whom the man was speaking, but he clearly wanted the manager of the restaurant to hear him. The woman sitting next to me leaned over and whispered, "Now there's a man who thinks he is more important than the rest of us."

I laughed when she said that and immediately thought of a story I had read about the famous actor Gregory Peck. As the story goes, Peck was once standing in line with a friend, waiting for a table in a crowded Los Angeles restaurant. They had been waiting for some time. The diners seemed to be taking their time eating and new tables weren't opening up very fast. They weren't even that close to the front of the line. Peck's friend became impatient, and he said to Peck, "Why don't you tell the maître d' who you are?" Peck responded with great chuckle. "No," he said, "if you have to tell them who you are, then you aren't."

When the woman I was sitting next to me saw me smiling she asked me what I was thinking. I told her the story about Gregory Peck. When she heard the story, she said, "Well, somebody ought to tell that impatient idiot that he 'ain't the somebody he thinks he is!'" After a pause she turned back to me and said, "His ego has apparently got the best of him and turned him into a common whiner!"

Now that comment made me laugh out loud! Thinking of the last time you had to wait in line for any long period of time, has your ego gotten the best of you so that you ended up becoming a whiner?

November 22
Unbroken Love

A rabbi recalled a time when one of his students asked him, "Why didn't the Lord provide enough manna to Israel for a year, all at one time? Would not that have been better so the people could store up the manna and draw on it whenever they needed it?"

The teacher said, "I will answer you by telling a story. Then you will understand. Once there was a king who had a son to whom he gave a yearly allowance, paying him the entire sum on the fixed date at the beginning of the year. It soon happened that the day on which the allowance was due was the only day of the year when the father ever saw his son."

"So, the king changed his plan and gave his son, day by day, that which was sufficient for the day; and then the son visited his father every morning. It was only when the son took the time to visit with his father that he learned just how much he needed his father's unbroken love, his companionship, his wisdom, and yes, his giving!"

The rabbi concluded his lesson by saying, "Thus God dealt with Israel and deals with us in our own daily walk." Do you make time every day to discover how much you need your Heavenly Father's unbroken love?

November 23
A Gratitude Magnet

During this season of Thanksgiving, I have been doing a gratitude list each evening before I go to bed. I think it's really interesting what I find to put on that list each night. Sometimes the things I am grateful for are the littlest things that happen during the day that might go completely unnoticed and be lost to me if I had not taken the time to run a gratitude magnet through the events of the day.

One of the things I recently put on my list was a little story that an elderly friend of mine sent me. In a note my friend wrote, "With Thanksgiving almost upon us, I though you would find this story a joy to read." Here is the story she sent me:

A little boy was asked what he was thankful for by his Sunday School teacher. It was Thanksgiving and the teacher was encouraging all the children to give personal expression to their feelings of gratitude. The little boy said that he was especially thankful for his glasses, and the teacher asked him why. Very quickly he answered, "Because my glasses keep the boys from hitting me and the girls from kissing me."

In this season of gratitude, why not run a "gratitude magnet" through your day's events and see what has been a blessing to you today?

November 24
What We Have Not Lost

Have you ever heard something that made you sit up and take notice? I had that experience the other day when I read about something that happened in a Baptist church during the Vietnam War. It happened during some of the darkest days of that war, when television news would list the number of American soldiers who had been killed that day. Sometimes they even showed pictures of those who had been killed.

One Sunday morning in that Baptist church, a mother stood before the congregation and announced that her son had died in the war. The church was overwhelmed with emotion as she spoke about how much she loved her son. Then, as she finished speaking, she announced that she was giving the church $10, 000.00 in gratitude for her son's short but wonderful life.

When the announcement was made of the generous donation, another mom in the congregation whispered to her husband, "Let's give the same amount for our boy!" Her husband said, "What are you talking about? Our son wasn't killed." "That's just the point," she said. "Let's give it as an expression of our gratitude to God that we still have our son with us!"

In this month during which we celebrate Thanksgiving, perhaps a good look around our lives will remind us of how blessed we are. We must be sure not to take our blessings for granted.

November 25
Something to Think About

I was reading about the crown jewels of England this past week when I came on some information that I found very interesting. According to my research, the Koh-I-Noor diamond, which is now part of the crown jewels, is one of the most spectacular in the world. It was given to Queen Victoria as a gift from a maharajah when he was a very young boy.

Later, when he had grown into a man, that same maharajah visited Queen Victoria again. He requested that the stone be brought from the Tower of London to Buckingham Palace. The maharajah took the diamond and, kneeling before the queen, gave it back to her, saying, "Your Majesty, I gave this jewel to you when I was a child, too young to know what I was doing. I want to give it to you again as a man, with all of my heart and affection and gratitude, now and forever, fully realizing all that I do and all that I give." Queen Victoria cried and said she was so very grateful for his gift that in the future she would always look at the diamond and be filled with gratitude.

Is there any gift you have been given that fills you with profound gratitude whenever you see it? Is there any person in your life who fills you with gratitude whenever you see them? That is something to think about for sure.

November 26
Understanding God

When I was in third grade, I was fascinated by a story that our religion teacher, a nun, told us about a great saint named Augustine. She told us he was a very smart man, and he was also a bishop who thought he knew a whole lot about God. Then she said, "But one day God sent a child about your age to tell him he didn't know everything about God!"

Now that got my attention. I listened very closely as she told us this story:

"Boys and girls, this is an ancient story about St. Augustine. That means it's very old and it is also true." Our teacher went on: "One day, Augustine took a break from writing about the Holy Trinity to take a walk along the seashore. There he came across a child, who was in the third grade. That child was sent from God. The boy was intently scooping up a pail full of water out of the ocean, then walking up the beach and dumping it out into the sand, then going back down to scoop out another pail of water to pour into the sand. That child kept running back and forth, doing the same thing."

"Augustine asked the child what he was doing. The child explained that he was emptying the sea out into the sand. When the bishop tried to gently point out that it wasn't possible to do that, the child replied, 'Ah, but I'll drain the whole ocean out way before you will ever understand the Trinity. God told me to tell you. There are some things about God we can never fully understand.'"

If you ever find yourself not fully understanding God and his ways, listen to that child whom God sent to Augustine.

November 27
Something to Remember at Thanksgiving

There is a famous incident from the ministry of Mother Teresa. Once, a child she picked up from the street began to cry as she hugged her. Mother Teresa could tell from the child's face that she was hungry. She wondered how many days it had been since that little one had eaten, but the child did not seem to know. She gave the child a piece of bread, and the child took the bread and, crumb by crumb, started eating it.
Mother Teresa said to her, "Eat, eat the bread. You are hungry." The little one looked at her and said, "I am afraid. When the bread will be finished, I will be hungry again."

I remember talking to a missionary who had been working in some of the poorest countries in the world. He told me at table one night that one of the most devastating things that happens to people during famines is, once they experience hunger on that level, they are never able to be free from the fear of starving. That fear stays with them for the rest of their lives.

As that missionary and I got ready to eat supper together, he looked at me and said, "When you have seen starving people, like I have, you can never, ever have a meal again without saying grace with all your heart. Few of us realize what a true blessing it is to have enough to eat." The missionary then looked at me and said, "Would you please say grace?"

Wow! I don't think I ever said a more heartfelt prayer over a meal as I did that night.

During this season when we celebrate Thanksgiving, perhaps we all might want to think more deeply about the "grace" we pray when we gather with our families to eat!

November 28
The Less You Speak

There is a Zen story that has a lot to teach us. According to that story, a great spiritual Master agreed to guide four monks into a deeper spiritual practice. He instructed them to meditate silently without speaking for two weeks. He instructed them to light a candle as a symbol of their practice and directed them to enter into a deep silence.

By nightfall on the first day, the candle flickered and then went out.

The first monk said: "Oh, no! The candle is out."

The second monk said: "We're not supposed to talk!"

The third monk said: "Why must you two break the silence?"

The fourth monk laughed and said: "Ha! I'm the only one who didn't speak."

The deep silence the Master had invited the four monks to keep was very short-lived. When the Master heard what occurred that very first night, he asked the monks what had happened to them. Each monk had his reason for breaking the silence. In fact, they all had different reasons, but each of the four monks shared his thoughts without filtering them — none of which improved the situation.

After listening to the four monks, the Master said he wished there had been five monks instead of four. He said, "If there had been a fifth, wiser monk, he most likely would've remained silent and kept meditating. By keeping the deep silence, he could teach you without a single word, without breaking his own quest for a deeper spiritual life. You must all remember this: talking inevitably leads to embarrassing yourself. Listening leads to learning."

Finally, the Master gave the four monks these words to keep in mind as they seek a deeper spirit: "The less you speak, the smarter you get. And, maybe not quite coincidentally, the smarter you get, the less you speak."

November 29
What Do You Know?

Once, there was a man whom everyone respected for his holiness and virtuous living. Whenever anyone asked him how he had become so holy, he always answered: "I know what is in the bible." Although no one ever saw him read his bible or even quote from the bible, they reasoned that the man was so good, he must really know what is in that holy book.

One day he had just given a talk on how to be good, when an a simple but kind person asked: "Well, can you tell me simply, what is in your bible?"

"In my bible," said the renowned man "there are two pressed flowers and a letter from my friend."

What do you think the crowd did when they heard what was in that famous man's bible? I am sure there were great roars of laughter. When I first heard that story, that was my reaction as well. What is interesting is what you begin to think about after you stop laughing.

That story dates from around the year 700 A.D. It was told over and over again through the ages because, as the monk who told it to me put it, "Every so often we all need a silly story to remind us that religious people can often be way too pompous and way to sober and serious. After all, at the center of our spiritual life, it is not what you know but rather who you know! It is about knowing God and his love. It is about being loved and about what we do with the love that has been showered on us."

After a bit of a pause, the monk added, "That story reminds us to not take ourselves too seriously!"

November 30
Maybe It's Time

One of my favorite passages from the writings of St. Paul is from his second letter to the Corinthians. In that letter, he describes having to deal with some personal difficulty, which he called a "thorn in the flesh" which was stealing his peace. He felt overwhelmed and defeated by it and he begged God to free him from it. After much prayer, he heard God speak to him saying, "And God said to me, 'My grace is sufficient for you, for my strength is made perfect in weakness."

It reminds me of an old story that the Desert Fathers would tell about our human frailty. They would say that we are like the old man riding down the road on a donkey while he carried a 200-pound sack of wheat on his shoulder. Someone asked him why he did not take the weight off his own shoulders and strap it to the donkey. "Oh, no!" he protested. "I couldn't ask the donkey to carry all that weight."

Many folks are carrying burdens today that they do not have to carry alone. It reminds me of one of my parishioners who was seriously ill but did not want to "burden" her family with it so she would not ask any of her children or grandchildren for help. When she told me that, I immediately told her the story of that old man and his 200-pound sack of wheat. In the end, she finally let me contact her children and grandchildren to ask for their help.

Do you have a "thorn in the flesh" or a "200 pound of wheat on your shoulder"? Perhaps it is time to ask for help.

December

December 1
Which Door?

There is a story about a samurai soldier, who came to a holy monk and asked, "Is there really a heaven and a hell?"

"Who are you?" the monk asked.

"I am a samurai," the soldier replied.

"You, a soldier!" exclaimed monk. "What kind of ruler would have you as his guard? Your face looks like that of a beggar."

The samurai became so angry that he began to reach for his sword, but monk laughed and said: "So you have a sword! Even your weapon is probably much too dull to cut off my head."

As the samurai soldier drew his sword the monk kindly remarked: "Here opens the door to hell!"

At these words the samurai, perceiving the monk's discipline and holiness, sheathed his sword, bowed, and asked forgiveness.

"Here opens the door to heaven," said the holy monk kindly.

Each day in each encounter we have with people we have the opportunity to open doors. By our actions and our words, we can either open a door to hell or we can open a door to heaven. Which door would you rather open?

December 2
Nobody in the Boat

Have you ever been irritated by those around you? I can't imagine anyone who has not had that experience. When I was praying this morning before Mass, an elderly woman came into church and made her way to the pew right in front of me.

As I was trying to maintain my meditation, the old woman opened her purse and began to sort out the various objects within it. She did this for ten minutes until she found a cough drop. She then quickly unwrapped it and put it in her mouth. I thought, "Now she will be quiet, and I can get back to my prayer."

Well, just as I finished a quieting exercise, she began to crunch and chew the cough drop! All at once it struck me as funny and I started laughing. Apparently thinking that I was coughing and not laughing, the woman turned to me and asked, "Do you need a cough drop?"

As I looked back on this morning's experience, I remembered that the Taoists have a famous teaching about an empty boat that rams into your boat in the middle of a river. According to their teaching, while you probably wouldn't be angry at an empty boat, you might well become enraged if someone were at its helm who carelessly rammed into your boat.

The point of the story is that the other people in your life who may have insulted you, hurt your feelings, or made you angry – are all in fact empty, rudderless boats. They were compulsively driven to act as they did by their own unexamined motives, therefore, they did not know what they were doing and had little control over it.

The Taoists teach that just as an empty boat that rams into us isn't targeting us, so too people who act unkindly are driven along by the unconscious forces of their own wounding and pain. Until we realize this, we will remain prisoners of our self-absorption, our past, and our need to be respected. All of this keeps us from opening to the more powerful currents of life and love that are always flowing through the present moment.

Those Taoists have great insights. The next time you find yourself being irritated by someone, think about that image of an empty boat ramming into your boat. No matter who it is who is irritating you, just remember there is probably nobody in that boat!

December 3
Be Careful

The Sufis have many stories they tell to teach folks important truths. One of those stories has much to teach about how to manage the challenges daily life can bring.

According to the story, there was a group of frogs traveling through the woods when suddenly, two of them fell into a deep pit. All the other frogs gathered around the pit and studied the situation closely.
When they saw how deep the pit was, they told the unfortunate frogs they would never get out. The two unfortunate frogs ignored the comments and tried to jump up out of the pit.

The other frogs kept telling them to stop, that they were as good as dead and they should just give up and be done with it. Finally, one of the frogs in the pit took heed to what the other frogs were saying and simply stopped. He lay down, gave up, and died.

The other frog continued to jump as hard as he could. Once again, the crowd of frogs yelled at him to stop the pain and suffering and just die. With that he jumped even harder and finally made it out. When he got out, the other frogs asked him, "Why did you continue jumping? Didn't you hear us?"

The frog explained to them that he was deaf. He didn't hear what they were saying. He thought they were encouraging him the entire time. He felt encouraged by them and was able to overcome his difficult situation.

The Sufi masters say that this story has two lessons for each of us: There is power of life and death in what we say to one another. An encouraging word to someone who is down can lift them up and help them make it through the day.
A destructive word to someone who is down can be what it takes to kill them. Be careful of what you say. Be careful that you speak life to those who cross your path.

December 4
Good Ideas and Thoughts

One of the most fascinating people in American history is Benjamin Franklin. He often reminded people that one should never let a good idea or thought go to waste. He believed that good thinking and good ideas could lead to some new inventions that would make life richer and more enjoyable.

If you examine Franklin's life, you will soon learn that he certainly did not let a good thought or idea go to waste. He was a prolific inventor and scientist who was responsible for numerous inventions. One was the Franklin stove: Franklin's first invention, created around 1740, provided more heat with less fuel. Another was bifocal glasses, because he was frustrated with having to use several pairs of spectacles to see clearly. Franklin wanted to save time and frustration so he developed bifocals that could be used for both distance and reading.

Franklin's inventions took on a musical bent when, in 1761, he invented what he called the armonica, a musical instrument composed of spinning glass bowls on a shaft. Both Ludwig van Beethoven and Wolfgang Amadeus Mozart composed music for the strange instrument. Franklin also came to invent a very comfortable rocking chair, the lightning rod, the American penny, and even a flexible catheter.

There is one other thing that Ben Franklin also discovered: The Gulf Stream. After a return trip across the Atlantic Ocean from London in

1775, he began to speculate about why the westbound trip always took longer. His measurements of ocean temperatures led to his discovery of the existence of the Gulf Stream. This knowledge served to cut two weeks off the previous sailing time from Europe to North America.

Just from this brief account of some of his inventions, it is certainly clear that Ben Franklin did not let any of his good thoughts or ideas go to waste. This might lead us to consider what we are doing with our own good ideas and thoughts. Are your good thoughts and ideas going to waste? Do you have good thinking that could make the world a better place?

December 5
A Pile of Odd Rocks?

Whenever I am asked to teach Christian spirituality, I most often begin with two definitions. The first definition is that spirituality is learning how to see. The second definition is simply this, prayer is learning how to hear. I was reminded of these definitions this week when I stopped for a red light on my way to the parish. As I sat waiting for the light to change, I noticed the bumper sticker on the car in front of me. In bold letters is proclaimed: "A pile of rocks ceases to be a pile a rocks when someone has a cathedral in mind." Isn't that a great quotation? One of the basic tenets of Christianity as it is lived out, or maybe just about every spirituality is that how we look at things, the way we see the world around us determines so much of how we will experience life every day.

So, when you come upon a pile of rocks, what do you see? Do you see just a pile of odd stones, or does your heart or soul allow you to see a future cathedral?

Or if you were to look in the mirror, what do you suppose you would see? Your eyes will take in your image, but what will your heart and soul see in that image? If you look at the members of your family, or at each of your friends, what do you see in them?

Your eyes will certainly take in their physical form, but what will your soul help you to see in each of them?

What do you see when you look out at the world through the news media or social media? When you look at the world through those eyes, do you see the world as a pile of odd rocks or are you able to see a future cathedral?

Much of the teaching of Jesus is about how we are invited to see the world and how we can choose to see each other. He taught his disciples how to see the hand of God in everyday life, and how to see the people around them as true brothers and sisters.

As I waited for that red light to change, I thought about that bumper sticker and came to the realization that when God looks at each one of us, I am certain the he doesn't see us as a pile of odd rocks, but rather as magnificent cathedrals.

December 6
Which One Are You?

A young man went to his mentor to ask a particular question. He asked, "Sir, how can I tell if I am a true disciple of Jesus or not?" The mentor replied, "Are you avoiding evil and trying to do good?" The young man replied, "I have done both, but I am still unsure if something is missing in my practice and discipleship."

The mentor then said, "I will tell you a story about two people. When you have listened carefully to the story, tell me which of the two people in the story is you."

The mentor then told this story: "Two people are lost in the desert. They are dying from hunger and thirst. Finally, they come to a high wall. On the other side they can hear the sound of a waterfall and birds singing. Above, they can see the branches of a lush tree extending over the top of the wall. Its fruit looks delicious. One of them manages to climb over the wall and disappears down the other side. The other, instead, returns to the desert to help other lost travelers find their way to the oasis."

After the young man heard the story, he realized what he must do and who he must become. Having read the story above, which one of the two people are you?

December 7
Learn What You Can

Have you ever tried to pray and been unable? Have you ever tried to meditate only to find yourself so distracted that you could find no peace at all? If so, perhaps this little parable from the Desert Fathers might be helpful.

A student went to his meditation teacher and said, "My meditation is horrible! I feel so distracted, or my legs ache, or I am filled with gas and am uncomfortable, or I'm constantly falling asleep. It's just horrible!"

"It will pass," the teacher said calmly. "Learn what you can."

A week later, the same student came back to his teacher. "My meditation is wonderful! I feel so aware, so peaceful, so alive! It's just wonderful!"

"It will pass," the teacher replied calmly. "Learn what you can from it."

December 8
How Do You Respond?

Some years ago, when the famous tennis player Arthur Ashe was dying of AIDS, someone wrote him a letter to ask him why God had selected him for such a terrible and devasting disease. Although he had received many letters, this one letter provoked him to send a response.

Ashe thoughtfully described how he had enjoyed his career in tennis and how blessed he felt to have been so successful. Then he said,

"When I was holding the winner's cup, I never asked God, 'Why me?' So today, in pain, I should not be asking God, 'Why me?' I have decided to be thankful to God for the 98% of my life that was full of good things."

When life hands you difficulties or sorrows, how do you respond?

December 9
Summing Up Your Life

One of my favorite people from American history is George Washington. He is a remarkable person who has much to teach us, and probably one of the most admired people in our nation's history. One sign of that is the number of things named for him. In fact, there are **189 things named after George Washington. There is** 1 state named for him, 7 mountains, 8 streams, 10 lakes, 33 counties, 9 colleges, and 121 towns and villages. That says a lot about how Washington has been regarded by his country over the years.

History says that he was 6 feet, 5 inches tall with red hair. He was very strong, and his soldiers described him as muscular. Thomas Jefferson once remarked that Washington was the finest horseman in North America, who had enormous strength and courage. He was considered physically intimidating.

As for his personality, those who knew Washington said that he was very cautious in friendship, saving that for very few people. Yet he was courteous to strangers. He spoke in a low, somewhat deep voice, and was a patient listener, which John Adams called a "gift." He rarely let his emotions show, and he kept counsel with few. He had a bad temper that often flared up during a battle but which he learned to control in adulthood.

Maybe most importantly, those who knew him knew said that he was not power hungry. He despised the public life and served as president only because he was virtually begged to do so. He is the only U. S. president to be elected unanimously, winning every electoral vote. Washington came to see slavery as cruel and wicked and was the first founding father to free slaves and help older slaves retire from a life of hard toil.

George Washington was truly a remarkable person. As I think about him, I am reminded of what a friend of mine said about him during a book club discussion I attended. The club had just finished reading a biography of the first president, and we were asked to sum up what we had learned from reading about his life. My friend summed it up by saying, "Washington taught us that leadership is not about power, but about serving people with all of your heart and soul."

I think that truly does sum up Washington's life; it also sums up any good person who wants to live the Gospel. Perhaps we should all ask ourselves, from time to time, if that description sums up our lives as well.

December 10
A Barking Dog

I was recently part of a 12-step meeting in which the discussion turned to stories that have helped people learn and grow in their efforts to recover from their addictions. Many stories were shared, and all of us present at the meeting were grateful for the shared wisdom. One of my favorite stories was told by an Indian man who had just come back from visiting his family in New Delhi. Here is what he shared.

"A friend of mine once went to see a very important government official in India. When they were walking on the grounds of the presidential palace, a large and fierce-looking dog tore the loincloth off a Hindu guru who was also present and, barking loudly, cornered him by a wall. Now, this guru had the reputation of being able to tame tigers with a glance, but he obviously had no such way with dogs, and he called out to my friend to do something."

"My friend shouted, 'A barking dog does not bite.' 'I know that and you know that,' the guru shouted back, 'but does the dog know that?'"

When the Indian man shared his story, someone in the group asked him, "So what does that little anecdote teach you?" The man smiled at us and said, "Just because you think you know something doesn't mean it can't hurt you!"

December 11
Difficult Times

Have you ever been through difficult times? What was it that got you through those times? When I have been through difficult times, what has gotten me through has been the realization that there is someone bigger than me who is looking out for me. As I say that, I am reminded of something I read recently about George Bush and Vladimir Putin.

Author Peggy Noonan told about a meeting between President George W. Bush and President Vladimir Putin of Russia. According to her, because it was their first meeting as world leaders, Bush wanted to be sure they connected and looked for depth of soul and character. He did not want it to be simply a political meeting.

Bush remembered a story he had read about Putin, that his mother had given him a Christian cross that Putin had blessed while he was in Jerusalem. Bush had been touched by the story and mentioned it to Putin.

Putin responded to that story and said he had taken to wearing the cross. One day, he set it down in a house he had been visiting. Strangely, the house burned down, and all Putin could think about was that his cross was lost in the rubble. He motioned for a worker to come to him so he could ask him to look for the cross. The worker walked over to Putin, stretched out his hand, and showed him the already recovered cross.

Putin told Bush "It was as if something meant for me to have the cross," inferring that he believed in a higher power. Bush said, "President Putin, that's what it's all about — that's the story of the cross. The story of the cross is that God intended it for you and for me. Perhaps there is hope for us and the world."

Even Vladimir Putin had a sense that there was something or someone bigger who was looking out for him. Have you ever felt the presence of God in that way? Look around you and pay close attention. It has been my experience that when we are in the darkest of times, God makes his presence felt.

December 12
The Half of it

Have you ever thought about what it will be like when we die? I think of it often and I began thinking about it more this past week because of what I have been reading.

I was recently reading about Marco Polo and all of his great adventures in which he saw and experienced incredible things. It is said that he often could not find the words to adequately describe what he had been through in his long journeys. When Marco Polo came back to Venice from his travels in Cathay, he immediately began to describe the incredible wonders he had seen there. People did not believe him and for the rest of his life many people tried to get him to confess that he had lied, or exaggerated, or simply made up the whole journey. Even as he lay on his deathbed people tried to get him to say that he had lied about the wonders he had described. His last answer was, "I have always told you the truth! But you must also know and I swear it to you, I never told the half of it! There were so many wonders!"

As I read about Marco Polo's excitement about what he had seen and experienced in the East, I began thinking of the people I know who have shared what they saw when they experienced what is known as a "near death experience". Over my more than 40 years as a parish priest, many people have shared with me what they saw, heard and felt while they were dead. One man actually put it just the way Marco Polo did when he returned from his great adventure – the man said to me, "I am certain that I saw Jesus when I was dead and I can't even explain the half of it! What I saw was amazing. There are no words for it!"

Saint Paul experienced something similar and this is what he said about it, "Eye has not seen, nor ear heard, neither have entered into the heart of man, the things which God has prepared for them that love him.'

I am not sure just what we will experience when we die, but I bet we will not even be able to tell the half of it!

December 13
Now Is the Time

I was at the public library recently when I came upon a curious but interesting anecdote from the life of Ernest Hemingway. The anecdote took place during the First World War. According to Hemingway himself, he had a near-death experience after he had been wounded during the war. He talked about it in a letter he wrote to his family while he was convalescing in Milan from a shrapnel wound.

The letter was dated October 18, 1918 and included this little tidbit: "All the heroes are dead. And the real heroes are the parents. Dying is a very simple. I have looked at death and really, I know."

In the letter, he described just what he experienced at the time: "A big Austrian trench mortar bomb, of the type that used to be called ash cans, exploded in the darkness. I know that I died then. I felt my soul or something coming right out of my body, like you'd pull a silk handkerchief out of a pocket by one corner. It flew around and then came back and went in again, and I wasn't dead anymore. I've looked at death, I have been dead, I really know."

Can you imagine what that must have been like for Hemingway? It surely frightened him. Perhaps you know someone who, like Hemingway, has known death, seen it, and been changed by it. Maybe even you have had your own experience of death. One thing is certain: whenever anyone has such an experience, they are never the same. They have been changed forever.

This reminds me of a man I know who recently died of cancer. As he was getting closer and closer to death, we would meet and have some cookies and conversation. I remember asking him what he had learned from his ten-year battle with cancer, and what it felt like to know that death was very near.

The man said, "Knowing that time is short makes you cut to the chase. My pain and suffering and my daily gaze into the certainty of the nearness of my death have taught me the great importance of taking the time you have to be kind to others. Looking death in the face means that I cannot look at any face without wanting to be kind to that person. For some people death is scary. For me it is simply a friend reminding me that time is running out. Now is the time to be kind!"

December 14
Life is an Adventure

I was in a mall the other day when I saw a poster that read:
"Remember, life is truly and adventure!
That got me thinking.

I recently read about something that happened to a famous Scottish biologist by the name of Alexander Fleming. In the summer of 1928, he did something that would change the course of history. It so happened that he was in such a hurry to get away for a vacation that he failed to clean up his lab when he had finished his last day of work. When he returned two weeks later, he found that some of his petri dishes had grown large batches of mold. As he was sorting through the dishes prior to throwing them in the trash, he noticed that the mold had invaded a petri dish in which he had been growing a very powerful bacteria culture. The mold had destroyed the bacteria. As he studied the mold, he soon realized that it was a kind of fungus that typically grows on bread. He was so intrigued that Fleming decided to write a scientific paper on that mold and how it could be used in practical ways. He wrote the paper, gave the mold a name, and then promptly went on with his life.

It was not until the time of the Second World War that a group of doctors looking for a way to cure or at least treat battle wound infections decided to try Fleming's mold. That mold's powers proved to be almost miraculous. It worked to cure even the most terrible infections. The doctors got it to manufacturers who got it to the front lines of the war. Countless lives were saved. It quickly became the most used antibiotic in the world.

Alexander Fleming's rush to get out of town for a vacation proved to be a godsend for the world. Fleming eventually shared in a Nobel Prize for his moldy discovery. When asked about his discovery of Penicillin, Fleming simply said, "One sometimes finds what one is not looking for." After a brief pause, he added, "It's a good thing to pay attention and notice things."

As I read about Fleming's "accidental" discovery, it got me thinking about how often every one of us will sort of "stumble in to a discovery" that can change our lives. We may not discover something as astounding as Penicillin, but we may discover talents we did not know we had. On the other hand, sometimes, a bad mistake can lead to a different way of seeing life or seeing ourselves. We may even stumble our way into a relationship that turns into a profound friendship or even into marriage. We never know when God might surprise us with a new discovery. This is what makes life a real adventure.

December 15
Problems

Have you ever had a problem that, no matter what you tried, nothing seemed able to solve it? I ask that question because recently, someone asked me if I had any advice that would help solve a family problem. When I asked about the nature of the problem, the woman said, "We have a stubborn child who annoys everyone. We are at wit's end."

As I was listening to her, I kept thinking of an old story that comes from the Middle East. Muslim mystics, known as Sufis, taught their students that difficult problems with unruly children can only be solved by a creative approach. Then they would tell this story:

There was once a small boy who banged a drum all day. No matter what anyone said, he wouldn't stop. Various people were called in by neighbors and asked to do something about the child. One by one, townsfolk came to warn the boy about his eardrums or that drums were only for sacred ceremonies. They gave him a book and meditation lessons. They even gave neighbors earplugs. Nothing worked.

Eventually, a smiling Sufi came along. Handing the boy a hammer, he said, "I wonder what's *inside* the drum?" It wasn't long before the drum banging stopped.

How creative are you in dealing with the problems that life might bring your way?

December 16
Have You?

There is traditional German folktale that has something important to teach us. According to that legend, there was a man whose ax was missing, and he suspected that his neighbor's son had stolen it.

As he watched the boy from afar, he noticed that the boy walked like a thief, looked like a thief, and yes, he even spoke like a thief.

Several weeks passed before the day when the man found his ax while digging in his valley. The next day he happened to notice his neighbor's son, and as he looked at him from afar, he saw that the boy walked and looked and even talked like any other child.

Those who retell the story usually conclude the story by asking one question of their listeners: "Have you ever been like the man who lost his ax?"

December 17
Beware

In the ancient world of the Middle East, this story was told by the sages: A wise man went out for a walk. and in the middle of that walk he met the Plague. Startled, the sage asked, "Where are you going?" Taken aback, the Plague answered, "To the big city. I have to kill five thousand people there." The sage was overwhelmed at that thought so he fled from the Plague.

In a few days the same wise man again met the Plague. The sage had heard from folks in the big city and was quite angry. He began to accuse the Plague, "You said that you'd kill five thousand people, but you've killed nearly fifty thousand!"

"No," objected the Plague. "I've killed only five thousand; the others became terrified and let that terror get in their heart. They all died from fear." This left the sage speechless.

The Plague spoken very quietly to the sage, "I do more damage with fear than I ever do with my poisons. You would be wise to pay attention to me. Beware of fear!"

December 18
What's Your Recipe?

I read about a tourist who was on vacation in the mountains. He loved the fresh, clean air and wholesome, natural life the mountains seemed to offer. One day, as the tourist was out on a hike to the top of a large hill, he met a very old looking man. Happy to meet someone from the area, he struck up a conversation.

"Have you lived here in these mountains your whole life?" the vacationer asked the man. "Yes, I have been in these hills since the day my maw gave birth to me," the man replied. Looking closely at the old man, the vacationer asked, "How is it you folks live to such a ripe, old age?"

"It's pretty simple," said the local man. "We drink home brew every day, smoke a couple of packs of cigarettes from our home-grown, mountain tobacco. We never exercise, and the only work we do is only what is necessary. That is pretty much the recipe for how we live around here. We are very content and happy too."

"That is amazing," the visitor said. "That is contrary to all of the commonsense rules we've taught about living a healthy life. Just how old are you, old timer?" "I'll be twenty-nine in July," the man replied.

After a pause the local man asked the vacationer, "By the way, what would you say your recipe is for how you live?"

December 19
What to Do with Your Life

Whenever I am part of high school or college retreat teams, I am often asked some very important questions. Many of the young men and women will pull me aside and ask, "How can I know what God wants me to do with my life?"

My response to that question is always pretty much the same. I first ask them this question: "Are you talking about what God wants you to do now or in the future?" Their usual reply is, "I need to know what God wants me to do in the future."

I usually pause to let them think, then I say that the best way to find out what God wants you to do in the future is to simply ask yourself this question: What should I be doing today?

Those young people always look a bit puzzled by that, so I tell them that if they ask that question every day and try to do what they think God wants them to do now, God will eventually lead them to the future he has in store for each one of them.

December 20
Winning

A Presbyterian minister who is a friend of mine told me about something he remembered from his seminary days. He said that toward the end of his last year of school, he was playing basketball with his friends in the campus gym. My friend looked at me and said, "You know how arrogant a graduate student can be as they are about to graduate, don't you? Well, I was certainly like that on the day I want to tell you about." Then he continued:

"That day, as we were playing basketball, I noticed that the man who cleaned the gym was sitting on the sidelines watching us. He was the janitor, an old black man with white hair, who was waiting patiently until we had finished playing. As he sat there watching, he was reading his bible. Full of myself, I went up to him and inquired, 'What are you reading?' The man did not simply say, 'the bible.' Instead, he answered, 'the Book of Revelation.'"

"With a bit of surprise, I asked, 'The Book of Revelation? That is the most difficult book of the bible for anyone to really understand. So, do you understand it?' 'Oh yes,' the man assured me. 'I understand it. It is plain to me!' 'You understand the Book of Revelation?' I replied. 'No one really understands it! Tell me, what does it mean?'

Very quietly, that old janitor answered, 'It means that Jesus is gonna win.'"

My minister friend turned to me and said, "Today, I believe God sent that humble man to remind me that my arrogance would be of no value to the Kingdom of God. That janitor knew more than all that I had learned in seminary. He knew the ultimate thing that the bible has to teach us. And do you know what that is? It is simply this: no matter how terrible things may look, in the end, Jesus is gonna win!"

December 21
The Christian Version

A guy made his way to the U. S. Post Office to buy some stamps for his Christmas cards. He thought it would be a quick in and out visit, but that was not to be. The line was enormous. When he got to the window, he asked for a sheet of Christmas stamps. The clerk handed him a brightly colored set showing lots of candles and emblazoned with the word "Kwanzaa."

"No," he said, "I'd like some Christmas stamps." The clerk looked a bit annoyed and rummaged around in the supply and pulled out some jolly snowmen and made ready to ring up the transaction.

"No," he said again, "I'd like some religious ones." Out came more candles, this time saying "Hanukkah." Before the guy could object, the clerk said, "How about these bright blue ones with the gold Arabic calligraphy proclaiming "Eid?"

By now the customer was really frustrated. "Actually," he said, "I was looking for the ones with the mother and child. I'd like some Christian Christmas stamps."

"Oh, you should have told me that you needed the Christian version!" the clerk said loudly.

There was a long silent pause as the clerk was getting change ready for the customer. Then the clerk said, "I'm surprised you didn't realize that Christians can't just horn in on Christmas, you know. There's a very big world out there and perhaps you don't need to be so touchy about it!"

As the customer left the post office he simply said, "She thinks Christians are 'horning in' on Christmas! How odd!"

December 22
A Flow of Grace

An astronomer, who is a member of one of those megachurches, went to talk to the man who was pastoring that church. The astronomer said, "Reverend, I have noticed in listening to you, that you minister-types always make the bible and being a Christian unnecessarily complicated with all your biblical exegesis, verse analysis, and theological and ecclesiastical doctrines. I think all of that stuff is of little value. It is quite simple to me: Do unto others as you would have others do unto you. That's all you need to know and all you need to do. So why do you gunk up the works with all of that study?"

The pastor thought for a second and then answered, "You know, I'm glad you raised that issue. If I stop to think about astronomy and astronomers, with all of your theories about an expanding universe and black holes and myriad galaxies, we don't need all that scientific mumbo jumbo. I think all of astronomy is actually quite simple. It seems to me that it can all be summed up in a few words: Twinkle, twinkle, little star. How I wonder what you are. Why do you astronomers gunk up the works with all of your studies and theories?"

That story always makes me laugh because my own training in Scripture warns against either over-simplifying what the bible teaches or making it more complicated than it needs to be. One of my teachers put it this way: "Reading and studying the Scriptures requires both solid study and an openness to the flow of God's grace that leads to understanding."

December 23
Making Them Disappear

I recently read an article in which the actor Anthony Hopkins described how he prepared for his role in the movie, "The Remains of the Day," where he plays a butler to a super-rich family. As a part of his research, Hopkins interviewed an actual butler. Here is what that butler told Hopkins: "My goal in life is complete and total obsequiousness, a skilled ability to blend into the woodwork of any room like a mere fixture, on a par with table lamps."

Hopkins said that the one sentence he will never forget is when this man said that you can sum up an excellent butler this way: "The room seems emptier when he's in it." What the butler meant was that his goal was always to do his work, like filling wine glasses, clearing plates and silverware without being noticed, and never needing to be thanked.

Anthony Hopkins remarked that as he sees it, a rich person who needs a butler must never take the butler for granted. If they begin to take the man for granted, they will begin the wholesale practice of ingratitude. Then he said, "That's just the problem with routine ingratitude: it makes people disappear."

If you were to take a few minutes to consider the people in your life right now, is there anyone that you take for granted so much that they disappear from your life?

December 24
Telling the Story

I saw a cartoon that I loved and immediately sent it to friends. In it, a little girl sits her baby brother on her lap and says that she is going to tell him the wonderful story of Christmas. Her story turns out to be a tad different than the one you or I have grown up with.

According to her version, Jesus was born just in time for Christmas up at the North Pole, surrounded by eight tiny reindeer and the round Virgin Mary. Then Santa Claus showed up with lots of toys and stuff and some swaddling clothes and baby food in little jars. The three wise men and elves all sang carols while the Little Drummer Boy and Scrooge helped Joseph, who was drinking eggnog, trim the tree. In the meantime, Frosty the Snowman saw this star and ran and jumped and played.

On this eve of your Christmas celebration, how would you describe what Christmas is and what it means to you?

December 25
The Real Santa

This is Christmas Day. I was sitting in church praying before morning Mass on the Third Sunday of Advent when a parishioner came up to me and said, "You have to read this story that my daughter sent me in a Christmas card." Here's the story:

A mom took her three little girls to a mall to do some Christmas shopping and to visit Santa, who was supposed to be there that day. While they were there, the kids had an opportunity to sit in Santa Claus' lap and tell him what they wanted for Christmas. When they had finished, Santa Claus asked them, "Will you do something for me on Christmas morning?"

The three little girls said, "Yes!" Then Santa Claus said, "I want you to be sure to sing 'Happy Birthday' on Christmas morning."

The little girls were surprised by this question and said that nobody in their family was having a birthday on Christmas Day. Their mother, who was standing by and listening to the conversation, said, "Come on, now, you guys know whose birthday is on Christmas!" One of the little girls suddenly remembered and exclaimed, "Oh yeah, it's Jesus' birthday!"

Santa Claus said, "That's right, so you be sure to sing happy birthday to Jesus on Christmas!" Then Santa kissed each of them on the top of their head and gave each one a candy cane.

As their mother led the three little girls away from Santa, she heard her youngest daughter tell her sisters, "I am sure that he is the real Santa and not some guy dressed up to look like him." One of her sisters said, "How do you know that?" "Because he seems to know Jesus and only the real Santa would know Jesus!" said the third sister.

If knowing Jesus is what qualifies one to be the "real" Santa, would *you* be a real Santa?

December 26
The Child in Us

On this day after Christmas, I am thinking of something that happened here in the United States during World War One. At the time, the war was in full swing, and Americans were facing a bleak Christmas season.

The government was considering a ban on toy buying that year. They hoped to convince parents to buy Liberty bonds instead. But before they made such a monumental decision, government officials arranged a special meeting with A.C. Gilbert, the inventor of one of the most popular toys in history, the Erector Set.

Erector Sets were toy construction sets with which children could build skyscrapers, spaceships, and anything else their minds could conceive. But what could a toy inventor say that would convince the government to save Christmas? Gilbert didn't have to say much. Before the meeting began, he pulled a batch of toys out of his briefcase, spread all of toy sets across the floor and simply said, "Have at it!"

Soon, all the government officials, including the Secretary of the Navy, were on the floor playing. There was no ban on toys that year. The toy maker just gave them the toys and the child in those government officials came out.

God the Father sent his Son on Christmas to bring out the child in each of us!

December 27
Consequences

Almost all religious traditions speak about the importance of awareness. Just being aware of the world around us can lead to incredible insights.

I remember taking a literature class back in college in which the professor was trying to teach us the importance of paying attention to what you choose to do. He said, "It is quite frightening when you realize that a simple, seemingly unimportant choice you make can spell disaster for other people we don't even know."

When we all looked puzzled by his statement, he read a passage from a Russian writer, Mikhail Chekhov. The passage was from one of that author's stories in which a peasant removes the bolts from railroad ties to use as weights on his fishing nets. The peasant is totally unaware of the fact that his seemingly trivial act will later cause the deaths of hundreds of unsuspecting railroad travelers.

Our teacher concluded his lesson by reminding us to become more aware of how our seemingly unimportant choices can have very serious consequences. After he said that, our professor got very quiet and, in a whisper, said, "pray for the gift of awareness."

December 28
Thinking Big

I heard a story about a banker, who had no children of his own but who took a strong interest in the little boy who lived next door. Every morning as they waited for their buses, the man would say to the little boy, "Son, whatever you do today, I want you to think big." For months, every morning, he would remind the boy, "Remember now, think big today."

One day when the boy was about eleven years old, the banker came out to find a big sign in the boy's front yard. The sign read: "Dog for sale -- $50,000." The banker drew a deep breath and then said, "Well son, you certainly have listened to my advice. You are surely thinking big asking such a high price for that dog." The boy just smiled.

Several days later, the banker came out and saw that the sign was not in the boy's front yard anymore. He said, "Hey, I see your sign is gone. Did you sell your dog?" "I sure did!" said the boy.

Now the banker was a little taken aback, so he asked, "Did you get your asking price?" The boy laughed and said, "I did a trade that was worth the same." "What do you mean?" the banker asked. "The girl down the street loved my dog so much that she traded me two $25,000 cats for him! Your advice about thinking big really works!"

I don't know who thought bigger, the boy or the girl down the street, but I love that story. It reminds me to take some time every now and then to consider just how "big" my thinking is.

The Buddhist concept of "beginner's mind" teaches that when we approach life as a "beginner," we have the freedom to ask all of the questions that come to mind, and we end up with a much broader view of things. It is probably a very wise thing for each of us to examine if we are thinking big enough to have a "beginner's mind."

December 29
Feeding Your Soul

As the year is approaching its end, I have been thinking about time and about getting older. When I think about getting older, I remember something I read about the famous mystery writer Agatha Christie.

When she was asked if she feared getting older, she just laughed and said, "No, I think that I will enjoy getting older. Did you know that I married an archeologist? You see I can look forward to getting older because there is a tremendous advantage to being married to an archeologist – for one thing, the older I get, the more interested he becomes in me!"

What is your attitude about getting older? It always amazes me how differently people see getting older. Many are frightened of the aging process, thinking that it means the end of a happy life or of independence. There are other folks who see getting older as an adventure to be embraced and something to enjoy.

I remember seeing Pablo Casals, the famous cellist, interviewed on "60 Minutes." The reporter asked Casals, who had just turned 93, if he still practiced playing the cello at his age. When Pablo Casals said yes, the reported asked, "Pablo, you are 93! Why do you need to practice?"

Casals thought for a moment, then replied, "Because, I finally think I am making some progress!" The reporter then asked him, "Do you spend a lot of time practicing?" Casals said, "I guess I spend five or six hours a day playing the cello. Music feeds my soul. My body may be 93, but my soul is forever young! Besides, can you think of a better way to spend my old age?"

As this year begins to wind down, ask yourself how you want to spend your old age. Is there anything that you are doing in your life today that feeds your soul?

December 30
Great Pearls of Wisdom

I recently had the opportunity to visit with a woman who had just celebrated her 99th birthday. She is such an amazing woman in that you would never suspect that she is as old as she is because she does not act like an old lady. When I asked her about her secret to staying young and happy, she simply said, "There are five things I have learned that I must keep if I want to live a happy, good life." She paused for a moment and then said, "Well, aren't you going to write these things down? My "five keeps" are real pearls of wisdom, so you should write them down!"

I did write them down and here they are:

1. Although your body is old, your mind does not have to be, KEEP developing it!
2. Your humor is one of the best things about you, so KEEP enjoying it!
3. Not all of your strength is gone, so KEEP using what you have left!
4. Opportunities to do new things and learn new things have not vanished, KEEP pursuing them!
5. God is alive and well, so KEEP seeking Him!

Aren't those great pearls of wisdom?

December 31
Your Nature

On this last day of the year, here is a simple story for your consideration: Two monks were washing their bowls in the river when they noticed a scorpion that was drowning. One monk immediately scooped it up and set it upon the bank. In the process he was stung. He went back to washing his bowl, and again the scorpion fell in. The monk saved the scorpion and was again stung.

The other monk asked him, "Friend, why do you continue to save the scorpion when you know it's nature is to sting?" "Because," the monk replied, "it is my nature to save."

As you stand on the last day of one year and on the eve of a whole new year, take some time to consider this question, "What is my nature? Is it my nature to sting, or is it my nature to save?" After you have answered that question, ask yourself one more question: "In this past year, have I been living according to my nature? In the coming year, will I live according to my nature?"